MW00830941

SHAKESPEARE AND THE ADMIRAL'S MEN

For most of the 1590s, the Admiral's Men were the main competitors of Shakespeare's company in the London theatres. Not only did they stage old plays by dramatists such as Christopher Marlowe and Thomas Kyd; their playwrights invented the genres of humours comedy (with *An Humorous Day's Mirth*) and city comedy (with *Englishmen for My Money*), while other new plays such as *A Knack to Know an Honest Man* and *The Downfall of Robert, Earl of Huntingdon* were important influences on Shakespeare. This is the first book to read the Admiral's repertory against Shakespeare's plays of the 1590s, showing both how Shakespeare drew on their innovations and how his plays influenced Admiral's dramatists in turn. Shedding new light on well-known plays and offering detailed analysis of less familiar ones, it offers a fresh perspective on the dramatic culture of the 1590s.

TOM RUTTER is Lecturer in Shakespeare and Renaissance Drama at the University of Sheffield. He is the author of *Work and Play on the Shakespearean Stage* (Cambridge, 2008) and *The Cambridge Introduction to Christopher Marlowe* (2012), as well as numerous journal articles and book chapters on early modern drama. He is a co-editor of the journal *Shakespeare*.

SHAKESPEARE AND THE ADMIRAL'S MEN

Reading Across Repertories on the London Stage, 1594–1600

TOM RUTTER

University of Sheffield

CAMBRIDGE
UNIVERSITY PRESS

CAMBRIDGE
UNIVERSITY PRESS

University Printing House, Cambridge CB2 8BS, United Kingdom

One Liberty Plaza, 20th Floor, New York, NY 10006, USA

477 Williamstown Road, Port Melbourne, VIC 3207, Australia

4843/24, 2nd Floor, Ansari Road, Daryaganj, Delhi – 110002, India

79 Anson Road, #06–04/06, Singapore 079906

Cambridge University Press is part of the University of Cambridge.

It furthers the University's mission by disseminating knowledge in the pursuit of education, learning, and research at the highest international levels of excellence.

www.cambridge.org
Information on this title: www.cambridge.org/9781107077430
10.1017/9781139924870

First published 2017

Printed in the United States of America by Sheridan Books, Inc.

A catalogue record for this publication is available from the British Library.

Library of Congress Cataloging-in-Publication Data
NAMES: Rutter, Tom, author.
TITLE: Shakespeare and the Admiral's Men : reading across repertories on the London stage, 1594-1600 / Tom Rutter, University of Sheffield.
DESCRIPTION: Cambridge ; New York, NY : Cambridge University Press, 2016. | Includes bibliographical references and index.
IDENTIFIERS: LCCN 2016029972 | ISBN 9781107077430 (hardcopy : alk. paper)
SUBJECTS: LCSH: Shakespeare, William, 1564-1616–Stage history–To 1625. | Shakespeare, William, 1564-1616–Stage history–England–London. | Admiral's Men (Theater company)–History. | Theatrical companies–England–London–History–17th century. | Theatrical companies–England–London–History–16th century.
CLASSIFICATION: LCC PR3095 .R88 2016 | DDC 822/.309–dc23 LC record available at https://lccn.loc.gov/2016029972

ISBN 978-1-107-07743-0 Hardback

Contents

Acknowledgements

This book was written with the aid of a semester's research leave from the School of English at the University of Sheffield and, before that, teaching remission enabled by the Humanities Research Centre at Sheffield Hallam University. I am grateful to both institutions (more specifically, Susan Fitzmaurice and Chris Hopkins) for this invaluable time, and more importantly for giving me the chance to work alongside some wonderful Renaissance scholars: Faith Acker, Annaliese Connolly, Nicky Hallett, Lisa Hopkins, Marcus Nevitt, Emma Rhatigan, Cathy Shrank, Matt Steggle and Rachel Stenner. I owe all of them a profound debt for offering friendship and intellectual stimulation on a daily basis and for the feedback they have given on my work in formal and informal settings alike. I am also grateful to my other colleagues at both universities for their society and support, especially Jill LeBihan, Steve Earnshaw and Graham Williams, and I have learned a great deal from my PhD students, Tony Prince, Melanie Russell and Chris Butler (to whose work on *As You Like It* I am indebted). Moving away from Sheffield, I would like to record my thanks to Andrew Gurr and Roslyn Lander Knutson, who, as well as setting many of the terms of the debates in which this book engages, have been unfailingly helpful, generous and supportive of my research into the Admiral's Men repertory. Lucy Munro also deserves credit (or blame) for drawing my attention to repertory studies as an approach to early modern drama when we were both doctoral students at the University of London.

While working on Shakespeare and the Admiral's Men, I have had invaluable opportunities to clarify my thinking about them and on related topics through writing articles published in *Medieval and Renaissance Drama in England, Shakespeare, Shakespeare Bulletin* and *Early Theatre*, and chapters published in *The Oxford Handbook of Early Modern Theatre, Working Subjects in Early Modern English Drama* and *Community-Making in Early Stuart Theatres*. Although none of that material is duplicated in this book, it has provided important groundwork for it, and my occasional citations of it are intended to reflect this rather than (I hope) stemming from personal vanity. I would also like to thank the Shakespeare Association of America, the Marlowe Society of America, the British Shakespeare Association, the Renaissance Society of America, the Irish Renaissance Society and the Cambridge Shakespeare Conference, as well as the organisers of the Community-Making in Early Stuart Theatres symposium at Åbo Akademi University, the Reforming Shakespeare conference at De Montfort University, the Global and Local Marlowes conference at King's College London, and the Spiritual and Material Renaissances seminar at Sheffield Hallam University for giving me the opportunity to present my research. In particular, I am grateful to Michelle M. Dowd, Kevin De Ornellas, Roger D. Sell, Deborah Cartmell, Gabriel Egan and (again) Lucy Munro and Lisa Hopkins for inviting me to contribute to the events they were convening. Helen Hackett generously read a portion of the manuscript and suggested several improvements. I am grateful to Sarah Stanton at Cambridge University Press for having faith in this project from the beginning, and the Press's anonymous readers for their invaluable feedback from proposal to clearance stage. For the deficiencies of this book I am fully responsible.

The licensing of the cover image was paid for in part by the Research Strategy Committee of the School of English at the University of Sheffield.

Finally, I would like to thank my wife Sophie and our children Cædmon and Aphra, for everything else.

Note on Dating

In some texts cited in this book, dates are given using the old-style dating system, in which the new year began on Lady Day (25 March). For example, Philip Henslowe records a performance of *1 Tamburlaine* on '30 of desemb[er] 1594', followed by a performance of *2 Tamburlaine* on 'j of Jenewary 1594'. (Except where indicated, all references to Henslowe are to R. A. Foakes's 2002 updating of his and R. T. Rickert's 1961 edition of *Henslowe's Diary* for Cambridge University Press. The text above appears on p. 26.) When referring to such instances, I use the form '1 January 1594–5' in order to acknowledge the way the date appears in the source while making clear that the reference is to the modern calendar year 1595. Direct quotations from Henslowe retain his wording.

Introduction

The title of this book, 'Shakespeare and the Admiral's Men', may require some explanation. Although, as Terence G. Schoone-Jongen shows in *Shakespeare's Companies*, disagreement still rages about the playing company or companies to which William Shakespeare may have belonged prior to joining the Lord Chamberlain's Men in 1594, one thing almost everyone agrees on is that he never belonged to the Admiral's Men.[1] The chapters that follow explore a different type of relationship: one not of company affiliation, but of reciprocal influence. I aim to show how, over the course of the 1590s, Shakespeare's work as a dramatist for the Lord Chamberlain's Men was informed by the plays that the Admiral's Men were staging at the Rose theatre, in terms of subject matter, theme, characterisation, treatment of materials and more; and how in turn, Admiral's Men dramatists drew on Shakespeare's work when writing new plays of their own. I follow this relationship up to 1600, the year in which the Admiral's Men relocated to the Fortune playhouse in Golding Lane. This and other important developments around that time, such as the move of the Lord Chamberlain's Men to the Globe (1599), the revival of the children's companies (1599–1600), and the growing willingness of the Privy Council to tolerate a third adult company (formally licensed in 1602), represent a reconfiguration of London's theatrical culture in ways that make the turn of the century an appropriate end point.[2]

---

[1] According to Schoone-Jongen, 'The Queen's Men, Strange's Men, Pembroke's Men, and Sussex's Men arguably constitute the four most prominent candidates', while John Southworth, *Shakespeare the Player: A Life in the Theatre* (Phoenix Mill: Sutton Publishing, 2000) is a rare recent example of a work that makes the case for Shakespeare's involvement with the Admiral's. Terence G. Schoone-Jongen, *Shakespeare's Companies: William Shakespeare's Early Career and the Acting Companies, 1577–1594* (Farnham: Ashgate, 2008), pp. 173, 190–5.
[2] A company made up of the servants of the Earl of Oxford and of the Earl of Worcester was licensed to perform at the Boar's Head on 31 March 1602. See *English Professional Theatre, 1530–1660*, ed. by Glynne Wickham, Herbert Berry and William Ingram (Cambridge: Cambridge University Press, 2000), pp. 108–10.

1

In some respects, the argument that Shakespeare's work in the 1590s was influenced by the Admiral's Men is not a new one. The Admiral's repertory included plays by Christopher Marlowe such as the two parts of *Tamburlaine*, *Doctor Faustus* and *The Jew of Malta*, not to mention Thomas Kyd's *The Spanish Tragedy*, and the importance of all of these to Shakespeare's dramatic development is generally accepted. Since 1990, the question of Marlowe's impact on Shakespeare has attracted book-length studies by James Shapiro and Robert A. Logan, not to speak of book chapters and journal articles, while *The Spanish Tragedy* is routinely cited as an influence on *Hamlet*.[3] However, during Shakespeare's time with the Lord Chamberlain's Men, neither Marlowe (who died on 30 May 1593) nor Kyd (who was buried on 15 August 1594) was in a position to supply the Admiral's Men with new material; their drama, not all of which had been originally written for that company in any case, survived in its repertory as old plays that could still attract audiences. From 1594 onwards, the contributors of new plays were dramatists like George Chapman, author of the first 'humours' comedy, *An Humorous Day's Mirth*; William Haughton, whose play *Englishmen for My Money* can be regarded as the first London-based city comedy; and Anthony Munday, whose *Earl of Huntingdon* plays supplied the template for subsequent literary treatments of Robin Hood – besides authors of plays such as *A Knack to Know an Honest Man* whose identities have been lost to posterity. Any discussion of Shakespeare in relation to the commercial environment in which he wrote during the latter part of the 1590s needs to recognise men like these as his competitors and fellow innovators.

In electing to read Shakespeare's dramatic output, not in relation to the work of an individual dramatist, but in relation to the repertory of the Admiral's Men as a whole, my practice both exemplifies and is informed by a strand of research into early modern drama that takes playing companies and their repertories as the object of its enquiry. This approach has a long pedigree, exemplified in the twentieth century by works such as T. W. Baldwin's *The Organization and Personnel of the*

---

[3] James Shapiro, *Rival Playwrights: Marlowe, Jonson, Shakespeare* (New York: Columbia University Press, 1991); Robert A. Logan, *Shakespeare's Marlowe: The Influence of Christopher Marlowe on Shakespeare's Artistry* (Farnham: Ashgate, 2007). Three recent discussions are Clara Calvo, 'Thomas Kyd and the Elizabethan Blockbuster: *The Spanish Tragedy*', in *Shakespeare and Contemporary Dramatists*, ed. by Ton Hoenselaars (Cambridge: Cambridge University Press, 2012), pp. 19–33; Richard Wilson, '"The Words of Mercury": Shakespeare and Marlowe', in *Shakespeare and Contemporary Dramatists*, pp. 34–53; and Thomas Cartelli, 'Marlowe and Shakespeare Revisited', in *Christopher Marlowe in Context*, ed. by Emily C. Bartels and Emma Smith (Cambridge: Cambridge University Press, 2013), pp. 285–95.

Shakespearean Company (1927), Robert Boies Sharpe's *The Real War of the Theaters* (1935) and Alfred Harbage's *Shakespeare and the Rival Traditions* (1952).[4] In the 1980s and 1990s, it gathered pace as texts such as Andrew Gurr's *Playgoing in Shakespeare's London* (1987), Roslyn Lander Knutson's *The Repertory of Shakespeare's Company 1594–1613* (1991) and Scott McMillin and Sally-Beth MacLean's *The Queen's Men and Their Plays* (1998) made their influence felt.[5] The reasons for this development are multiple and varied, as I have discussed at greater length elsewhere.[6] Gurr and Knutson were (amongst other things) contributing to existing scholarly debates: in Gurr's case about the demographics of playgoing, in that of Knutson about the extent to which different acting companies followed similar business models.[7] I would also suggest that the increased enthusiasm, from the 1980s onward, for historicist approaches to early modern drama found useful materials in repertory-oriented studies, since the acting company represented a place where dramatic writing came into contact with other practices such as patronage, censorship, repertory management and playgoing and with the commercial pressures of the marketplace.[8] Knutson's book, for example, sought to identify the principles upon which acting companies bought and commissioned plays, while McMillin and MacLean identified political reasons behind the formation of the Queen's Men in 1583.[9] In a period when critics were keen to relate the drama to the new social and economic formations of Elizabethan capitalism, or to identify the workings of power in dramatic literature, a theatre history oriented towards acting companies offered a way of grounding their analysis in the material practices of the entertainment

---

[4] T. W. Baldwin, *The Organization and Personnel of the Shakespearean Company* (Princeton: Princeton University Press, 1927); Robert Boies Sharpe *The Real War of the Theaters: Shakespeare's Fellows in Rivalry with the Admiral's Men, 1594–1603: Repertories, Devices and Types* (New York: Modern Language Association of America, 1935); Alfred Harbage, *Shakespeare and the Rival Traditions* (New York: Macmillan, 1952).

[5] Andrew Gurr, *Playgoing in Shakespeare's London* (Cambridge: Cambridge University Press, 1987); Roslyn Lander Knutson, *The Repertory of Shakespeare's Company 1594–1613* (Fayetteville: University of Arkansas Press, 1991); Scott McMillin and Sally-Beth MacLean, *The Queen's Men and Their Plays* (Cambridge: Cambridge University Press, 1998). Citations in the current study are from the second edition (1996) of Gurr.

[6] Tom Rutter, 'Repertory Studies: An Overview', *Shakespeare*, 4 (2008), 352–66.

[7] Gurr's book responds to Ann Jennalie Cook's *The Privileged Playgoers of Shakespeare's London, 1576–1642* (Princeton: Princeton University Press, 1981), which in turn served as a rejoinder to Harbage. Knutson takes issue with a view of the Admiral's Men that she associates with F. G. Fleay and others, and which I discuss later in this chapter.

[8] This is well illustrated by the contents of a landmark collection of 1997, *A New History of Early English Drama*, ed. by John D. Cox and David Scott Kastan (New York: Columbia University Press, 1997), which includes separate chapters on all of these topics.

[9] Knutson, *Repertory of Shakespeare's Company*, pp. 15–55; McMillin and MacLean, pp. 1–36.

industry. At the same time, the influence of post-structuralist theorists such as Michel Foucault, who interrogated and historicised the role of the author, provided a theoretical rationale for moving away from the individual dramatist as the object of enquiry, as Lucy Munro recognised in a 2003 article that sought to theorise a 'repertory approach' to early modern drama. This shift of focus seemed particularly appropriate to the study of the early modern theatre, partly because of its inherently collaborative nature but also because it was not a culture that necessarily privileged dramatists above theatre companies: witness the title pages of printed plays, which almost always name the acting company but do not necessarily specify a playwright.[10] Finally, I would suggest, the *Records of Early English Drama* (REED) project conducted from the University of Toronto since the late 1970s uncovered a wealth of archival material, and collated material already known to scholars, in a way that made it possible to analyse the professional habits (in particular the touring patterns) of individual companies much more extensively than had previously been the case. The results of this are evident in the third chapter of McMillin and MacLean's book, which discusses the touring habits of the Queen's Men and stresses the importance of travel for the company, and they can also be seen in the more recent work of MacLean (with Lawrence Manley) and Gurr on individual companies.[11]

The potential of a company-oriented approach to generate new insights is illustrated by a wealth of monographs that have appeared since 2000 and that share an interest in companies and their repertories while remaining diverse in their focuses and methodologies. Mary Bly's *Queer Virgins and Virgin Queans on the Early Modern Stage* offers a history of the King's Revels Company of child players, identifying a distinctive corporate style in their plays' bawdy comic heroines and 'queer puns'.[12] Knutson's *Playing Companies and Commerce in Shakespeare's Time* addresses the question of commercial relationships between companies: she argues that these were less competitive than is sometimes supposed, and she reads allusions to the contemporary theatrical scene in plays such as *Hamlet*, Ben Jonson's

---

[10] Lucy Munro, 'Early Modern Drama and the Repertory Approach', *Research Opportunities in Renaissance Drama*, 42 (2003), 1–33 (pp. 1–2, 6–14).

[11] McMillin and MacLean, pp. 37–83; Lawrence Manley and Sally-Beth MacLean, *Lord Strange's Men and Their Plays* (New Haven: Yale University Press, 2014), pp. 247–79; Andrew Gurr, *The Shakespeare Company, 1594–1642* (Cambridge: Cambridge University Press, 2004), pp. 54–69; *Shakespeare's Opposites: The Admiral's Company 1594–1625* (Cambridge: Cambridge University Press, 2009), pp. 72–81.

[12] Mary Bly, *Queer Virgins and Virgin Queans on the Early Modern Stage* (Oxford: Oxford University Press, 2000), p. 6.

Poetaster and Thomas Dekker's *Satiromastix* as strategic rather than aggres-sive.[13] Gurr has offered company histories both of the Lord Chamberlain's and of the Admiral's Men, examining their commercial strategies, staging practices, touring habits, finances, repertories, patronage and more. Munro's history of the Children of the Queen's Revels surveys their relationship with the Blackfriars audience, their role in the development of tragicomedy, and their dramatists' innovations in the genre of tragedy.[14] Schoone-Jongen summarises the critical debate over Shakespeare's company affiliations prior to the Lord Chamberlain's Men. A collection of essays on the Queen's Men edited by Helen Ostovich, Holger Schott Syme and Andrew Griffin testifies to the range of topics a company-oriented approach can embrace, including contributions on touring, patronage, playing spaces, printing and performance, as well as critical discussions of individual plays.[15] Brian Walsh, too, focuses on the Queen's Men, stressing their importance in shaping 'the historical and theatrical imagination of Shakespeare', while James Marino suggests that Shakespeare's plays on subjects previously treated by the Queen's Men and others were rewritings undertaken with the aim of asserting his company's rights over the material.[16] Two studies focus on specific playhouses and, consequently, the companies who performed there: Mark Bayer's *Theatre, Community, and Civic Engagement in Jacobean London* considers the Fortune and Red Bull theatres, homes of the Admiral's successor companies the Prince's / Palsgrave's Men and of Queen Anne's Men, while Eva Griffith offers a history of the Red Bull.[17] Bart van Es in *Shakespeare in Company* approaches Shakespeare's writing after 1594 in the light of his position as sharer in the Lord Chamberlain's Men, arguing that his close familiarity with the men who would perform his plays had a decisive effect on his writing.[18] Most recently, Lawrence Manley and Sally-Beth MacLean's study of *Lord Strange's Men and*

---

[13] Roslyn Lander Knutson, *Playing Companies and Commerce in Shakespeare's Time* (Cambridge: Cambridge University Press, 2001).

[14] Lucy Munro, *Children of the Queen's Revels: A Jacobean Theatre Repertory* (Cambridge: Cambridge University Press, 2005).

[15] *Locating the Queen's Men, 1583–1603: Material Practices and Conditions of Playing*, ed. by Helen Ostovich, Holger Schott Syme and Andrew Griffin (Aldershot: Ashgate, 2009).

[16] Brian Walsh, *Shakespeare, the Queen's Men, and the Elizabethan Performance of History* (Cambridge: Cambridge University Press, 2009), p. 3; James Marino, *Owning William Shakespeare: The King's Men and Their Intellectual Property* (Philadelphia: University of Pennsylvania Press, 2011).

[17] Mark Bayer, *Theatre, Community, and Civic Engagement in Jacobean London* (Iowa City: University of Iowa Press, 2011); Eva Griffith, *A Jacobean Company and its Playhouse: The Queen's Servants at the Red Bull Theatre (c. 1605–1619)* (Cambridge: Cambridge University Press, 2013).

[18] Bart van Es, *Shakespeare in Company* (Oxford: Oxford University Press, 2013).

Their Plays offers a comprehensive account of that company including their career in and outside London, the probable contents of their repertory, the distinctive qualities of their plays and their relationship with their patron.

When one surveys this increasingly populous field, the obvious question arises of what the current study has to add to it. Its distinctiveness rests in a combination of factors. Firstly, rather than focusing on the repertory of a single playing company it seeks to chart an evolving and reciprocal relationship. Neither Shakespeare, as a Lord Chamberlain's Men dramatist, nor the playwrights working for the Admiral's Men operated in a hermetically sealed environment determined by the boundaries of their repertory: they were demonstrably open to each other's innovations, such that one can see (for example) *A Midsummer Night's Dream* responding to plays in the Admiral's repertory (as I shall argue in Chapter 2) and going on to influence the author of the Admiral's play *Captain Thomas Stukeley* (as I shall argue in Chapter 3). Secondly, it attempts to combine an approach informed by the findings of theatre historians with a set of priorities that are, above all, critical. On the one hand, I hope that it sheds light on the way in which dramatists for different companies drew on each other's work; on the other, I hope that in doing so it reveals new features of the plays of Shakespeare and his contemporaries, highlighting the artistic choices they made and the aesthetic effects generated by their adherence to and rejection of earlier practice. To this extent, although I follow the practice of 'repertory studies' in using playing companies as my organising principle, treating Shakespeare as a Lord Chamberlain's Men dramatist and Chapman, Haughton, Munday and the rest as Admiral's Men dramatists, I retain a sense of authorial agency, whether of dramatists working individually or collaboratively, while recognising that this agency was shaped by other forces including the repertorial policies of companies themselves, the decisions made by actors when preparing a play for the stage, the various processes involved in getting a play into print, and the changes a play might undergo during its afterlife in the repertory.

One obvious objection to my approach relates to the decision to consider a number of Admiral's Men dramatists, but only Shakespeare among the dramatists writing for the Lord Chamberlain's Men during the 1590s. Surely, the argument might run, this is an unholy combination of two different theoretical models, one focused on the acting company and another focused on an individual playwright. Moreover, in privileging Shakespeare above other Lord Chamberlain's Men dramatists, and indeed over the Admiral's Men dramatists who are not named in the title of my book, I could be accused of perpetuating a bardocentric model of theatre history of the very kind that repertory studies seeks to question: McMillin and MacLean, for example, begin their study of the Queen's Men by observing that only partial attention has been given to that company by 'scholars with other stories to tell, stories that concern Shakespeare and the 1590s'.[19] I accept the justice of this accusation, although I would note that in the above list of monographs since 2000 some seven incorporate Shakespeare in their titles, suggesting that practitioners of repertory studies have found it harder to get out of his shadow than they might like. This may indicate authors' awareness of the utility of Shakespeare in bookselling terms, but (more kindly) it may also be attributed to an understanding that when navigating unfamiliar territory of the kind that company-oriented surveys often enter, it is useful to have some familiar points of reference such as Shakespeare offers. The reader's prior knowledge of *The Merchant of Venice* offers an easier way in to *A Knack to Know an Honest Man* than does, say, *Fair Em*, which may be equally unfamiliar. Furthermore, a discussion of 'Shakespeare and the Admiral's Men' can be defended as an honest response to the fact that the tally of Lord Chamberlain's Men plays up to 1600 that have survived in print is dominated by Shakespeare: other than his twenty-two (or thereabouts), only *A Larum for London*, *A Warning for Fair Women* and Ben Jonson's two humours plays can be securely attributed to the company, along with, more speculatively, *Fair Em* and *Mucedorus*.[20] There is no Lord Chamberlain's Men equivalent of Henslowe's diary that might give us a sense of the many other plays, since lost, which presumably comprised the company's repertory. Accordingly, to focus explicitly on Shakespeare avoids the misleading impression that the plays under discussion comprise a representative sample of what his company was performing during the 1590s. For similar reasons, I have chosen to focus on the Admiral's Men rather than including other London companies such as Pembroke's Men, who staged the lost and notorious *Isle of Dogs* in 1597, or the servants of the sixth Earl of Derby, to whom Thomas Heywood's *Edward IV* was

---

[19] McMillin and MacLean, p. 1.
[20] A plausible list of Shakespeare's Lord Chamberlain's Men plays to 1600 might include *As You Like It*, *The Comedy of Errors*, *Hamlet*, *1 Henry IV*, *2 Henry IV*, *Henry V*, *Julius Caesar*, *King John*, *Love's Labour's Lost*, *The Merchant of Venice*, *The Merry Wives of Windsor*, *A Midsummer Night's Dream*, *Much Ado about Nothing*, *Richard II* and *Romeo and Juliet*, along with plays probably written for other companies that came into the Lord Chamberlain's repertory: the three parts of *Henry VI*, *Richard III*, *The Taming of the Shrew*, *Titus Andronicus* and *The Two Gentlemen of Verona*. See Knutson, *Repertory of Shakespeare's Company*, pp. 179–209.

ascribed when it was printed in 1599.[21] A comprehensive history of the
1590s theatre would certainly need to take account of both companies,
but neither has left behind a sufficiently substantial repertory to allow for a
sustained comparison with Shakespeare's work.[22]

Above all, though, I hope to achieve two things by considering
Shakespeare's plays alongside the repertory of the Admiral's Men.
The first is to add to our understanding of this outstandingly canonical
figure. Recent studies have highlighted the influence that works in the
repertory of the Queen's Men, in particular, exerted upon Shakespeare's
development: Walsh, for example, argues that 'Shakespeare seizes on
the consciousness of history as a construct' that he finds in Queen's Men
history plays and 'experiments with different ways in which this notion
can be used to assess the concept of history', while Janet Clare demonstrates
the persistent influence of Queen's Men plays upon Shakespeare throughout his career (as with *The Famous Victories of Henry the Fifth* and Shakespeare's *Henry IV* and *Henry V* plays).[23] However, less attention has been
paid to the new plays that were appearing during Shakespeare's first years
with the Lord Chamberlain's Men. Although specific instances of intertextuality have been addressed, such as the similarities between *A Midsummer
Night's Dream* and Anthony Munday's *John a Kent and John a Cumber*
(which may be the Admiral's play *The Wise Man of West Chester*), a more
comprehensive study is yet to appear.[24] The nearest thing is Martin
Wiggins's *Shakespeare and the Drama of His Time*, a short but wide-ranging
monograph that efficiently and convincingly locates Shakespeare's development in relation to emerging dramatic trends such as the humours comedy
of the late 1590s (as I discuss in Chapter 4).[25] However, the broad chronological sweep of Wiggins's book, and its interest in plays staged by a variety
of companies, distinguishes it from my own, whose narrower focus allows a
lengthier discussion of individual dramas.

That leads me to the second thing I hope this book will achieve, which
is to give sustained critical attention to plays that seldom receive it. In some

---

[21] Thomas Heywood, *The First and Second Partes of King Edward the Fourth*, 'As it hath diuers times
beene publiquely played by the Right Honorable the Earle of Derby his seruants' (London, 1599;
STC: 13341).
[22] On the importance of companies beyond the Lord Chamberlain's and the Admiral's Men, see
Knutson, *Playing Companies and Commerce*, pp. 8–9.
[23] Walsh, p. 109; Janet Clare, *Shakespeare's Stage Traffic: Imitation, Borrowing and Competition in
Renaissance Theatre* (Cambridge: Cambridge University Press, 2014), pp. 144–64.
[24] I. A. Shapiro, 'Shakespeare and Mundy', *Shakespeare Survey*, 14 (1961), 25–33; Nevill Coghill,
Shakespeare's Professional Skills (Cambridge: Cambridge University Press, 1964), pp. 42–60.
[25] Martin Wiggins, *Shakespeare and the Drama of His Time* (Oxford: Oxford University Press, 2000).

cases, as with *A Knack to Know an Honest Man*, this may be due to their anonymity, which prevents them from being easily classified in a literary system that still tends to privilege the role of the author. In others, as with the plays of Anthony Munday, it may be because they are perceived as the work of minor dramatists. But even Admiral's Men plays of acknowledged importance are not always discussed with the level of detail one would expect: in his essay on Chapman in *The Cambridge Companion to Shakespeare and Contemporary Dramatists*, for example, Paul Franssen notes the significance of *An Humorous Day's Mirth*, observing that it 'antedates the fashion for the "humours" play, usually associated with Ben Jonson, by a year', only to pass on immediately to other topics. Shona Mcintosh's survey of 'Recent Studies in George Chapman (1975–2009)' was able to find only two critical essays on this landmark play.[26] In the current study, as well as discussing the impact of such plays on Shakespeare – and his on their authors – I have tried to offer a more general discussion of their themes, language, stagecraft and politics, with the aim of conveying some impression of the range of theatrical material offered by the Admiral's Men between 1594 and 1600. This makes no claims to exhaustiveness: I do not refer, for example, to the anonymous *Look About You* printed as an Admiral's Men play in 1600, which Gurr discusses at length in *Shakespeare's Opposites*, or to Thomas Dekker's *The Shoemaker's Holiday*, perhaps the Admiral's Men play of this period that has the greatest claim to canonical status after the work of Marlowe and Kyd (although I have touched on its relationship with *Henry V* elsewhere).[27] My choice of material has been shaped by the extent to which I have been able to identify instances of intertextuality between Admiral's Men plays and the work of Shakespeare: thus, in Chapter 1 I focus on their 1594 play *A Knack to Know an Honest Man*, a drama set in Venice that pits two faithful friends against a vengeful moneylender, which has obvious points of affinity with *The Merchant of Venice*. More specifically, I argue that this anonymous play brought together material from earlier works including Marlowe's *The Jew of Malta* (which was playing alongside it in the Admiral's repertory), the Lord Strange's Men play *A Knack to Know a Knave* and a much earlier drama,

---

[26] Paul Franssen, 'George Chapman's Learned Drama', in *Shakespeare and Contemporary Dramatists*, pp. 134–48, pp. 134–35; Shona Mcintosh, 'Recent Studies in George Chapman (1975–2009)', *English Literary Renaissance*, 41 (2011), 219–44.

[27] Gurr, *Shakespeare's Opposites*, pp. 59–71; Tom Rutter, *Work and Play on the Shakespearean Stage* (Cambridge: Cambridge University Press, 2008), pp. 88–96.

Richard Edwards' *Damon and Pythias*, in ways that Shakespeare would find dramatically enabling and which proved to be commercially successful.

In the next two chapters, I continue to argue that as well as being directly influenced by Marlowe plays in the mid-1590s repertory of the Admiral's Men, Shakespeare learned from the work of dramatists who had themselves reshaped Marlovian materials. In Chapter 2 I focus on *Doctor Faustus*, another play that discernibly influenced Shakespeare's dramaturgy of the 1590s. As with *The Jew of Malta* and *The Merchant of Venice*, I argue that Shakespeare's practice in integrating aspects of this tragedy into the comic *A Midsummer Night's Dream* followed the example of playwrights including Anthony Munday in *John a Kent and John a Cumber*, as well as non-Admiral's dramatists such as Robert Greene. In Chapter 3 I discuss Shakespeare's *Henry IV* plays in relation to George Peele's *The Battle of Alcazar* and the anonymous *Captain Thomas Stukeley*, two plays whose response to Marlowe is more complex and creative than the critical label 'sons of *Tamburlaine*' would suggest. Both of them undermine the rhetoric and values of Marlowe's protagonist in ways that resemble Shakespeare's practice; the former unquestionably predates *Henry IV*, and if the latter does not, then its verbal closeness to Shakespeare has implications for the dating of Part I. *Stukeley* also responds to aspects of its non-dramatic context – the Nine Years' War, the career of the Earl of Essex – in ways that parallel features of the *Henriad*.

Although it is uncertain whether *Captain Thomas Stukeley* responds to *Henry IV* or vice versa, my final chapters demonstrate that by the late 1590s, the direction of influence between Shakespeare and the Admiral's Men had unquestionably become two-way, with plays such as William Haughton's *Englishmen for My Money* and Henry Porter's *The Two Angry Women of Abington* incorporating pieces of dialogue and stage business that allude to *Romeo and Juliet* and *The Merchant of Venice* (amongst others). I discuss these plays alongside *The Merry Wives of Windsor*, which shares their English setting, non-aristocratic milieu and interest in women's free choice in marriage, and which, like them, has affinities with the 'humours' comedy inaugurated by Chapman in 1597 with *An Humorous Day's Mirth*. Furthermore, I use the points of contact between all four plays as a means towards highlighting any differences between the ways in which Shakespeare and Admiral's Men dramatists treated comparable materials that might point to an identifiable company style or outlook. Along similar lines, my final chapter considers whether the Admiral's Men repertory articulates a consistent religious position, a topic I explore by examining plays about two controversial figures: *Sir John Oldcastle*, whose protagonist is a Lollard martyr, and Anthony Munday and Henry Chettle's *Robert, Earl of Huntingdon* plays, which feature the folk-hero Robin Hood. I also examine the relationship between these plays and Shakespeare's *Henry IV*, whose Falstaff was originally named Oldcastle, as well as his *As You Like It*, whose depiction of forest exile openly alludes to the Robin Hood story.

Before my discussions of individual plays, however, the remainder of this Introduction prepares the ground by setting out in more detail the scholarly controversy on a question that is of crucial importance to the book as a whole: the extent to which different playing companies possessed distinctive corporate identities, and the factors that may or may not have produced these, including patronage, audience membership and business practices. Any study that sets out to identify patterns of influence across theatrical repertories is, to some extent, presupposing the coherence of those repertories as bodies of work. Accordingly, the paragraphs that follow survey the existing debate on this topic, which informs my readings of the Admiral's Men's repertory, and of Shakespeare's plays, over the chapters that follow.

Corporate Identity and 'House Style'

In their preface to *The Queen's Men and Their Plays*, McMillin and MacLean articulate an assumption that is basic to much repertory-oriented criticism. They argue that in the wake of Andrew Gurr's *The Shakespearian Playing Companies* (1996), which offers separate histories for the major companies of the period, 'Each company of note now needs to be studied in detail and with an eye for its own special characteristics', and they explain that for the Queen's Men these include 'its acting style, its staging methods, its kinds of versification, its sense of what constituted a worthwhile repertory of plays'.[28] This agenda is based upon a principle that they take to be axiomatic: 'organizations within a profession always develop identities of their own, widely recognized features which stand out from the procedures they share with the other organizations'. In the main part of their book, the authors identify some of the distinctive qualities of the Queen's Men, including the primacy of touring in their business model, the extent to which they were favoured by court, their plays' claim to be

---

[28] McMillin and MacLean, p. xii. See also Andrew Gurr, *The Shakespearian Playing Companies* (Oxford: Clarendon Press, 1996).

telling a true, Protestant-inflected history of England and the greater importance accorded visual motifs in their plays (as opposed to poetic subtlety) in comparison with the work of Shakespeare or Marlowe.[29]

This assumption has proved an extremely enabling one, for reasons that have already been noted in this introduction. By shifting the focus from the dramatist to the playing company, it arguably reflects the priorities of early modern theatrical culture, which did not privilege playwrights over players as modern criticism often has. It opens up space for the discussion of practices that originated as much, or more, in the company as in the playwright, such as acting style, staging and repertory management. And by linking the content of that repertory both to paying audiences and to noble patrons, it offers a means of locating dramatic production in relation to the wider social and political currents of early modern England. The specific notion that each major company had its own 'special characteristics', however, is not beyond dispute. In her contribution to the later collection on the Queen's Men edited by Ostovich, Syme and Griffin, Knutson raises questions about the usefulness of the concept of 'house style', particularly when it comes to assigning plays of unknown auspices to one or another repertory: 'How do I differentiate those plays in the immediate family of the Queen's Men from those that are second and third cousins because of that company's influence? And . . . how much of a house style is the result of the dramatists' sense of identity rather than that of the company?' Knutson proceeds to show how qualities McMillin and MacLean take to be characteristic of the Queen's Men 'are present in non-Queen's Men plays of the 1580s'; that being the case, 'how is it possible to put any weight on these characteristics as signs of a play owned by the Queen's Men?'[30] While not dismissing the notion of house style altogether, Knutson does suggest that it carries a risk of circularity: if we go looking for characteristics of different acting companies in their extant works, there is a high chance that we will find them. Perhaps the appropriate lesson to draw from this is that the student of dramatic repertories needs to combine an alertness to their possible distinctive qualities with an awareness that such qualities may be a mirage created by the topography of the discipline itself.

A graphic example of the potential for circularity to afflict the discussion of early modern acting companies, one of particular relevance to the

[29] McMillin and MacLean, pp. xiii, 6, 17, 33, 123.
[30] Roslyn Lander Knutson, 'The Start of Something Big', in *Locating the Queen's Men*, pp. 99–108 (pp. 99–100, 102).

Admiral's Men, is represented by the so-called diary (more properly an account book) kept by the theatre owner and manager Philip Henslowe and preserved in the archives of Dulwich College (founded by his son-in-law, the actor Edward Alleyn). This is the single most important surviving document concerning the day-to-day operations of the London theatre of Shakespeare's time, including details of play receipts, payments on behalf of the Admiral's Men and other companies to playwrights and to the Master of the Revels, and transactions relating to the construction of new theatre buildings and the acquisition of props, to give but a few examples. Thanks to Henslowe's diary, we are aware of dozens of early modern plays otherwise lost to posterity. However, the unambiguously financial priorities of this document have been hard to stomach for those wishing to maintain a more idealised image of the early modern drama.[31] The late Victorian commentator F. G. Fleay, shortly after describing the manuscript as 'the most valuable relic of all that we possess concerning the Elizabethan stage', went on to insist that its value 'lies not, as I have seen it asserted, in its showing us what the inner arrangement of Shakespeare's company must also have been, but in setting before us the selfish hand-to-mouth policy on which its principal rivals were guided'. He argued that the diary shows how Henslowe kept 'his actors in subservience and his poets in constant need by one simple method, viz., by lending them money and never allowing their debts to be fully paid off'; by contrast, the policy of the Lord Chamberlain's Men

> was the exact opposite to that of their rivals. Managed by the housekeepers or principal sharers, whose interest was that of the whole company, and not by an independent employer whose object was to fill his own pocket, they sought to produce plays of lasting interest, which would bear revival and be a perennial source of income. They employed few poets, and paid them well.[32]

Fleay's argument links company organisation, repertorial practices and quality of output. Henslowe's diary shows him making money from gate receipts at the theatres he owned and through advancing money to actors and playwrights alike. Shakespeare's company, it is presumed, being less dependent on external capital, were motivated by higher aesthetic values,

---

[31] For more substantial histories of critical response to Henslowe, see the Introduction to *Henslowe's Diary*, ed. by R. A. Foakes [and R. T. Rickert], 2nd edn (Cambridge: Cambridge University Press, 2002), pp. xxviii–xliv; Carol Chillington Rutter, *Documents of the Rose Playhouse* (Manchester: Manchester University Press, 1984), pp. 1–5; and Roslyn Lander Knutson, *Repertory of Shakespeare's Company*, pp. 15–20.
[32] Frederick Gard Fleay, *A Chronicle History of the London Stage 1559–1642* (London: Reeves & Turner, 1890), pp. 95, 117–18.

and consequently focused on quality rather than quantity in their production of plays. Fleay's remarks were quoted at length, and with substantial agreement, by W. W. Greg in his important 1904–8 edition of Henslowe, while in *The Elizabethan Stage* E. K. Chambers, although wary of making statements about the quality of the Admiral's repertory, commented on 'the disadvantages under which a company in the hands of a capitalist lay, in respect of independence and economic stability'.[33]

As Bernard Beckerman pointed out in 1962, however, there is simply no evidence beyond 'an idolatrous love of Shakespeare' to support the argument that 'Shakespeare's plays were of such popularity that they could be repeated again and again while other companies had to change their bills daily'.[34] The fact that no other theatre owners or company managers left an equivalent to Henslowe's diary that survived the passage of time cannot allow us to assume that they were actuated by different motives; as R. A. Foakes and R. T. Rickert reasonably conclude in the Introduction to their own edition of the diary, 'the evidence suggests that they were all capitalists'.[35] Furthermore, the difference in financial organisation by which Fleay, Greg and Chambers appear to set such store – the measure of independence the Lord Chamberlain's Men enjoyed as a result of actors owning their own playhouse – was not a reality until 1599, when Cuthbert and Richard Burbage had to resort to share capital to finance the building of the Globe.[36] The view of the Admiral's Men as profoundly dissimilar to the Lord Chamberlain's in their commercial habits and outlook is based largely on lack of unambiguous documentary evidence to the contrary, and some wishful thinking.

The currently accepted wisdom is that the practices of the Admiral's Men in regularly acquiring new plays and reviving successful old ones, rotating these plays while keeping them in production for a number of months, and duplicating their own successes as well as those of other companies, were typical rather than exceptional, not least because of the commonsense assumption that an outfit that did not operate in this way could not have survived in a competitive market.[37] However, just because the Admiral's Men and the Lord Chamberlain's Men followed comparable business practices, it does not follow that their plays must have resembled each other in style or content. Here we encounter a problem already

---

[33] Walter W. Greg, *Henslowe's Diary*, 2 vols (London: A. H. Bullen, 1904–8), vol. II, p. 112; E. K. Chambers, *The Elizabethan Stage*, 4 vols (Oxford: Clarendon Press, 1923), vol. I, p. 368.
[34] Bernard Beckerman, *Shakespeare at the Globe 1599–1609* (New York: Macmillan, 1962), p. 14.
[35] *Henslowe's Diary*, p. xxxvii.   [36] *English Professional Theatre*, p. 493.
[37] Knutson, *Repertory of Shakespeare's Company*, pp. 15–55.

mentioned in this introduction: the fact that most of the extant plays from the Lord Chamberlain's 1590s repertory are by Shakespeare, while the surviving Admiral's plays, and those referred to by Henslowe, are by a range of authors writing in a wide variety of genres and styles. A natural assumption is that Shakespeare's plays do not illustrate the full repertorial range of his company, and that just as the Admiral's staged plays on, for example, biblical themes, so would the Chamberlain's have done in order to capitalise on their evident appeal to playgoers.[38] Nevertheless, in the absence of definitive evidence, it is impossible to be entirely sure about this. Furthermore, while Knutson has argued that commercial pressures encouraged companies 'to have dramatists duplicate the successes in other companies' repertories, both in subject matter and form', other critics have identified factors that may have given a distinctive flavour to plays in the Admiral's repertory.[39]

One question that has attracted some critical attention is that of whether the Admiral's Men collectively held a specific political allegiance that was reflected in their drama, perhaps as a result of their patronage by Charles Howard (1536–1624), second Baron Howard of Effingham and, from 1585, Lord Admiral of England. This argument was made in *The Real War of the Theaters* (1935) by Robert Boies Sharpe, who identified Howard as a supporter of William Cecil's party at Court and a militant Protestant and anti-Catholic (as suggested by his support for the execution of Mary, Queen of Scots), and Lord Chamberlain Henry Carey as more tolerant, 'looked on by the Queen as a suitable representative of the milder Catholic sympathisers and influencer of the more dangerous ones'. Not only are Sharpe's accounts of alliances at Court somewhat over-simplified, however; he assumes a level of animosity between the Chamberlain's and the Admiral's Men, stemming from a 'bitter personal enmity between the Burbadges and the Alleyns and their violent quarrel at the Theatre in 1591', that is no longer generally accepted.[40] Furthermore, his readings of the plays themselves are not always convincing or consistent: for example, his statement that the Admiral's history plays 'seem to have been of the romantic and legendary type in their dealing with English history' while the Chamberlain's 'had a remarkable repertory of patriotic, warlike English history plays, calculated by their martial and dynastic characteristics to delight their courtly audiences, in which the war party headed by Essex

---

[38] Knutson, *Repertory of Shakespeare's Company*, p. 66.   [39] Ibid., p. 7.
[40] Sharpe, pp. 11–12, 5; Knutson, *Playing Companies and Commerce*, pp. 1–20.

was strongly represented' sits oddly with his presentation of Howard as Protestant hawk, as well as reading Shakespeare's histories as more patriotic than some later critics have been inclined see them. Finally, he makes comments about the two companies' audiences that seem to rest on assumptions for which no evidence is offered: he writes of playgoers at the Rose, 'various hints and deductions suggest that they were a somberer, more dowdy, more citizen-like lot than gave tone and color to the assemblage at the Theatre or the Cross Keys', but does not identify the hints and deductions in question.[41]

Problematic as Sharpe's arguments may be, a more nuanced case can be made for the political influence of patrons on company repertories. In his study *Theatre and Reformation*, Paul Whitfield White emphasises the way Protestant statesmen used the theatre as a means of spreading Reformation doctrine and anti-Catholic satire. The classic example is Thomas Cromwell's support during the 1530s for the former Carmelite friar and future Bishop of Ossory John Bale, who both wrote and acted in plays such as *King John* (which stresses the medieval monarch's conflicts with Rome and attributes his death to poisoning by a monk) and *Three Laws* (which personifies a range of vices in the form of Catholic clergy).[42] Although plays treating on 'matters of religion or of the governance of the estate of the Commonwealth' were ostensibly prohibited in 1559, 'Plays dealing explicitly with theological and ecclesiastical issues were printed or written for performance by professional troupes throughout the sixties and well into the seventies'.[43] White mentions *Mary Magdalene*, *The Tide Tarrieth No Man* and *New Custom*, and wonders whether such plays were performed by the companies belonging to individuals known to have supported Protestant 'preachers, pamphleteers and printers' such as the Duchess of Suffolk and the Earls of Warwick and of Leicester.[44] In their book on the Queen's Men, McMillin and MacLean identify similarly political considerations as lying behind the creation of that company, apparently at the behest of the Queen's Principal Secretary Sir Francis Walsingham, in March 1583: they hypothesise that in addition

---

[41] Sharpe, pp. 39, 19.
[42] White surmises that other Henrician and Edwardian companies such as the players of the Earl of Oxford (father of Spenser's dedicatee), the Duke of Somerset, the Lord Admiral Edward Clinton, and the Marquess of Dorset probably also staged Reformist drama. Edward VI's own players performed a lost interlude in 1549 that required a seven-headed dragon, and it is difficult to see how this could have been anything other than a play critical of Rome. Paul Whitfield White, *Theatre and Reformation: Protestantism, Patronage, and Playing in Tudor England* (Cambridge: Cambridge University Press, 1993), pp. 43, 58, 49.
[43] *English Professional Theatre*, p. 51; White, p. 59.   [44] White, p. 62.

to supplying the court with a cheap and reliable form of entertainment, the Queen's Men were supposed to serve as an embodiment of court-based national culture while on tour, carrying 'royal influence throughout the realm' and staging plays that articulated a Tudor Protestant ideology.[45]

One reason why the arguments of McMillin and MacLean are relevant to this study is because Charles Howard may himself have been involved in the formation of the Queen's Men. As Andrew Gurr points out, in March 1583 Thomas Radcliffe, third Earl of Sussex, who as Lord Chamberlain might have been expected to take a leading role in decisions relating to the provision of court entertainment, was terminally ill, and he would die in June. Howard had experience in the role of Lord Chamberlain, having deputised for Sussex during an earlier illness in 1574–5, and would be formally appointed to it ten months later.[46] He also had a family connection to the man given a royal warrant 'To choose out a company of players for her majesty', Master of the Revels Edmund Tilney: they shared a grandmother, Agnes Tilney, the second wife of the second Duke of Norfolk.[47] Howard may already have been on good terms with Walsingham by this time: his biographer Robert Kenny quotes frequently from their correspondence, and in a letter to the Earl of Leicester of 1585 Walsingham would write that Howard had 'always showed himself forward to further all good causes' and deserved to deputise as Justice in Eyre during Leicester's absence in the Low Countries.[48] He was thus well positioned to influence the creation of the new company, and apparently sympathetic to the Protestant-nationalist position that McMillin and MacLean associate with the Queen's Men. As Lord Chamberlain, Howard seems to have protected them, objecting in 1584 (along with Vice-Chamberlain Sir Christopher Hatton) to an attempt at the 'suppressing and pulling down of the Theatre and Curtain' playhouses, apparently the current venues of the Queen's and the Earl of Arundel's Men.[49] All of this invites the question of whether Howard's patronage of his own group of players was conducted with a similarly political aim in mind, a question that will be addressed in the discussion of *Sir John Oldcastle* and other plays in Chapter 5.

---

[45] McMillin and MacLean, pp. 13, 26–7.

[46] James McDermott, 'Howard, Charles, second Baron Howard of Effingham and first earl of Nottingham (1536–1624)', in *Oxford Dictionary of National Biography* (Oxford: Oxford University Press, 2004); online edn, January 2008 www.oxforddnb.com/view/article/13885 (accessed 29 July 2015).

[47] Gurr, *Shakespearian Playing Companies*, p. 198; Robert W. Kenny, *Elizabeth's Admiral: The Political Career of Charles Howard Earl of Nottingham 1536–1624* (Baltimore: Johns Hopkins Press, 1970), p. 4. For the text of the warrant, see *English Professional Theatre*, p. 208.

[48] Kenny, p. 98. [49] *English Professional Theatre*, p. 346.

It is questionable, though, whether any coherent political or religious sympathies in the repertory of the Admiral's Men would primarily reflect the agenda of Charles Howard himself. As John Cocke later wrote in his Theophrastian 'character' of 'A common Player' in 1615 (by which time the London companies had members of the royal family as their patrons), 'howsoeuer hee pretends to haue a royall Master or Mistresse, his wages and dependance proue him to be the seruant of the people'.[50] Cocke's words suggest that playing companies' output would have been influenced more by their assumptions about what would appeal to playgoers day in, day out far more than by the behests of Privy Councillors. This raises the question of whether demographic variations between the audiences of different companies might have led to differences between the types of play they staged. In contrast to Sharpe's division between the 'citizen-like lot' at the Rose and the 'tone and color' in evidence at the Theatre, more recent commentators have tended to argue for similarity and overlap, at least during the 1590s. Alfred Harbage noted in 1952 that 'Although the plays other than Shakespeare's surviving from the Chamberlain's repertory are few, yet *Alarum for London, Warning for Fair Women, Thomas Lord Cromwell* and *The Merry Devil of Edmonton* are precisely of the kind and quality of those represented by the Admiral's Men', implying that the two companies attracted similar audiences with similar tastes, while Michael Hattaway's study *Elizabethan Popular Theatre* is less interested in the differences between the companies that staged the plays he discusses in detail (*The Spanish Tragedy, Mucedorus, Edward II, Doctor Faustus* and *Titus Andronicus*) than in their shared status as 'popular drama' in contrast to the plays of the children's companies, for example.[51] Andrew Gurr, too, writes that in a theatrical environment dominated by two playing companies, 'regular attendance by the same people at the suburban playhouses where the two companies performed was inevitable'.[52] However, the revival of companies of child actors at the end of the decade in expensive, indoor theatres at St Paul's and the Blackfriars, staging plays that claimed to be aimed at the social elite, has been seen by some as having implications for the social allegiances of adult companies too.[53]

[50] John Stephens, *Essayes and Characters: Ironicall, and Instructive* (London, 1615; STC: 23250), pp. 296–7.
[51] Harbage, p. 88; Michael Hattaway, *Elizabethan Popular Theatre: Plays in Performance* (London: Routledge and Kegan Paul, 1982), p. 1.
[52] Gurr, *Shakespeare's Opposites*, p. 33.
[53] Tom Rutter, *Work and Play on the Shakespearean Stage* (Cambridge: Cambridge University Press, 2008), pp. 99–106.

Brian Gibbons argues that 'progressively after 1600 many of the plays performed by the King's Men at the Globe shared the satiric and intellectually questioning mood' of child company plays, aligning him with Harbage's position that of the adult companies, Shakespeare's was 'most interested in absorbing the Blackfriars clientele'.[54] This may well be a correct interpretation, but it has to rely on evidence drawn from the plays themselves rather than from external sources: it is not until at least the mid-1610s that we see the Fortune and the Red Bull (home of Queen Anne's Men) being associated with rusticity, spectacle and non-gentle audiences including '*Apple-wives* and Chimney-boyes'.[55] The question for theatre historians is when to date the beginnings of this split between the Chamberlain's and the other adult companies. In *Playgoing in Shakespeare's London*, Gurr finds Admiral's Men plays around the turn of the century expressing attitudes towards marriage, as well as a Protestant view of England's history and destiny, that he associates with citizen audiences, and distinguishes them from the views implied by plays in the Chamberlain's repertory; however, this view appears to have been modified in his more recent book on the Admiral's Men.[56] Less guardedly, Richard Helgerson distinguishes Shakespeare's history plays, which he sees as 'concerned above all with the consolidation and maintenance of royal power', from the histories staged by the Admiral's Men, which 'give their attention to the victims of such power'. Helgerson could be accused here of eliding the difference between individual playwrights and their respective companies: he writes of 'the Henslowe history plays' rather than those of Munday, Chettle, Dekker or any other playwright, and of the efforts of 'Shakespeare and his company' 'to exclude and to alienate the popular, the socially marginal, the subversive, and the folk', even though he does not refer to any histories by other Lord Chamberlain's dramatists (including the anonymous *Thomas Lord Cromwell*, which would appear closer to the position he ascribes to the Admiral's dramatists). One event to which Helgerson refers, though – James Burbage's

---

[54] Brian Gibbons, *Jacobean City Comedy*, 2nd edn (London: Methuen, 1980), p. 14; Harbage, p. 89. See also Andrew Gurr, *Playgoing*, 2nd edn, pp. 151–69, although Gurr is more cautious in proposing this view in *Shakespeare Company*, pp. 137.

[55] John Tatham, *The Fancies Theater* (London, 1640; STC: 23704), sig. H2v. Gurr also quotes Thomas Tomkis's Cambridge play *Albumazar* (1615), where a rustic character refers to 'the Plaies I see at the Fortune and the Red Bull, where I learne all the words I speake and understand not', and John Melton's description in *Astrologaster* (1620) of *Doctor Faustus* at the Fortune, where 'a man may behold shagge-hary'd Devills runne roaring over the Stage with Squibs in their mouthes, while Drummers make Thunder in the Tyring-house, and the twelvepenny Hirelings make artificial Lightning in their Heavens'. See Gurr, *Playgoing*, pp. 179, 238, 243, 259–60.

[56] Gurr, *Playgoing*, pp. 153–6; *Shakespeare's Opposites*, pp. 180–1.

purchase in 1596 of property in the Blackfriars with the intention of opening
a playhouse there – may be read as indicating a long-term intention to take
the Lord Chamberlain's Men upmarket by giving them access to a small,
indoor theatre, although this aim was not realised until about 1610.[57] Nevertheless, even after this date the company continued to perform at the Globe,
and rebuilt it after it burned down in 1613, suggesting that it was not only the
Henslowe companies that remained committed to performing before socially
diverse audiences.[58]

   Arguments about the social and political allegiances of different adult
companies, at least in the Elizabethan era, thus touch on individually
suggestive points while remaining unsettled overall. One point of difference
for which there is rather more evidence, however, relates to a dominant
figure in the Admiral's history, namely their star actor Edward Alleyn.
Alleyn – who performed with the Admiral's in the late 1580s, again between
1594 and 1597, and once again for a short period from 1600 – was closely
involved in the running of the Rose theatre with Henslowe (whose step-
daughter he married in 1592), and the two men jointly invested in the
building of the Fortune at the end of the decade. Thomas Nashe wrote in
1592 that 'Not *Roscius* nor *Aesope* ... could euer performe more in action,
than famous *Ned Allen*', and in his 1633 prologue to Marlowe's *The Jew
of Malta* Thomas Heywood would remember how 'in *Tamburlaine*, / This
Jew, with others many', he won 'The attribute of peerless'.[59] Alleyn's success
in charismatic roles such as these seems to have been aided by considerable
height, a powerful voice and a magnetic stage presence, judging by contemporary allusions: the epithet 'stalking' is frequently associated with Tamburlaine, and the satirist Everard Guilpin would describe a braggart in 1598 as an
imitator of another of Alleyn's roles, Cutlack the Dane:

> Clodius me thinks lookes passing big of late,
> With Dunstons browes, and Allens Cutlacks gate:
> What humours haue possest him so, I wonder,
> His eyes are lightning, and his words are thunder.[60]

---

[57] Richard Helgerson, *Forms of Nationhood: The Elizabethan Writing of England* (Chicago: University of Chicago Press, 1992), pp. 234, 139, 245, 226. On the date when the King's Men moved to the Blackfriars, see J. Leeds Barroll, 'Shakespeare and the Second Blackfriars Theatre', *Shakespeare Studies*, 33 (2005), 156–70.

[58] Andrew Gurr, 'Venues on the Verges: London's Theater Government between 1594 and 1614', *Shakespeare Quarterly*, 61 (2010), 468–89 (p. 479).

[59] Thomas Nashe, *Pierce Penilesse His Supplication to the Diuell* (London, 1592; STC: 18371), sig. H3v; Thomas Heywood, 'The Prologue to the Stage, at the Cockpit', in Christopher Marlowe, *The Jew of Malta*, ed. by N. W. Bawcutt (Manchester: Manchester University Press, 1978), p. 193.

[60] See Andrew Gurr, 'Who Strutted and Bellowed?', *Shakespeare Survey*, 16 (1963), 95–102 (p. 99).

As Susan Cerasano argues, not only is it the case that 'the Tamburlaine craze shaped Alleyn's artistic career'; 'Alleyn's continued presence within the Lord Admiral's Men molded the Rose repertory for almost a decade', encouraging the company to commission or acquire plays that would be well served by his particular gifts such as *Tamar Cham*, *Phaeton* and *Hercules*. Cerasano notes that while the mid-1590s repertory of the Admiral's Men 'included a broad range of kinds of plays ... , the performance schedule gave more space to tragedies, histories (of all kinds), and to heroic romances than it did to comedies'. Even after Alleyn's departure from the stage in 1597, the Admiral's were reviving plays in which he had originally played the lead roles, and of course they still possessed the associated props and costumes.[61] Alleyn's distinctive acting style, then, seems to have had a decisive influence on his company both during and after his career as an actor.

In 1601–2 Alleyn sold the Admiral's Men his playbooks for *Mahomet*, *The Wise Man of West Chester*, *Vortigern*, *The French Doctor*, *The Massacre at Paris*, *Crack Me This Nut*, *Philip of Spain*, *Longshanks* and *Tamar Cham*, facilitating these plays' ongoing performance, and this leads me on to one last factor that may have contributed to an Admiral's Men 'company style': the influence of plays already in their repertory upon audiences, actors and dramatists alike.[62] Gurr has emphasised the importance in this respect of Marlowe's plays in particular: although *The Massacre at Paris* and *The Jew of Malta* (at least) had previously been performed by other companies, once acquired by the Admiral's Men they, *Tamburlaine* and *Doctor Faustus* 'continued as the beating heart of the company's repertory' along with *The Spanish Tragedy*.[63] Holger Schott Syme has cast doubt on the financial centrality of these plays, pointing out that after 1594 the Admiral's made less money from them than from their new, non-Marlovian plays and that they were performed less and less frequently (and lucratively) as the decade went on.[64] Nevertheless, there are other types of importance than the financial, as Paul Menzer suggests when noting the willingness of the Admiral's Men to revive their Marlowe plays at the new Fortune. Such plays were by now part of their heritage, their 'corporate history'.[65]

---

[61] Susan Cerasano, 'Edward Alleyn, the New Model Actor, and the Rise of the Celebrity in the 1590s', *Medieval and Renaissance Drama in England*, 18 (2005), 47–58 (pp. 50–2).
[62] See *Henslowe's Diary*, pp. 180–1, 184, 187, 204–5, 217.   [63] Gurr, *Shakespeare's Opposites*, p. 171.
[64] Holger Schott Syme, 'The Meaning of Success: Stories of 1594 and Its Aftermath', *Shakespeare Quarterly*, 61 (2010), 490–525 (p. 500).
[65] Paul Menzer, 'Shades of Marlowe', *Marlowe Studies: An Annual*, 1 (2011), 181–92 (pp. 190–1).

Furthermore, the familiarity of such plays made them common ground for playgoers and playmakers, a fertile source of allusion and intertextuality. When the hero of the anonymous play *Captain Thomas Stukeley* (probably first performed by the Admiral's Men in 1596) boasts, 'Were it my fortune could exceed the clouds, / Yet would I bear a mind surmounting that' (5.118–9), the audience is surely expected to see him as a disciple of the same company's Tamburlaine, who asserted that Nature 'Doth teach us all to have aspiring minds'.[66] Several things, it might be suggested, may be going on here: the Admiral's Men, for whom *Tamburlaine* has been a long-lived success, have acquired another play with an aspirant hero in the Tamburlaine mould; a playwright or playwrights, anticipating the demand for such a play, has written one; Edward Alleyn, who has performed arrogant heroic roles to acclaim, is taking on another; the audience is (hopefully) enjoying seeing him do so, as well as appreciating a moment of intertextual shorthand that underscores the resemblance. All of these factors and more, it may be, combine to encourage the production of plays that partake in a distinctive 'house style'.

And yet, of course, the influence of *Tamburlaine* was not restricted to the Admiral's Men. In a play dating from perhaps a year or two later, *2 Henry IV*, Shakespeare has Pistol talk of 'hollow pampered jades of Asia', garbling a line from the second part of Marlowe's play.[67] It may be objected that something different is happening here from what we see in *Stukeley*: the aim is to make Pistol appear, not a heroic aspirant, but a histrionic braggart not unlike Guilpin's Clodius. Perhaps Shakespeare is even having a joke at Marlowe's expense: as Alexander Leggatt suggests, 'No one was writing plays like *Tamburlaine* any more, and you could raise a laugh by quoting it.'[68] Before writing off the allusion as parody, though, perhaps we should remember that *Henry IV* is, like *Tamburlaine*, a two-part history play; its young hero, moreover, will reappear in a heroic drama that critics have repeatedly likened to Marlowe's.[69] Shakespeare, then, would appear to be less structurally independent of Marlowe than his

[66] *The Stukeley Plays*, ed. by Charles Edelman (Manchester: Manchester University Press, 2005); Christopher Marlowe, *Tamburlaine the Great*, ed. by J. S. Cunningham (Manchester: Manchester University Press, 1981), Part I, 2.7.20.

[67] William Shakespeare, *The Second Part of King Henry IV*, ed. by Giorgio Melchiori (Cambridge: Cambridge University Press, 1989), 2.4.131; Marlowe, *Tamburlaine*, Part II, 4.3.1.

[68] Alexander Leggatt, 'The Companies and Actors', in *The Revels History of Drama in English*, vol. III: *1576–1613*, by J. Leeds Barroll, Alexander Leggatt, Richard Hosley and Alvin Kernan (London: Methuen, 1975), pp. 97–117 (p. 103).

[69] See Shapiro, *Rival Playwrights*, pp. 81–5, 97–101, 143–67; Sara Munson Deats, 'Mars or Gorgon? Tamburlaine and Henry V', *Marlowe Studies: An Annual*, 1 (2011), 99–124.

comic use of Pistol might suggest. Can we be so confident, for that matter, that the *Stukeley* dramatist is simply rehashing *Tamburlaine* and that he is not, like Shakespeare, using it to ironic effect at Stukeley's, and/or Marlowe's, expense? And can we be sure that it is only to Marlowe, and not to the *Stukeley* dramatist, that Shakespeare is responding?

Questions like these take us back to the problem of circularity identified earlier in this section: when making statements about company style and dramatic influence, it can be hard to avoid reproducing our own preconceptions about what the plays in a particular repertory ought to be like, and about who ought to be influencing whom. It is too much to hope that the chapters that follow can be wholly immune from this tendency. Nevertheless, in tracing the relationships between Shakespeare and the Admiral's Men I aim to offer interpretations that read plays in their company context without allowing that context to determine their meaning, and to recognise the reality of dramatic repertories while acknowledging that influence works between them as well as within them.

CHAPTER I

'How might we make a famous comedie'
From *A Knack to Know an Honest Man* to *The Merchant of Venice*

> In the name of god Amen begininge the 14 of
> maye 1594 by my lorde admeralls men
>
> Rd at the Jewe of malta 14 of maye 1594 . . . . xxxxviij s

Thus runs the first record of the Admiral's Men in Philip Henslowe's diary: a performance of *The Jew of Malta* for which Henslowe notes the receipt of 48 shillings. The performance presumably took place at the Rose theatre, where from 19 February 1591–2 onward Henslowe had recorded performances by a series of companies: Lord Strange's Men until 1 February 1593–4, other than a plague-induced hiatus from 23 June to 28 December 1592; then, after another gap due to plague, the Earl of Sussex's Men from 27 December 1593 to 6 February 1593–4; and finally, 'the Quenes men & my lord of Susexe to geather' from 1 to 8 April 1594.[1] The arrival of the Admiral's, however, marked the start of a residency at the Rose that would continue until they moved to the Fortune in 1600 – a long-term attachment that seems to have been an entirely new phenomenon in English theatre history. Even the Lord Chamberlain's Men, who along with the Admiral's enjoyed from this time until the end of the decade an unusual degree of official protection and favour, did not experience this level of stability, leaving the Theatre in 1598 after their dispute with Giles Allen over the lease. The Admiral's performance of *The Jew of Malta* on 14 May 1594 therefore seems to offer a logical starting point for this book.

In some respects, though, 1594 is less of a new beginning than it might at first appear. For one thing, its watershed status has been questioned by Roslyn Knutson, who identifies and disputes a prevailing view of it as the year in which 'theatrical commerce moved out of turmoil into the calm and stability of a politically controlled marketplace' under the direction

---

[1] Philip Henslowe, *Henslowe's Diary*, ed. by R. A. Foakes [and R. T. Rickert], 2nd edn (Cambridge: Cambridge University Press, 2002), pp. 16–21.

24

of aristocratic patrons like Charles Howard.² For another, the Admiral's Men unquestionably had a history prior to their tenure at the Rose: a playing company under Howard's patronage had performed a lost play called *Tooley* at court on 27 December 1576, and another called *The Solitary Knight* on 17 February 1577, before going on to tour the eastern counties of England.³ More recently, they had acquired the services of the dramatist Christopher Marlowe, whose *Tamburlaine the Great* was credited to the Admiral's Men when it appeared in print in 1590, and of the actor who by 1592 was eminent enough to inspire Thomas Nashe's comparison of him to Roscius and Aesop, Edward Alleyn (see Introduction).⁴ Admittedly, by the time Nashe wrote his encomium Alleyn himself seems to have been performing with the servants of Ferdinando Stanley, Lord Strange; the remainder of the Admiral's Men apparently left London, with companies of that name touring England and the continent. Nevertheless, the outfit that appears in Henslowe's records on 14 May 1594 did have some members in common with the earlier Admiral's (the returning Alleyn, Richard Jones, James Tunstall), and thus represented continuity as well as novelty in respect of its 1580s incarnation.⁵ Finally, the company's residence at the Rose was not uninterrupted: from 3 June to 13 June 1594, Henslowe records a series of performances by 'my Lorde Admerall men & my Lorde chamberlen men' in the playhouse at Newington Butts in the modern-day Elephant and Castle district to the south of the Rose (which was closed for reasons unknown). Given these various circumstances, 14 May 1594 cannot be seen as representing a straightforward break with the past either for the Admiral's Men or for the Elizabethan theatre in general.

Despite these caveats, however, there is a strong reason for choosing 1594 as a *terminus a quo* for this study. Because it marks the year when,

---

² Roslyn L. Knutson, 'What's So Special about 1594?', *Shakespeare Quarterly*, 61 (2010), 449–67 (pp. 449–50). In particular, Knutson takes issue with the hypothesis of Andrew Gurr that Lord Admiral Charles Howard and Lord Chamberlain Henry Carey in 1594 engineered a 'duopoly' whereby their companies would be given the same pre-eminent status that the Queen's Men had possessed from 1583. See Andrew Gurr, 'Three Reluctant Patrons and Early Shakespeare', *Shakespeare Quarterly*, 44 (1993), 159–74; *The Shakespearian Playing Companies* (Oxford: Clarendon Press, 1996), pp. 65–9; *The Shakespeare Company 1594–1642* (Cambridge: Cambridge University Press, 2004), pp. 1–10; 'Henry Carey's Peculiar Letter', *Shakespeare Quarterly*, 56 (2005), 51–75; *Shakespeare's Opposites: The Admiral's Company 1594–1625* (Cambridge: Cambridge University Press, 2009), pp. 1–19; 'Venues on the Verges: London's Theater Government between 1594 and 1614', *Shakespeare Quarterly*, 61 (2010), 468–89.
³ E. K. Chambers, *The Elizabethan Stage*, 4 vols. (Oxford: Clarendon Press, 1923), vol. II, p. 134–5.
⁴ Christopher Marlowe, *Tamburlaine the Great* (London, 1590; STC: 17425).
⁵ *Henslowe's Diary*, p. 21; Gurr, *Shakespearian Playing Companies*, pp. 234–7.

rejoined by Alleyn, the Admiral's Men started performing at the Rose theatre, it is the point at which – thanks to Henslowe's diary – we begin to have some sense of their day-to-day activities. It is also the approximate point from which Shakespeare can clearly be linked to a specific acting company, the Lord Chamberlain's Men. For the purposes of this book, then, it is the year from which it becomes practicable to trace a reciprocal relationship between Shakespeare as an actor-dramatist writing for the Lord Chamberlain's Men, and the evolving repertory of the Admiral's. The current chapter considers what seems to be the earliest extant new play staged by the Admiral's Men after the theatres reopened in 1594, *A Knack to Know an Honest Man*, and argues for its significance as an influence on Shakespeare's early work for the company to which he had recently moved.

*

Over the months that followed their brief period at Newington Butts, the Admiral's Men developed a repertory at the Rose that combined old plays that had previously been performed there by other companies (such as *The Jew of Malta*, *The Massacre at Paris* and *The Ranger's Comedy*), old plays that apparently belonged to the Admiral's already (*Mahomet*, *Tamburlaine* and *Doctor Faustus*) and new plays including *Galiaso*, *Philipo and Hippolito*, *The Second Part of Godfrey of Bouillon*, *The Merchant of Emden*, *Tasso's Melancholy*, *The Venetian Comedy*, *Palamon and Arcite* and *The Love of An English Lady*. The earliest new play to have survived, however, is 'a Knacke to Know a noneste' (printed in 1596 as *A Knack to Know an Honest Man*), first performed on 22 October 1594.[6] The play earned 40 shillings (£2) on its first performance, less than *Galiaso* (£3 4s.), *Philipo and Hippolito* (£3 2s.), *The Second Part of Godfrey of Bouillon* (£3 11s.), *The Merchant of Emden* (£3 8s.), *Tasso's Melancholy* (£3 4s.) and possibly *The Love of an English Lady*.[7] However, *A Knack to Know an Honest Man* (whose authorship is unknown) was to become highly lucrative for Henslowe and the Admiral's Men: Henslowe recorded receipts of 599 shillings over twenty-one performances, putting it fifth in the league table of 'Top-grossing productions in Henslowe's Diary' compiled by Holger Schott Syme.[8] Its publication two years after its first appearance may be taken as one gauge of its popularity; another is the entry in the

---

[6] *Henslowe's Diary*, pp. 22–5.
[7] Henslowe records 47s. 'Rd at venesyon & the love of & Ingleshelady', making it unclear how many plays' takings are being referred to.
[8] Holger Schott Syme, 'The Meaning of Success: Stories of 1594 and Its Aftermath', *Shakespeare Quarterly*, 61 (2010), 490–525 (p. 507). *A Knack to Know an Honest Man* comes behind 'The Wise

Stationers' Register by John Danter on 5 November 1594 for 'a ballad wherin is shewed a knacke how to knowe an honest man from a knaue', presumably designed to capitalise on the play's success.[9] No ballad seems to be extant, although the play does end with a rhyme about how 'to know a perfect honest man' (l. 1786), but a prose work (which does not resemble the play) appeared in 1596 entitled *The Triall of True Friendship or Perfit Mirror, Wherby to Discerne a Trustie Friend from a Flattering Parasite. Otherwise, A Knacke to Know a Knaue from an Honest Man.*[10] The play is apparently alluded to in Thomas Middleton and Thomas Dekker's *The Roaring Girl*, staged by the Admiral's successor company the Prince's Men in 1611, when Gallipot asks, exposing Laxton's amorous intrigues with Mistress Gallipot, 'I pray who playes a knacke to know an honest man in this company?'. Either the Prince's Men expected their audiences to remember the old play, or they may recently have revived it, much as the King's Men revived *Mucedorus* in 1610.[11]

Even if only because it is the earliest extant new play staged by the Admiral's Men after their move to the Rose, and because of its evident success in their repertory, *A Knack to Know an Honest Man* would merit study. As this chapter will argue, however, it was also a highly innovative offering that combined elements drawn from the earlier play *A Knack to Know a Knave* and from the first play the Admiral's performed at the Rose, Christopher Marlowe's *The Jew of Malta*, with a friendship theme derived ultimately from Cicero but more immediately from Richard Edwards's 1564 drama *Damon and Pythias*. After the next sections of this chapter, which survey the use of these materials by the anonymous dramatist or dramatists behind *A Knack to Know an Honest Man* (whom I will refer to for convenience as 'the *Knack* dramatist'), I will go on to argue that the blend that resulted discernibly affected the development of Shakespearean comedy in the mid 1590s, influencing *The Merchant of Venice* in details of location, theme and structure. My argument is intended to modify the dominant view of Shakespeare's sources for this play, which tends to focus

---

Man of West Chester', 'Seven Days of the Week', *The Blind Beggar of Alexandria*, and 'The Comedy of Humors', usually identified with *An Humorous Day's Mirth.*

[9] See *A Knack to Know an Honest Man*, ed. by H. De Vocht (Oxford: Malone Society, 1910), p. vi. Quotations from the play refer, by line, to this edition.

[10] M. B., *The Triall of True Friendship or Perfit Mirror, Wherby to Discerne a Trustie Friend from a Flattering Parasite* (London, 1596; STC: 1053).

[11] Thomas Middleton and Thomas Dekker, *The Roaring Girle* (London, 1611; STC: 17908), sig. I4v. The title page of the 1610 edition of *Mucedorus* advertises it as 'Amplified with new additions, as it was acted before the Kings Maiestie at White-hall on Shroue-sunday night': *A Most Pleasant Comedie of Mucedorus* (London, 1610; STC: 18232).

on non-dramatic materials (in particular Italian prose fiction) and on *The Jew of Malta*: although Marlowe's influence on *The Merchant of Venice* is not in doubt, the reshaping of Marlovian materials in *A Knack to Know an Honest Man* anticipates Shakespeare to a striking extent. Finally, I shall briefly suggest that an appreciation of *A Knack to Know an Honest Man*'s influence on Shakespeare brings into focus other ways in which *The Merchant of Venice* is informed by its non-Marlovian dramatic precursors, as well as significant ways in which Shakespeare chooses to depart from the pattern set by the earlier play.

A Knack to Know an Honest Man and the Commercial Theatre

Although *A Knack to Know an Honest Man* has gained a little critical attention recently in books by Tim Fitzpatrick, Peter Hyland and Kevin Quarmby, it remains relatively marginal to most discussions of 1590s drama; a plot summary may therefore be helpful.[12] The play is set in Venice and centres on the merchant Brisheo and his son-in-law Lelio, who kills his former friend Sempronio in a duel for attempting to seduce his wife. Brisheo helps Lelio, who has been condemned to death, abscond from Venice, but Sempronio's uncle and heir Servio succeeds in getting Brisheo banished and his goods confiscated. Over the course of the play, the dramatic focus shifts between a variety of points. We see Sempronio, who in fact is not dead but has been miraculously healed by a hermit and disguised as the semi-allegorical figure Penitent Experience, deliver a series of critiques of Venetian society. We see Servio's persecution of Lelio and Brisheo, less out of loyalty to Sempronio than out of the desire to obtain his enemies' estates. Following Brisheo's banishment, we observe the fortunes of his destitute sons, who are imprisoned for wounding

---

[12] Fitzpatrick discusses the creation of dramatic space through speech, and the use of stage doors: Tim Fitzpatrick, *Playwright, Space and Place in Early Modern Performance: Shakespeare and Company* (Farnham: Ashgate, 2011), pp. 98–100, 41, 156, 194. Hyland briefly mentions the apparent use of a wig as a means of disguise: Peter Hyland, *Disguise on the Early Modern English Stage* (Farnham: Ashgate, 2011), p. 48. Quarmby refers to the play as part of the context for Thomas Middleton's treatment of the disguised ruler trope in *The Phoenix*: Kevin A. Quarmby, *The Disguised Ruler in Shakespeare and His Contemporaries* (Farnham: Ashgate, 2012), p. 155. Less recently, G. K. Hunter describes the play as an example of the 'shift of morality form towards romantic adventure': G. K. Hunter, *English Drama 1586–1642: The Age of Shakespeare*, Oxford History of English Literature, vol. VI (Oxford: Clarendon Press, 1997), p. 369. Jeremy Lopez considers the play's use of disguise: Jeremy Lopez, *Theatrical Convention and Audience Response in Early Modern Drama* (Cambridge: Cambridge University Press, 2003), p. 127. In a 2006 article I relate the play's depiction of merchants to its Venetian location: Tom Rutter, 'Merchants of Venice in *A Knack to Know an Honest Man*', *Medieval and Renaissance Drama in England*, 19 (2006), 194–209.

the Duke's son when he attempts to rape Lelio's daughter (their niece) but set free by Servio's daughter Phillida, who is in love with one of them. Having left Venice, they force Lelio to return there for punishment so that Brisheo may be redeemed, thus incurring the wrath of their father, for whom the tie of friendship with Lelio outweighs his relationship with his family. The climax of the play is a series of trial scenes in which various characters ask to be executed in the place of others: Phillida in her father's place (for letting the prisoners go free), and then in turn Brisheo's sons, Brisheo himself, and Sempronio in the place of Lelio, until Sempronio is permitted by the hermit to reveal his true identity and all are pardoned.

A Knack to Know an Honest Man is sometimes referred to as a sequel to the earlier play *A Knack to Know a Knave*, which Henslowe records being performed by Lord Strange's Men seven times during June 1592 and December–January 1592–3 and which was printed in 1594.[13] This is only half-true, however: not only were the plays performed by different companies (the Admiral's never staged *Knave*), but there is no link between them in terms of plot or characters, so it makes more sense to see *A Knack to Know an Honest Man* as a play 'intentionally similar in title' to its predecessor for commercial reasons.[14] In marked contrast to the later play's modern Venetian setting, *A Knack to Know a Knave* is a kind of morality play-cum-estates satire set in tenth-century England during the reign (957–75) of King Edgar. In one of its main plots, the courtier Ethenwald falls in love with the woman he is meant to be wooing on Edgar's behalf; in the other, the character Honesty (as Alan Dessen points out, the role that most firmly 'connects the play with the morality tradition') exposes the crimes of a flattering courtier, a coneycatcher, a grasping farmer and a moneylending priest before sentencing them all to punishments of extravagant violence and sadism.[15]

Beneath the surface difference, however, there is a continuity of sorts. *A Knack to Know an Honest Man*'s debt to the morality idiom of the earlier play is evident in the character Sempronio, who as Penitent Experience vows to live in poverty in Venice as 'a cynike pure' (l. 315), promising that the tongue he misused in trying to seduce Annetta 'Shall labour to releeue the innocent' (l. 303). Much as Honesty exposes the coneycatcher for bearing false witness, and the courtier for receiving bribes, Sempronio's

---

[13] *Henslowe's Diary*, pp. 19–20. *A Knack to Know an Honest Man* is described as a sequel by Hunter, p. 368, and Quarmby, p. 155.

[14] Roslyn Lander Knutson, *The Repertory of Shakespeare's Company 1594–1613* (Fayetteville: University of Arkansas Press, 1991), p. 52.

[15] Alan C. Dessen, 'The "Estates" Morality Play', *Studies in Philology*, 62 (1965), 121–36 (p. 130).

disguise as Penitent Experience allows him to see that his uncle Servio is 'an arrant couetous knaue' (l. 555) pursuing Lelio out of avarice rather than family loyalty, and to observe the senator Marchetto's attempts to seduce Lelio's wife with the comment 'I, here's a knacke to know an arrant knaue' (l. 475). More encouragingly, when Sempronio sees Annetta refusing to give in to Marchetto's advances he notes, 'Here's first a knacke to know an honest Lady' (l. 456), and he approves Brisheo's willingness to die with his sons rather than Lelio alone being punished with the words 'Here is a knacke to know an honest man' (l. 1692).[16] The motif of an allegorically named character distinguishing knaves from honest men thus links the play to its predecessor. In a metadramatic twist, though, it is repeatedly stressed that Sempronio is not an allegorical type but a human individual pretending to be an allegorical type, as when the sight of Annetta and her daughter Lucida makes him enraged at the thought of his former crimes:

> SEMPRONIO Fie on Sempronio that was so vnkind.
> FORTUNIO Fond man, why does thou so torment thy selfe?
> SEMPRONIO I beate Sempronio for abusing thee,
>   Thou loose vnbridled man, the cause of harmes,
>   Pardon Annetta, pardon Lucida.
> LUCIDA What ailes this aged man he stormeth so?
> FORTUNIO Some lunasie surpriseth me I feare,
>   Art thou Sempronio?
> SEMPRONIO This is Annetta, that Lucida, thou Fortunio,
>   But I am not Sempronio, but penitent experience. (ll. 423–32)

While Honesty is never anything but Honesty, 'a plaine man of the country' with '*a Knacke to know a Knaue*' (ll. 79, 72), Penitent Experience/Sempronio works both as a stock morality figure and as a character in a realistically conceived urban environment: the fact that he 'Speakes in parables', as Fortunio notes, is cause for comment rather than an accepted convention (l. 394). At moments such as that quoted above, where the character is aware of himself both as Sempronio and as 'not Sempronio', his palpable unease in his new identity helps to create an illusion of psychological depth.

The simultaneous coexistence in *A Knack to Know an Honest Man* of two sets of conventions, one derived from the allegorical morality tradition and another that treats Sempronio as a named human individual, is one of the features that the play shares with *The Jew of Malta*, whose presence in the Admiral's repertory during the preceding months has already been

---

[16] The honest man/knave tags, or variants on them, also appear at lines 381, 584, 814, 1338, 1380 and 1782–1804.

noted. Various commentators have observed how Marlowe's play treats Barabas as a Vice-like figure (for example, in his revelation of his villainy to the audience in the first scene of the play) but also encourages us to view him in ways that are incompatible with this, whether as a 'sympathetic victim of Christian treachery' (as David Bevington puts it) or as an 'instrument of satire' (in Ruth Lunney's words) who reveals the moral inadequacy of the Christians around him.[17] *A Knack to Know an Honest Man* adopts a similar strategy, juxtaposing Sempronio's identity as a specific Venetian with his status as a type of the penitent sinner, although the conceit of the magically enforced disguise allows him to occupy the allegorical role within a dramatic logic that is generally realistic.

This sense of Sempronio as individual rather than, or as well as, type, is accentuated by another feature that *A Knack to Know an Honest Man* shares with Marlowe's play: its location within a specific and vividly conceived urban environment. *The Jew of Malta*'s setting is advertised from the title onwards, and in the opening scene Barabas's soliloquies and his dialogues with the merchants conjure up an image of Malta as a trading centre to which argosies from Alexandria come 'smoothly gliding down by Candy shore ... through our Mediterranean sea' (1.1.46–7).[18] Marlowe's Malta is enmeshed in sixteenth-century international politics, governed by the Knights of the Order of St John and buffeted by Spanish and Ottoman competition for control of the Mediterranean. We are repeatedly reminded that *A Knack to Know an Honest Man* is, similarly, set in a centre of Mediterranean trade: when we first meet the merchant Brisheo, he is sending his servant with 'the master of my barke to vnlode the wares' (l. 245), the same ship is used to engineer Lelio's escape (ll. 489–92, 508–14), and we see a merchant reading in a letter that 'Your merchandise are solde, and we haue sent / Bils of Exchange to receiue the monie' (ll. 824–5). Venice in this play is ruled by a Duke and Senators; we see part of 'the feastiuall of holy Marke' during which 'our Lordes of Venice wonted bee, / To sacrifice in triumph to the sea' (ll. 746–7) (although in fact the doge's symbolic marriage to the sea took place on Ascension Day). The two plays are set in comparable locations appropriate

---

[17] David M. Bevington, *From 'Mankind' to Marlowe: Growth of Structure in the Popular Drama of Tudor England* (Cambridge, MA: Harvard University Press, 1962), p. 223; Ruth Lunney, *Marlowe and the Popular Tradition: Innovation in the English Drama before 1595* (Manchester: Manchester University Press, 2002), p. 113.

[18] Christopher Marlowe, *The Jew of Malta*, ed. by N. W. Bawcutt (Manchester: Manchester University Press, 1978). Subsequent references are to this edition.

to their depiction of characters engaged in maritime trade, and in both cases the setting helps to particularise the action and characters.

Indeed, when one turns to the plays' action and characters the affinities between *A Knack to Know an Honest Man* and *The Jew of Malta* become considerably more striking. Servio, the villain of the later play, is a moneylender (ll. 241–3) whose persecution of Lelio and Brisheo is motivated both by vengeance and avarice: as he tells his disguised nephew, he has obtained through Sempronio's death 'annual rents two thousand pounds, / The worth in plate of twice so many more', and he confides, 'Ile tell thee, euerie daie throughout the yere, / Ile loose a kinsman to possesse so much' (ll. 531–2, 534–5). His daughter, however, falls in love with Brisheo's son Orphinio, and sets him and his brother free when they are in Servio's custody following the wounding of Fortunio. Just in case the audience has missed the parallel with Barabas, who says he has been a moneylender (2.3.192–200) and whose daughter Abigail is in love with his enemy, the Christian Don Mathias, the characters are given dialogue that echoes Marlowe's play. Servio's response to Phillida's letting Orphinio and Zepherius escape is to banish her with the words 'Packe thou to hell thou wretch, come not in my sight, / But get thee gone' (ll. 1178–9), combining two lines from Barabas's mock-banishment of Abigail when she pretends to have become a nun, 'Away, accursèd, from thy father's sight' (1.2.349) and 'No, come not at me! If thou wilt be damned, / Forget me, see me not, and so be gone' (360–1). The same scene is quoted when Phillida, offering her own life in exchange for Servio's as punishment for the prisoners' escape, describes herself as 'The hapless daughter, of this haplesse man' (l. 1316); Abigail tells the Abbess she is 'The hopeless daughter of a hapless Jew' (1.2.316).

The similarities of setting, character and plot between *A Knack to Know an Honest Man* and *The Jew of Malta* could be understood simply as an attempt to reproduce a highly successful formula: although Marlowe's play was not 'ne' when Strange's Men first performed it at the Rose on 26 February 1591–2, it remained a durable presence in the repertories of a series of companies, and was performed twenty times by the Admiral's Men between 14 May 1594 and 21 June 1596. (The later play's setting may also reflect a contemporary fashion for Venice as a dramatic location: *The Venetian Comedy* had been performed some half dozen times over the two months before *A Knack*'s premiere.)[19] The verbal similarity between Phillida's line and Abigail's, however, implies an element of pastiche or

---

[19] *Henslowe's Diary*, pp. 16, 21–7, 34, 36–7, 47. On 'ne', see pp. xxxiv–xxxv.

homage rather than simple imitation, and this self-consciousness may suggest one way of reading the play's opening, which depicts three shepherds discoursing in a field soon to be unexpectedly sullied with Sempronio's blood:

> CORIDON. Here walke Menalchus on this grassie plaine,
> And while the wanton lambes feed on these downes,
> And hide them in the thickets from the Sunne,
> That shine on Venus stately builded towers,
> Discourse to aged Antimon and me,
> The dolefull historie and that drierie tale,
> That earst befell in fatall Arcadie,
> How poore Amintas persht in his loue. (ll. 4–12)

It is not entirely clear where in relation to the 'stately builded towers' of Venice the 'grassie plaine' is located, but we are certainly somewhere within the conventions of pastoral poetry, given the reference to Arcadia and the shepherds' nomenclature. The role of the shepherds is simply to witness the duel, and they soon disappear from the play other than a brief reappearance by Antimon two scenes later to give garbled testimony about it to the Duke and two senators. In this opening scene, however, the idiom is not clownish, but very much that of Virgil's Fifth Eclogue, where Mopsus and Menalcas shelter in a cave and, while their kids feed, Mopsus sings his elegy for Daphnis. In Virgil, the name Amyntas appears as that of a rival poet, the only one, Menalcas says to Mopsus, who 'claims to sing as well as you' ('solus tibi certat Amyntas'); in the play, Amintas appears to have taken the role of Daphnis as the subject of Menalchus's lament.[20]

Perhaps too much should not be read into this brief episode: inviting one of their number to sing an elegy is the very thing that one would expect a stereotypical group of shepherds to be doing when included as a plot device within an Renaissance play. However, it may be significant that the premiere of *A Knack to Know an Honest Man* on Wednesday, 22 October 1594, appeared as the culmination of a very Marlovian week at the Rose: *Tamburlaine* the preceding Wednesday and Friday, *The Jew of Malta* on the Monday and *Doctor Faustus* on the Tuesday. (*Palamon and Arcite* – perhaps another play with a friendship theme, if it was based on Chaucer's 'Knight's Tale' – was played on Thursday and *The French Doctor* on Saturday; there was no play on Sunday.) The only moment in Henslowe where we see anything similar to this is around the first

---

[20] Virgil, *The Pastoral Poems*, tr. by E. V. Rieu (Harmondsworth: Penguin, 1954), pp. 60–1.

performance of the revived *2 Tamburlaine* on 19 December 1594, where a remarkable six out of a sequence of nine plays are by Marlowe.[21] This does not look coincidental, and one wonders both whether the scheduling of Marlowe plays in the lead-up to *A Knack to Know an Honest Man* reflected an awareness of the play's affinities with *The Jew of Malta* (in line with the repertorial practices identified by Roslyn Knutson) and, more specifically, whether the promised elegy to Amintas at the opening of the play was meant to be understood as a reference to the late playwright, who would be remembered as a 'dead shepherd' at the end of the decade in Shakespeare's *As You Like It*.[22]

Although this reading of the start of *A Knack to Know an Honest Man* is highly speculative, the play's setting in a Mediterranean trading nation and its 'usurer's daughter' plot are more tangible points of contact with *The Jew of Malta*. An important difference between the two plays, however, is the way *A Knack to Know an Honest Man* offers a set of positive values that are opposed to those of the greedy and vengeful Servio. A common critical observation on *The Jew of Malta* is that while Barabas's Jewishness might seem to give him outsider status in Malta, his cynical materialism in fact makes him the embodiment of the real priorities of the hypocritical society around him: his activity is 'at once alien and yet central to the life of the community', as Stephen Greenblatt puts it.[23] Christians in the play may profess superior values but tend to use them as a mask for *realpolitik* (like Fernese) or avarice and lust (like the friars). In *A Knack to Know an Honest Man*, however, while no religious difference demarcates the gentile Servio from those around him, he is clearly set up to be contrasted as an 'arrant couetous knaue' (l. 555) with the faithful friends Lelio and Brisheo. The ideal of friendship, indeed, and the literature associated with it, is a noticeable influence on *A Knack to Know an Honest Man* that distinguishes it profoundly both from *The Jew of Malta* and from *A Knack to Know a Knave*.

---

[21] *Henslowe's Diary*, pp. 25–6.

[22] William Shakespeare, *As You Like It*, ed. by Michael Hattaway (Cambridge: Cambridge University Press, 2009), 3.6.80. Knutson notes the company's tendency to premiere new plays with Marlovian associations alongside performances of the appropriate Marlowe plays: the three days before the first performance of the second part of *Hercules*, for example, saw stagings not only of part I but also of the two parts of *Tamburlaine*, another two-part play about an aggressively heroic figure. Roslyn L. Knutson, 'Marlowe Reruns: Repertorial Commerce and Marlowe's Plays in Revival', in *Marlowe's Empery: Expanding His Critical Contexts*, ed. by Sara Munson Deats and Robert A. Logan (Cranbury, NJ: Associated University Presses, 2002), pp. 25–42 (p. 35).

[23] Stephen J. Greenblatt, 'Marlowe, Marx, and Anti-Semitism', *Critical Inquiry*, 5 (1978), 291–307 (p. 292).

A Knack to Know an Honest Man and the Literature of Friendship

A number of critics have stressed the importance of classically derived notions of friendship in sixteenth-century humanist literary culture, the most important source of these being Cicero's *De amicitia*, whose first modern edition was published in 1481. As Tom MacFaul puts it, Cicero's ideas of friendship 'dominated Humanist thought and verse (and even drama) for most of the sixteenth century', and were popularised in texts such as Erasmus's *Adagia* (1525) and Thomas Elyot's *Boke of the Governour* (1531), which 'can be seen as the key text in the English Renaissance discovery of friendship'. MacFaul describes the model thus:

> a friend is a second self with whom one shares everything, friends are virtuous and similar to one another, and the friend is chosen after long and careful assessment of his virtues; the purpose of such friendship is the promotion of virtuous thought and action; it may contribute to the public sphere, but it is ultimately independent of it.[24]

Idealistic as this notion sounds, Lorna Hutson and Alan Stewart are among the critics who have stressed its practical usefulness to Humanist writers – for example, as a means of binding them in a shared mastery of persuasive rhetoric, or as offering a means of negotiating relationships with literary patrons without casting themselves in a pedagogic role.[25] Nevertheless, the centrality of Cicero to grammar school curricula in the sixteenth century gave the ideas of *De amicitia* an extremely wide currency, making them a natural point of reference for such dramatists as Ulpian Fulwell, who uses the text to illustrate the title of *Like Will to Like* (1568): 'Cicero in his book *de amicitia* these woords dooth expresse, / Saying nothing is more desirous then like is vnto like.'[26] Furthermore, stories of faithful friendship such as those of Titus and Gisippus (adapted by Elyot from Boccaccio) and Damon and Pythias (discussed by Cicero in *De officiis*) provided writers from John Lyly to Richard Edwards with narrative material from which to craft their own literary engagements with the theme.[27]

---

[24] Tom MacFaul, *Male Friendship in Shakespeare and his Contemporaries* (Cambridge: Cambridge University Press, 2007), pp. 9, 6.

[25] Lorna Hutson, *The Usurer's Daughter: Male Friendship and Fictions of Women in Seventeenth-Century England* (London: Routledge, 1994), p. 60; Alan Stewart, *Close Readers: Humanism and Sodomy in Early Modern England* (Princeton: Princeton University Press, 1997), pp. xxxi–xxxii.

[26] Ulpian Fulwell, *An Enterlude Intituled Like Wil to Like Quod the Deuel to the Colier* (London, 1568; STC: 11473), sig. A2r.

[27] On Titus and Gisippus, see Hutson, pp. 52–86; MacFaul, pp. 68–72, discusses Lyly's *Euphues* (1578) as a rewriting of this narrative.

Given the familiarity of *De amicitia* to those with a grammar school education, it is perfectly possible that the *Knack* dramatist knew Cicero's text directly. The alternative title of Cicero's dialogue, *Laelius de amicitia*, which reflects the fact that its principal speaker is Gaius Laelius, presumably gave the character Lelio his name. Furthermore, the rationale for counterpointing the moneylender Servio with the faithful friends Lelio and Brisheo may have been suggested by Cicero's words on the disinterested nature of true friendship:

> For as men of our class are generous and liberal, not for the purpose of demanding repayment – for we do not put our favours out at interest, but are by nature given to acts of kindness – so we believe that friendship is desirable, not because we are influenced by hope of gain, but because its entire profit is in the love itself.[28]

Not only is true friendship distanced from the idea of putting 'favours out at interest'; it is associated with the gentlemanly class, Servio's symbolic exclusion from which is implied by his name and its connotations of servility.

Notwithstanding these apparently direct allusions to Cicero, however, Ciceronian ideas about friendship also make their way into *A Knack to Know an Honest Man* via another source text: Richard Edwards's play *Damon and Pythias*, written for the Children of the Chapel Royal in 1564 for court performance, printed in 1571 and reprinted in 1582. The title characters of this play enjoy an ideal friendship that is conceived in terms clearly derived from Cicero: their shared servant Stephano thinks 'they have but one heart between them' (5.32), and 'all their whole doings do fall to this issue: / To have no respect but only to virtue' (5.23–4).[29] When they visit Syracuse 'As men that come to see the soil and manners of all men of every degree' (7.70), Damon is arrested for spying, on the word of the flattering parasite Carisophus, and condemned to death by the tyrant Dionysius. He is allowed back to Greece to settle his affairs on condition that Pythias stand as surety for him. When the appointed day arrives and Damon has not yet returned, Pythias greets with 'joy' (15.108) the prospect of being executed in his friend's stead, only for Damon to

---

[28] Marcus Tullius Cicero, *De senectute, De amicitia, De divinatione*, tr. by William Armistead Falconer (London: Heinemann; New York: Putnam's Sons, 1923), p. 143.

[29] *Damon and Pythias* in *The Works of Richard Edwards: Politics, Poetry and Performance in Sixteenth-Century England*, ed. by Ros King (Manchester: Manchester University Press, 2001). Subsequent references are to this edition. Stephano's lines recall Cicero's view that the 'friendship cannot exist except among good men' (p. 127) and that the virtuous man seeks out 'another whose soul he may so mingle with his own as almost to make one out of two' (p. 189).

turn up at the last moment and the two friends each to demand to die in place of the other. Amazed at the sight of this 'strange friendship' (15.200), Dionysius spares Damon and Pythias, renounces tyranny and vows, 'True friendship will I honour unto my life's end' (15.243).

There are obvious broad structural similarities between *Damon and Pythias* and *A Knack to Know an Honest Man*, in particular the way they both culminate in scenes involving two faithful friends each pleading to be executed in the other's place. The conversion of Dionysius is echoed in a scene midway through *A Knack to Know an Honest Man* where the exiled Lelio and Brisheo, fighting for opposing armies, refuse to participate in single combat and succeed in reconciling their generals through the sheer spectacle of their amity: 'Shall wee contend for tytles wretchedly, / While meaner men contend in perfect loue', 'Medesa Duke of Florence' asks 'Forsa Duke of Myllan' (ll. 953–4). Beyond this, though, there are a number of textual parallels between the two, including a repeated use by Edwards of the knave/honest man binary: it is said of a flattering courtier, 'such knaves in presence / We see oft times put honest men to silence' (1.121–2), and again of courtiers in general, 'In a troop of honest men, some knaves may stand you know, / Such as by stealth creep in under the colour of honesty, / Which sort, under that cloak, do all kind of villainy' (11.66–8). Comparison with *Damon and Pythias* also clarifies an otherwise mystifying episode in *A Knack to Know an Honest Man* where Sempronio/ Penitent Experience says of a senator who was aided by Brisheo in the past but who refuses to help his indigent sons,

> Ha ha ha, a worldling right, the poets song
> Was well applied in this,
> For like the antes they eate the gaine of mens wealth,
> But flye them lyke the fiends when they are falne,
> These Cicero and Aristotle tearm'd a troope of seruile
> Base dishonest men. (ll. 809–14)

There is no obvious source in Aristotle or Cicero for the image of ants who eat the gain of men's wealth, but it may be a very free translation of a line from Horace (*Epistles*, 1.2) as it appears in *Damon and Pythias* when the good courtier Eubulus speaks of 'the caterpillers of all courtes – "*et fruges consumere nati*"' (10.215). The phrase means something like 'and born to consume the fruits [of the earth]', but given the context in *Damon and Pythias* one can see how the later dramatist might have misconstrued it. Another oddity of *A Knack to Know an Honest Man* that makes more sense in the light of *Damon and Pythias* is Lelio's decision, when he returns to

Venice to redeem Brisheo, to adopt the disguise of a collier singing 'VVill you buy any Coles, fine small Coles' (l. 1383): the comic character Grim the Collier was evidently a memorable feature of Edwards's play, supplying the title to William Haughton's drama of *c.* 1600, *Grim the Collier of Croydon*, and still remembered by an Oxford don some eight decades later.[30]

A Knack to Know a Knave had explored the knave/honest man dichotomy in terms of social morality; *Damon and Pythias* showed the *Knack to Know an Honest Man* dramatist how it might also be explored in terms of friendship. Modern historians of humanist friendship literature highlight the anxiety it produced as to whether professions of friendship were sincere or mere empty rhetoric: of how to 'distinguish the false frankness from the true', as Hutson puts it.[31] This problem is, to some extent, anticipated by Cicero, who writes that 'We ought … to choose men who are firm, steadfast and constant, a class of which there is a great dearth; and at the same time it is very hard to come to a decision without a trial, while such a trial can only be made in actual friendship.'[32] Edwards explores the problem by contrasting to Damon and Pythias the courtiers Aristippus and Carisophus, whose friendship is expedient, insincere and temporary. Its fragility is exposed when Dionysius starts to suspect Carisophus of flattery and Aristippus refuses to vouch for him: 'To swear for your honesty, I should lose mine own' (14.19). When Carisophus objects that 'A friend ought to shun no pain to stand his friend in stead' (14.29), Aristippus explains that theirs was no true friendship because 'The chiefest link lacked thereof' (14.32), namely honesty: friendship is 'Between the honest only, for "*Amicitia inter bonos*", says a learnèd man' (i.e. Cicero) (14.38). The equivalents in *A Knack to Know an Honest Man* are Sempronio, once part of a pair of 'faithfull friends' (l. 39) but revealed as untrustworthy by his attempt to seduce his friend's wife, and the senators who owe favours to Brisheo but refuse to help his penniless sons, illustrating Cicero's dictum that fickle friends are revealed when 'they either hold a friend of little value when their own affairs are prosperous, or they abandon him when his are adverse'.[33] It is precisely in response to a friend's misfortune, by contrast, that the true nature of Brisheo's friendship for Lelio reveals itself: 'When is the time for friends to shew themselues, / But in extremitie' (ll. 281–2).

A major point of difference between the two plays, however, is that while *Damon and Pythias* is largely positive in its treatment of friendship,

---

[30] See *The Works of Richard Edwards*, p. 89.   [31] Hutson, p. 6.   [32] Cicero, p. 173.
[33] Cicero, p. 175.

opposing it to the morally compromised nature of life at court, *A Knack to Know an Honest Man* emphasises its potential to generate conflicts of interest. It achieves this by the simple expedient of giving its faithful friends wives and children – responsibilities with which Damon and Pythias are unencumbered. Accepting banishment as his punishment for helping Lelio escape, Brisheo makes it entirely clear that he regards his duty to his friend and son-in-law as more important than that to his children:

> First Lelio mongst our chiefest citizens,
> Made me his father, and his vowed friend:
> Next, to defend my daughter from defame.
> He ventured life, And shall a little pelfe,
> These two yong boyes, make me forget my friend,
> That ventured life and vertue for my sake?
> No, I loue my Lelio, do what fortune can. (ll. 577–83)

While Sempronio's comment 'Why here's a knacke to know an honest man' (l. 584) invites us to respond positively towards Brisheo's willingness to leave his family and his trust that his sons' 'diligence' (l. 598) will earn them a living, it is alarming to see his responsibilities as a father so casually dismissed. Another indication that Brisheo's priorities may be questionable comes when his sons, on the run after injuring Fortunio, try to make Lelio return to Venice in the hope that Brisheo's exile may be overturned. On discovering their project, Brisheo's response is to disown them:

> These are not Brishios sons, bids Lelio hence:
> These are not Brishios sonnes that draw their swords:
> Thou [i.e. Lelio] art my son, these two are fortunes slaues;
> Avant vaine boyes, come not in my sight,
> By heauen and heauens adorning sunne,
> These are no sonnes of mine that sinne so much. (ll. 1246–51)

The inconsistency of his position is reinforced by his referring to them as 'manslayers' (l. 1255), which skirts round the fact that it is Lelio's willingness to commit murder that has produced the situation they find themselves in. The play's position on the behaviour of Brisheo thus appears equivocal: it seems simultaneously to applaud his honesty amid a city stuffed with the venal, the vengeful and the hypocritical, and to suggest that the humanist ideal of friendship hits problems as soon as it makes the move from affectionate letters between classically educated men to a real world in which people have conflicting responsibilities. This problematising of friendship is of a different order to that which Jennifer Richards finds in *Damon and Pythias*, where the title characters' idealism is 'humorously undercut' by the practical wisdom of their servant Stephano.[34]

The provision of male characters with wives and children also allows for the climax of *A Knack to Know an Honest Man* to be worked out in accordance with the conventions of romantic comedy, in contrast with *Damon and Pythias*, which culminates in the morally edifying spectacles of Dionysius's conversion, Carisaphus's expulsion from court and the freeing of Stephano. Not only does Servio's daughter Phillida end up with Orphinio; the reintegration of the penitent Sempronio within the circle of friendship to Lelio and Brisheo is reinforced by bonds of matrimony, as the Duke observes 'how Lelio hand in hand / Ioynes Sempronio with his Lucida'. The dominant order Alan Stewart portrays humanist writers as rejecting – 'structured through male bonding, which perpetuated itself through the exchange of women in marriage' – is still very much evidence in this humanist-inspired play.[35]

It is impossible to reconstruct the exact nature of *A Knack to Know an Honest Man*'s evident appeal to theatregoers in the 1590s. However, the preceding sections have attempted to identify some of the ways in which the play reworked existing materials into a distinctive new format. From *A Knack to Know a Knave* it derived a title, a fictional project of going through society uncovering wrongdoers, and – at least in relation to one character, and to a partial extent – an allegorical approach to characterisation. However, drawing on *The Jew of Malta* it gave these characteristics a modern and exotic location, as well as a plot strand featuring a usurer and his daughter. Finally, against the immorality identified by Sempronio and practised by Servio it counterpoised Ciceronian values of faithful friendship exemplified in *Damon and Pythias*, a play with which it has numerous affinities. These enabled it to engineer a happy ending, in which the friends are saved and the usurer's daughter married, quite at odds with Marlowe's more sardonic conclusion. In the section that follows, I will make the further argument that this combination of materials was a significant influence upon Shakespeare's design of *The Merchant of Venice*, a play conventionally dated to 1596 and hence presumably written when the popularity of *A Knack to Know an Honest Man* was at its height.[36]

---

[34] Jennifer Richards, 'Male Friendship and Counsel in Richard Edwards' Damon and Pythias', in *The Oxford Handbook to Tudor Drama*, ed. by Thomas Betteridge and Greg Walker (Oxford: Oxford University Press, 2012), pp. 293–308 (pp. 303–5). McFaul (p. 95) also finds *Damon and Pythias* gently mocking the friendship ideal as well as upholding it.

[35] Stewart, p. xxiii.

[36] Salarino's reference in the opening scene to his ship, 'my wealthy Andrew', is usually taken as referring to a Spanish galleon captured by the Earl of Essex at Cadiz, although it is of course possible

The Merchant of Venice and *A Knack to Know an Honest Man*

In critical discussion of the sources of *The Merchant of Venice*, *A Knack to Know an Honest Man* has not been prominent. For one thing, commentators tend to place emphasis not on dramatic works, but on the prose narratives from which Shakespeare is understood to have derived his plot, including three collections in particular: Giovanni Fiorentino's *Il pecorone* (printed in Italian in 1558), the source of the main plot; Richard Robinson's translation of the *Gesta Romanorum* (1595), the source of the casket test; and *Il novellino* by Masuccio Salernitano (1575), from which Shakespeare takes the Jessica–Lorenzo subplot.[37] For another, when the attempt is made to locate Shakespeare's play in relation to the drama of its time, the example to be singled out is invariably Christopher Marlowe's *The Jew of Malta*; mention has sometimes been made of a lost play called *The Jew*, but lack of information about its contents has discouraged recent critics from identifying this as a source.[38]

The privileged status of *The Jew of Malta* as dramatic influence on *The Merchant of Venice* is hardly surprising. While, given the dissimilarity in plot between the two, M. M. Mahood is justified in saying that Marlowe's play 'is not, in the conventional sense, a source' of *The Merchant of Venice*, Shakespeare's treatment of Jewish characters in his play is undeniably informed – albeit not in any straightforward way – by Marlowe's highly successful drama, which by 21 June 1596 had been performed thirty-six times since February 1592.[39] As John Russell Brown notes, there are a number of 'Verbal parallels between the two plays', including such keywords as 'simplicity' and 'sufferance' in the idiolects of Shylock and Barabas.[40] Furthermore, there are similarities between particular episodes as noted by Mahood, such as the way both Shylock and Barabas argue that expropriation

---

that the line is a later interpolation. William Shakespeare, *The Merchant of Venice*, ed. by M. M. Mahood (Cambridge: Cambridge University Press, 2003), p. 1. References to the text of *The Merchant of Venice* use this edition.

[37] William Shakespeare, *The Merchant of Venice*, ed. by Jay L. Halio (Oxford: Clarendon Press, 1993), pp. 13–20; *Narrative and Dramatic Sources of Shakespeare*, vol. I: *Early Comedies, Poems, 'Romeo and Juliet'*, ed. by Geoffrey Bullough (London: Routledge and Kegan Paul; New York: Columbia University Press, 1957), pp. 445–514.

[38] See E. A. J. Honigmann, 'Shakespeare's "Lost Source-Plays"', *Modern Language Review*, 49 (1954), 293–307 (pp. 297–8); William Shakespeare, *The Merchant of Venice*, ed. by John Russell Brown (London: Methuen, 1955), pp. xxix–xxx.

[39] *The Merchant of Venice*, ed. Mahood, p. 8; *Henslowe's Diary*, pp. 16–26, 34, 36–7, 47.

[40] *The Merchant of Venice*, ed. Brown, p. xxxi. 'Simplicity' appears in *The Jew of Malta* at 1.2.162 and in *The Merchant of Venice* at 1.3.35; 'sufferance' in *The Jew of Malta* at 1.2.240 and in *The Merchant of Venice* at 3.1.55.

of goods is tantamount to killing, and the way Jessica's throwing down her father's jewels to Lorenzo recalls Abigail's throwing down of Barabas's lost treasure to him.[41] And in a more general sense, the argument can be made that Shakespeare was influenced by Marlowe's presentation of Barabas as 'a real person as well as a figure of horror', in Geoffrey Bullough's words, with 'a case against the Christians whose profession is "policy", "And not simplicity as they suggest"', and by whom he is ill-treated.[42] As Robert A. Logan puts it, from the first two acts of *The Jew of Malta* 'Shakespeare may have learned generally or reaffirmed his understanding of how possible it is to invest a stock character with individualizing human traits'.[43]

Even more cautious critics such as Jay L. Halio, who emphasises the differences between Barabas's 'comic villainy' and Shylock's status as 'the first stage Jew in English drama who is multi-dimensional and thus made to appear human', tend to agree that Marlowe influences Shakespeare in one important respect: through the character of Abigail, who 'may have first led Shakespeare to think of a daughter for Shylock'.[44] While the Jew in *Il pecorone* has no daughter, Shakespeare in *The Merchant of Venice* is able to achieve significant and complex dramatic effects through delineating Shylock's relationship with Jessica: his love for her, and her desertion of him, give him a vulnerability that elicits our compassion, even as they motivate the vengefulness that can tend to alienate us. Barabas's shift from love for his 'one sole daughter, whom I hold as dear / As Agamemnon did his Iphigen' (1.1.136–7), as he ominously puts it, to murderous hatred for 'her / That like a fiend hath left her father thus' (3.4.104–5) is clearly the precursor, as evidenced by Shakespeare's echoing of the line 'O my girl, / My gold, my fortune, my felicity' (2.1.47–8) in the words Solanio attributes to Shylock: 'My daughter! O my ducats! O my daughter!' (2.8.15). Marlowe's play can thus be seen as the stimulus for Shakespeare's decision to add the story of the Neapolitan miser and his daughter, as taken from *Il novellino*, to that of Ansaldo, his adopted son Gianetto, and the Jewish moneylender as taken from *Il pecorone*, as well as directly influencing specific points of language and characterisation.

However, as the previous sections of this chapter have shown, *The Merchant of Venice* was not, in fact, the first play of the 1590s to bring

---

[41] *The Merchant of Venice*, ed. Mahood, pp. 7–8.
[42] *Narrative and Dramatic Sources*, vol. I, pp. 454–6.
[43] Robert A. Logan, *Shakespeare's Marlowe: The Influence of Christopher Marlowe on Shakespeare's Artistry* (Aldershot: Ashgate, 2007), p. 129.
[44] *The Merchant of Venice*, ed. Halio, pp. 9, 19.

together a 'faithful friends' plot and a 'usurer's daughter' plot: *A Knack to Know an Honest Man*, itself a play palpably influenced by *The Jew of Malta*, had already done so. This does not, of course, make *A Knack to Know an Honest Man* a narrative source of *The Merchant of Venice* in the same way that *Il pecorone*, the *Gesta* and *Il novellino* are – or even a source in the way that *The Jew of Malta* is, given that the verbal parallels that can be identified between Shakespeare's play and Marlowe's are not in evidence in *A Knack*. However, as the following paragraphs will attempt to argue, the play does influence Shakespeare's in different ways: in terms of setting, denouement, idiom and theme; and above all, as an example of how Marlovian materials might be reshaped in a manner suited to the theatrical environment of the mid 1590s.

Arguably, the similarity of setting – Venice, in contrast to the Malta of Marlowe's play – is the least significant of these, since the tale from *Il pecorone* that is the direct source for *The Merchant of Venice* has the same location. It is noteworthy, however, that Shakespeare and the *Knack* dramatist use this setting in comparable ways, drawing on two aspects in particular of Venice's contemporary reputation. The first relates to its association with judicial impartiality. As David McPherson writes, the idea of 'Venice the Just' was one component of the 'Myth of Venice' that prevailed in other European countries during the early modern period: 'an aspect of *La Serenissima*'s political wisdom was said to be its extraordinarily impartial and severe justice'.[45] *The Merchant of Venice* repeatedly alludes to this notion in presenting the Duke as subservient to the rule of law: 'The Duke cannot deny the course of law', Antonio accepts at 3.3.26, and Shylock invokes 'your charter and your city's freedom' in insisting that he must have his bond (4.1.39; see also 3.2.276–8). Near the beginning of *A Knack to Know an Honest Man*, the First Senator responds to Servio's tearful plea for justice for Sempronio with a speech that makes specific claims for the city's impartiality:

> Our senators in Venice are well schoold in such haps,
> And can doome of things, not by thy teares,
> Or sorrow working wordes,
> But by the truth and estimate of acts. (ll. 162–5)

Both plays' interest in themes of justice and mercy gains point through their setting in this particular location (although Venice's claim to be a just

---

[45] David C. McPherson, *Shakespeare, Jonson, and the Myth of Venice* (Newark: University of Delaware Press; London: Associated University Presses, 1990), pp. 27–8.

republic is severely tested later on in *A Knack to Know an Honest Man* when the Duke unilaterally creates a new law to exempt his son from punishment for the attempted rape of Lucida (ll. 1374–8)).

Another aspect of Venice's contemporary reputation that is apparent in both plays is its status as a city built on trade, where – in contrast to English social theory, if not practice – the gentle class engaged in merchandise. As one of the speakers puts it in John Ferne's dialogue *The Blazon of Gentrie* (1586):

> Merchaundizinge, is no competent, or seemelye trade of lyfe, for a gentleman: Yet custome in some Countryes, and with some Nations, hath preuailed to the contrarye.
>
> For the Gentlemen of Venice . . . tradeth merchandize: yea, the degree of knighthood (saith *Pogius*) deemeth it best fitting their honors, to be Merchants, a most vile and base iudgement.[46]

Both plays capitalise on the lack of stigma attached to trade in Venice, depicting friendships between merchandising and non-merchandising gentlemen who are understood to be social equals. Brisheo may be first seen discussing financial dealings and ordering the unloading of his ship (ll. 235–47), but there is no incongruity in the fact that Lelio, one of 'our chiefest citizens' (l. 577), has married his daughter and calls him 'father' (for example at ll. 257, 935 and 1219). Similarly, in *The Merchant of Venice* an international merchant can have as his 'noble kinsman' (1.1.57) 'a soldier and a scholar' who has belonged to the entourage of the Marquis of Montferrat (1.2.93–4).

Such friendships have no equivalent in *The Jew of Malta*, and indeed, the second way I would identify in which the *Knack* dramatist anticipates Shakespeare is in adding a pair of friends who are set up in contrast to the self-interested figure of the usurer. Although this structural opposition is, admittedly, another feature of *The Merchant of Venice* that comes from its narrative source in *Il pecorone*, Shakespeare attributes to it a thematic significance very similar to that which it possesses in *A Knack to Know an Honest Man*. In the earlier play, the dialogue in which Servio reveals to the disguised Sempronio how he has gained materially from Sempronio's death seems designed to expose him as a false friend, a word that the speakers sardonically repeat:

---

[46] John Ferne, *The Blazon of Gentrie* (London, 1586; STC: 10825), pp. 72–3. For more examples of this aspect of Venice's reputation, see Rutter, 'Merchants of Venice'.

SEMPRONIO Soft gentle friend, a word or two with you,
  From whence proceed these troubles that arise?
SERVIO For yong Sempronios death, my honest friend . . .
  I haue annuall rents two thousand pounds,
  The worth in plate of twice so many more,
  A few such breakfasts friend, would make me rich . . .
SEMPRONIO Wipe out that water from thy eies my friend.
SERVIO VVhat ayleth me?
SEMPRONIO VVhy thou art blind and canst not see. (ll. 521–3, 530–2, 544–6)

Servio's hypocrisy in feigning righteous indignation at Sempronio's death makes his use of the vocabulary of friendship parodic, much as Shylock abuses the language of friendship (as McFaul notes) in offering to 'extend this friendship' (1.3.161) of the flesh-bond to Antonio:

> I would be friends with you, and have your love,
> Forget the shames that you have stained me with,
> Supply your present wants, and take no doit
> Of usance for my monies, and you'll not hear me. (1.3.131–4)[47]

Shylock's speech comes in response to Antonio's insistence that a usurer cannot, by definition, be a true friend: 'when did friendship take / A breed of barren metal of his friend?' (1.3.125–6). Their exchange emphasises the structural importance to the play of the opposition between disinterested friendship and the financially motivated lending of money at interest – even if Shylock's motivation is ultimately shown to be more than simply materialistic, in that he refuses multiples of the sum he lent in order to 'have my bond' (4.1.87).

The structuring of *A Knack to Know an Honest Man* around the exposure of false friends, and the revelation of true ones, is another feature that reappears in *The Merchant of Venice*. The earlier play begins by depicting two 'faithfull friends' (l. 39), Lelio and Sempronio, who have become enemies through Sempronio's alleged attempt on Annetta's virtue. In the remainder of the play, the solicitude of Servio for the dead Sempronio is revealed as self-interest while Brisheo demonstrates true friendship to Lelio in adversity by accepting banishment on his behalf; by contrast, two Senators whom Brisheo helped in the past refuse to aid his sons when they fall on hard times. In *The Merchant of Venice*, of course, the wrecking of Antonio's ships serves as a plot device that exposes the malice underlying Shylock's professions of friendship, placing him in a

---

[47] See McFaul, p. 161.

position in which he is able to avenge Antonio's racism and his daughter's loss, as well as revealing the willingness of Antonio to die for Bassanio.

Antonio's venturing of a pound of flesh is clearly not Shakespeare's invention but is derived from *Il pecorone*. One detail that Shakespeare does add, however, is an anatomical lexicon that adds specificity to his forfeit. Although in the first instance Shylock says that the pound of flesh is to come from 'what part of your body pleaseth me' (1.3.144), by Act 4 it is the flesh 'Nearest his heart' (4.1.250; see also 229), allowing Antonio to pun painfully on paying the debt 'with all my heart' (4.1.277). Bassanio throws more body parts into the mix by offering to pay the debt tenfold 'On forfeit of my hands, my head, my heart' (4.1.208), an offer that is absent from *Il pecorone* (which is rather vague about where the pound of flesh is to come from). In a play about love and friendship, it is appropriate that the metaphorical or symbolic heart that one gives in love should be literalised in the way that Antonio suggests; in a play about relations between Christians and Jews, as David Schalkwyk and Julia Lupton have noted, Shylock's gesture may also be read as a literalisation of St Paul's notion of the circumcision of the heart as a 'universally available' covenant understood to differentiate Christianity from Judaism in Romans 2: 29.[48] But the language of hands, heads and hearts in the context of male friendship also recalls *A Knack to Know an Honest Man*, where Lelio volunteers to lose his 'head, or heart, or any part' for Brisheo's sake in returning to Venice (l. 1216) and Brisheo offers to redeem his sons from punishment by giving a hand for each (shades of *Titus Andronicus* here) before going on to say of Lelio, 'take for this my body, hart, and all' (l. 1641).

The long courtroom scene in which Brisheo makes his offer is, along with the combination of a 'faithful friends' plot and a 'usurer's daughter' plot, perhaps the most substantial detail that *A Knack to Know an Honest Man* seems to contribute to *The Merchant of Venice*. In *Il pecorone*, the equivalent episode is very brief. The disguised lawyer, who rather than arbitrating is speaking on Ansaldo's behalf, begins by telling him to come forward and inviting the Jew to fulfil his claim; as the Jew advances, the lawyer invokes the drop-of-blood clause. The narrative allows little time for suspense to be created, in marked contrast to the three hundred lines before Portia's 'Tarry a little' (4.1.301) that include the Duke's entreaties, Shylock's self-justification, the arrival of the lawyer and his clerk, Portia's

---

[48] David Schalkwyk, 'The Impossible Gift of Love in *The Merchant of Venice* and the Sonnets', *Shakespeare*, 7 (2011), 142–55 (p. 143). Schalkwyk cites Julia Lupton, *Citizen Saints: Shakespeare and Political Theology* (Chicago: University of Chicago Press, 2005), esp. pp. 24, 99–100.

speech on mercy and Shylock's rejection of it, her judgement and Antonio's last speech to Bassanio. *A Knack to Know an Honest Man*, however, includes not one but two courtroom scenes: one (ll. 1294–1381) in which the Duke threatens to torture Servio for letting Orphinio and Zepherius escape, only to be prevented by Sempronio bringing in a penitent Fortunio who explains how they prevented him from committing rape, and a second (ll. 1465–1805) in which first Orphinio and Zepherius and then Brisheo ask to die in Lelio's place before the hermit allows Sempronio to reveal that he is not, in fact, dead at all. As has already been argued, this long, suspenseful climax seems to have been inspired by the comparable scene in *Damon and Pythias*; its influence on *The Merchant of Venice* is suggested, not only by the speeches mentioned above in which friends offer their literal hearts for each other, but by two other details in particular.

The first concerns the treatment of Servio, in particular the sequence where Servio brings the captured Lelio before the Duke and Senate to claim his reward. Annetta and Lucida beg the Duke to have mercy on Lelio, and then, when this does not succeed, demand that they should receive the reward and Servio be punished for failing to give Lelio up immediately; Lucida gets the reward and Servio imprisonment. The lines in which Lucida pleads that 'mercy Prince, should moderate the Lawes' and that 'VVho spareth none, doth hate to Iustice adde' (ll. 1523, 1525) may, as Robert Boies Sharpe argued in 1935, have influenced Portia's more famous speech on mercy, although direct points of contact are hard to find.[49] More suggestive, it seems to me, is the way in which Lucida tricks Servio into requesting a legal severity that rebounds upon himself. As she says to the Duke, 'Your lawes command, that on the first surpryse, / VVho met with Lelio should disclose him strayght, / But Seruio three daies space did keepe him close' (ll. 1552–4). So, as one Senator observes, 'the Foxe was taken in the net, / And nygardnes was caught by sutteltie' (ll. 1559–60). A female character asks for mercy before turning Servio's own legalism against him: the pattern recurs in Shakespeare, albeit worked out with more elegance.

While it is appropriate that Shylock's downfall results from a literal-minded application of the agreement that he insists on fulfilling to the letter – he is to have a pound of flesh, but no less and no more – it also exposes the limitations of such literalism, however. As Portia insists, 'in the

---

[49] Robert Boyes Sharpe, *The Real War of the Theatres: Shakespeare's Fellows in Rivalry with the Admiral's Men, 1594–1603; Repertories, Devices, and Types* (Boston: Heath; London: Oxford University Press, 1935), pp. 22–3.

course of justice, none of us / Should see salvation. We do pray for mercy' (4.1.195–6): Shylock's lack of mercy is set up in contrast to the unmerited divine grace that 'droppeth as the gentle rain from heaven' (4.1.181). In so far as he disregards the letter of the bond, to that extent will he resemble the deity that Portia describes (leaving aside the question of how merciful the Christians themselves are in their eventual treatment of Shylock). His refusal to do so makes him the representative of a legalism analogous to the justice that would reward sin with death but for the grace of God; accordingly, whatever Portia's flaws as a human being (her racism towards Morocco and her lack of sympathy for Antonio's relationship with Bassanio come to mind, not to speak of her treatment of Shylock), the scene places her intervention in the fate of Antonio in parallel to the intervention of divine mercy in the eternal fate of mortals.[50] The discomfiture of Shylock is both cynical and miraculous.

This sense of the miraculous is the second thing that I would argue Shakespeare derives from the climax of *A Knack to Know an Honest Man*. Lelio's position is apparently impossible: he has been condemned to death for a murder that even he does not know he has not committed, and his supposed victim is magically prevented from revealing himself. Only magic can untangle this, and when it intervenes it is in a form that Sempronio identifies with one of the three theological virtues: 'O Charitie is come, I see him now', he says as the hermit finally enters (l. 1708). The hermit describes his action in relieving Sempronio of his guise as Penitent Experience in terms clearly meant to imply St Paul's Letter to the Ephesians:

> DUKE Hermit why dallies thou?
>   Sempronio was yong, but this is olde,
>   Sempronio was dead, but he doth liue.
> HERMIT Old Sempronio now is young againe,
>   And dead Sempronio now doth liue,
>   Behold him Lelio, dost thou know him now? (ll.1713–18)

In divesting Sempronio of whatever costume is meant to represent his aged guise as Penitent Experience, the Hermit literalises the Pauline injunction 'that ye cast of, concernyng the conuersation in time past, the olde man, whiche is corrupt through deceiueable lustes. And be renewed in the spirit

---

[50] For an example of a reading of the trial scene as depicting Antonio as a type of fallen man, 'Shylock as the embodiment of the Old Law' who 'represents justice', and Portia as 'permitting the Law to demonstrate its own destructiveness', see Barbara K. Lewalski, 'Biblical Allusion and Allegory in *The Merchant of Venice*', *Shakespeare Quarterly*, 13 (1962), 327–43 (pp. 339, 341). For a theologically alert complication of Lewalski's reading, see Stephen Marx, *Shakespeare and the Bible* (Oxford: Oxford University Press, 2000), pp. 103–24.

of your minde. And put on the new man, which after God is created in righteousnes and true holines (Ephesians 4: 22–4, Geneva version). The climactic action is represented in terms that seem intended to recall the working of divine grace – as is the case with the (literal) redemption of Antonio, and indeed, as D. J. Palmer has argued, as is later the case with King Henry V's casting off of the 'old man' Falstaff at the end of *2 Henry IV*.[51] While, incidentally, Damon in Edwards' play attributes Dionysius's softening to 'the immortal gods that did your heart so move' (15.234), the classical setting discourages explicitly Christian allegorising of this sort; the Pauline overtones to the Hermit's transformation of Sempronio are the addition of the *Knack* dramatist.

It has to be admitted that none of the similarities identified in the above paragraphs represents unequivocal proof of influence in the way that the shared features of the language of *The Jew of Malta* and *The Merchant of Venice* do. The Venetian setting, the friends willing to die for each other, the courtroom scene in which the moneylender is hoisted by his own petard – none of these, by itself, proves that Shakespeare knew *A Knack to Know an Honest Man* and used it in shaping his own Venetian comedy. Cumulatively, however, they represent a way of responding to Marlowe's play that is too close to Shakespeare's to be coincidental. Rather than a Barabas-like character dominating the play, he is counterbalanced by a pair of friends whose love is set up in contrast to his materialistic values. Following a tense climactic scene, they are rescued from death by a near-miraculous intervention that is presented in quasi-religious terms. Furthermore, it might be noted, rather than the usurer killing his daughter, she succeeds in outwitting him and getting the man of her choice. (The duel between Lelio and Sempronio from which both ultimately emerge alive could also be read as a reversal of the duel between Mathias and Lodowick in which both end up dead, but this is one feature of *The Jew of Malta* that does not turn up in *The Merchant of Venice*.) What all this amounts to is summed up by the disguised Sempronio's lines, 'O were there one could find Sempronio out, / How might we make a famous comedie' (ll. 1674–5). The *Knack* dramatist redeploys Marlovian character types and structural relationships between characters, but in place of 'The Famous Tragedy of the Rich Jew of Malta' (to quote the 1633 title page) generates a romantic comedy – a genre that was becoming increasingly popular by

[51] D. J. Palmer, 'Casting off the Old Man: History and St. Paul in "Henry IV"', *Critical Quarterly*, 12 (1970), 267–83.

the mid 1590s, as Roslyn Knutson observes.[52] In refashioning Marlovian materials into a form more in tune with prevailing dramatic fashion, he set an example that Shakespeare would elect to follow.

The Merchant of Venice and 1590s Comedy

This chapter has attempted to put forward an argument that Shakespeare's achievement in *The Merchant of Venice*, while undoubtedly influenced by *The Jew of Malta* as well as drawing on prose narrative sources, was also informed by the innovations of the dramatist or dramatists behind *A Knack to Know an Honest Man*. In turn, this exemplifies what will be a recurrent theme of this book: that reading Shakespeare's plays in relation to the repertory of the Admiral's Men can help us to construct a novel picture of 1590s drama in which the familiar landmarks are supplemented by new features that come into view. It can also help us to identify possible relationships between plays that are not typically linked: if we grant that *The Merchant of Venice* may have been influenced by *A Knack to Know an Honest Man*, for example, that raises the question of whether the work on which the latter play draws, *A Knack to Know a Knave* (in which Shakespeare may well have acted, if he was a member of Lord Strange's Men), might be another appropriate point of comparison. That might shed light on one peculiarity of *The Merchant of Venice*, namely Shylock's recourse to what Stephen Orgel describes as 'Puritan ways of speaking and arguing'.[53] Venetian Jew though he is, Shylock repeatedly manifests stereotypically Puritan attitudes such as hatred of masques as 'shallow foppery' (2.5.34), his decision to part with the 'huge feeder' Lancelot Gobbo on the grounds that 'Drones hive not with me' (2.5.44, 46), and his use of thrifty proverbs like 'Fast bind, fast find' (2.5.52) in a way that Jonson, Chapman and Marston would come to satirise in Touchstone in *Eastward Ho*. It so happens that both *Knack* plays, though they do not contain Jewish characters, satirise moneylenders who are depicted in unmistakeably Puritan terms. *Honest Man*'s Servio ascribes the capture of Brisheo's sons to 'God and my industrie', and subsequently laments their escape with the words 'I am a reprobate and cast away' (ll. 1113, 1177), thus betraying an ongoing concern about whether he is

---

[52] Knutson points out that 'Of the fifty-two new plays that the Admiral's men brought into production from June 1594 to July 1597, at least thirty-three were comedies (or seem to have been)', while tragedies were 'far fewer'. *The Repertory of Shakespeare's Company 1594–1613*, pp. 41, 44.

[53] Stephen Orgel, 'Shylock's Tribe', in *Shakespeare and the Mediterranean: The Selected Proceedings of the International Shakespeare Association World Congress, Valencia, 2001*, ed. by Tom Clayton, Susan Brock and Vicente Forés (Newark: University of Delaware Press, 2004), pp. 38–53 (p. 46).

one of the elect. In *A Knack to Know a Knave*, the moneylending Priest, as David Bevington notes, is explicitly identified as 'a "Precisian" or Puritan, perhaps the first so lampooned on the popular stage'.[54] He justifies his refusal to give money to a beggar with the injunction, 'Read the blessed saying of S. Paul, which is, thou shalt get thy liuing with the sweat of thy browes, and he that will not labour is not worthie to eat', explaining that he refrains from charitable giving because 'the Spirit doth not mooue me thereunto: and in good time, looke in the blessed Proverb of Salomon, which is, good deeds do not iustify a man, therfore I count it sinne to giue thee any thing'.[55] His citation of the book of Proverbs as grounds for rejecting the doctrine of justification by works is theologically dubious, but the salient point is made by Honesty: 'See how he can turne and wind the Scripture to his owne vse' (ll. 1636–7). Antonio, of course, will complain that Shylock can 'cite Scripture for his purpose' (1.3.98). The Puritanism of Shakespeare's Jew may be a legacy of his antecedents in the *Knack* plays.

Reading *The Merchant of Venice* alongside *A Knack to Know an Honest Man* uncovers telling similarities, though it is also revealing for the opposite reason: it throws some of Shakespeare's creative decisions into relief, demonstrating the kind of play that he chose not to write. For example, the earlier play ends at what one might have thought the more obvious moment: with the courtroom scene, once Sempronio's identity has been revealed, the prisoners freed, Servio forced to give up his ill-gotten gains, and various characters married off. Shakespeare, notoriously, prolongs the play into a final act that may be seen either as 'an expression of harmony ... completely without irony about the joy it celebrates', in C. L. Barber's words, or as giving expression to some of the play's unresolved conflicts and tensions.[56] Furthermore, *A Knack to Know an Honest Man* reveals another highly problematic aspect of the play – Shylock's Jewishness – to be, from a structural point of view, unnecessary. To state the obvious: it was evidently quite possible, in the 1590s, to write a romantic comedy set in Venice that pitted two friends against a vengeful moneylender without making that moneylender Jewish.[57] In keeping

---

[54] David Bevington, *Tudor Drama and Politics: A Critical Approach to Topical Meaning* (Cambridge: Harvard University Press, 1968), p. 228.

[55] *A Knack to Know a Knave*, ed. by G. R. Proudfoot (Oxford: Malone Society, 1964), ll. 1622–4, 1632–5.

[56] C. L. Barber, *Shakespeare's Festive Comedy: A Study of Dramatic Form and its Relation to Social Custom* (Princeton: Princeton University Press, 1959), p. 187. For a less idealised view of the final act, see Catherine Belsey, 'Love in Venice', *Shakespeare Survey*, 44 (1992), 41–53.

[57] The *Knack* plays, one of which is set in England and both of which include non-Jewish moneylenders, in this respect constitute exceptions to Lloyd Edward Kermode's argument that

Shylock as Jewish (as in *Il pecorone* and *The Jew of Malta*), Shakespeare notoriously involves his play in early modern and later controversies over race and religion. More narrowly, he facilitates a further peculiarity of the play's denouement: that Shylock is simultaneously excluded from the victorious Christian community and, paradoxically, forced into it through being made to become a Christian. As Edward Berry puts it, 'the act of forcible conversion transforms the quintessentially Shakespearean gesture of comic inclusiveness into macabre self-parody': 'in his case incorporation is worse than ostracism'.[58]

A final aspect of the play's ending that is highlighted through comparison with *A Knack to Know an Honest Man* is the position of Antonio. As we have seen, not only do the friends in the earlier play have wives before the action commences; at the end, the unmarried and penitent Sempronio is re-incorporated within the masculine community of friendship through marriage to Lucida. Shakespeare could easily have achieved something comparable for Antonio by, for example, marrying him (rather than Gratiano) to Nerissa; he shows himself quite willing to countenance such an abrupt pairing-off in *The Winter's Tale* in the case of Paulina and Camillo, and indeed, the betrothal of Gratiano and Nerissa is itself entirely unheralded by anything in the play's dialogue. By leaving Antonio unmarried, however, Shakespeare accentuates the contrast between the heterosexual pairings and Antonio's feelings for Bassanio. In *A Knack to Know an Honest Man*, the friendship of Brisheo and Lelio may conflict with Brisheo's duty towards his family, but it is essentially reinforced, not threatened, by their marriages in so far as Brisheo is Lelio's father-in-law. In *The Merchant of Venice*, however, the ring-trick seems designed to force Bassanio and Antonio to concede that their friendship has been supplanted by Bassanio's marriage to Portia: as Alan Sinfield notes, 'The seriousness of the love between Antonio and Bassanio is manifest, above all, in Portia's determination to contest it.'[59] In offering his soul as surety that Bassanio 'Will never more break faith advisedly' (5.1.253), Antonio acknowledges that the faith Bassanio owes Portia supersedes the obligations of friendship: 'th' unhappy subject of these quarrels' (5.1.238) has to accept his place on

---

dramatic representations of usury in the late sixteenth century follow an Anglicising trajectory, with the stage usurer evolving 'from foreign Jew to English non-Jew'. Lloyd Edward Kermode, 'After Shylock: The "Judaiser" in England', *Renaissance and Reformation*, 20.4 (1996), 5–26 (p. 6).

[58] Edward Berry, 'Laughing at "Others"', in *The Cambridge Companion to Shakespearean Comedy*, ed. by Alexander Leggatt (Cambridge: Cambridge University Press, 2002), pp. 123–38 (p. 126).

[59] Alan Sinfield, 'How to Read *The Merchant of Venice* Without Being Heterosexist', in *Alternative Shakespeares Vol. II*, ed. by Terence Hawkes (London: Routledge, 1996), pp. 122–39 (p. 126).

the margins rather than the play reasserting the bonds of male friendship as *A Knack to Know an Honest Man* does.

To identify *A Knack to Know an Honest Man*, then, as an influence on *The Merchant of Venice* is not merely to recognise the extent to which Shakespeare was influenced by contemporary theatrical fashion and drew on the structures and tropes of 1590s comedy. It also emphasises his willingness to subvert those structures and tropes to create distinctive and disquieting dramatic forms.

CHAPTER 2

'Hobgoblins abroad'
From *Doctor Faustus* to *A Midsummer Night's Dream*

In the previous chapter, I argued that critical accounts of *The Merchant of Venice* that identify Marlowe's *The Jew of Malta* as the play's principal dramatic antecedent, though justified as far as they go, are too limited in their scope. While the intertextual relationship between these two dramas is undeniable, in matters of setting, generic identity, thematic content and more Shakespeare also seems to have drawn on the highly popular Admiral's Men play of 1594, *A Knack to Know an Honest Man*. Recognising this does not mean discarding our sense of Shakespeare as a creative artist who responded on a very individual level to the innovations of his illustrious predecessor, Marlowe; but it should complicate that perception of him, and allow us to see Shakespeare also as a professional dramatist influenced by recent trends and developments in play-making.

The current chapter adopts a comparable approach in that it argues for the dual effect on Shakespeare's dramaturgy of an old play by Marlowe that lived on in the Admiral's repertory, and of newer plays that themselves reworked and reimagined Marlovian materials. The Marlowe play is *Doctor Faustus*, which apparently joined the Admiral's repertory in September 1594 but which must have been written before Marlowe's death on 30 May 1593 at the very latest, perhaps significantly earlier. The Shakespeare play is *A Midsummer Night's Dream*, a comedy whose Marlovian elements have recently been emphasised by Meredith Skura; its absolute terminal date is 1598, when it is mentioned by Francis Meres in *Palladis Tamia*, but it is typically dated to 1595–6.[1] The other plays, however, pose a number of problems. They include Robert Greene's *Friar Bacon and Friar Bungay*, a play that has been variously assumed either to precede or to follow *Doctor Faustus*, but which evidently has some sort of relationship to it; *Friar*

---

[1] Francis Meres, *Palladis Tamia: Wits Treasury* (London, 1598; STC: 17834), fol. 282r; on the date, see William Shakespeare, *A Midsummer Night's Dream*, ed. by R. A. Foakes, updated ed. (Cambridge: Cambridge University Press, 2003), p. 1. References to Shakespeare's play use this edition.

Bacon's sequel, *John of Bordeaux*; *A Knack to Know a Knave*, already mentioned in Chapter 1; and *John a Kent and John a Cumber*, which exists in the form of a manuscript signed by Anthony Munday and subscribed in another hand with a date that different commentators have read as 1590, 1595 and 1596. The relationship of this last play to the Admiral's Men play *The Wise Man of West Chester*, regularly recorded by Henslowe between 1594 and 1597, is yet another source of debate.

These uncertainties of dating and identification make any discussion of the relationship between the plays somewhat perilous. On the one hand there is a risk of circular argument, whereby assumptions are made (about the order in which plays appeared and who staged them) that produce readings that in turn are used to justify in retrospect the original, problematic assumptions, giving them more weight than they deserve. On the other hand, flatly ruling out speculation over topics whose basic details are uncertain seems an extreme position to take, especially in a field like early modern theatre history where so much information that we might wish to have is lacking: in the interests of saying anything at all, it is sometimes necessary to entertain hypotheses that may be unverifiable. Where this becomes inadmissible is when the critic allows hypothesis to calcify, unacknowledged, into fact – a tendency I have tried to resist. The current chapter therefore attempts to do two things: to lay out clearly a conservative reading of the available data, and to offer a somewhat more speculative interpretation, while distinguishing scrupulously between the two.

Some explanation also needs to be offered for the fact that, even leaving aside the debate over *The Wise Man of West Chester* and *John a Kent and John a Cumber*, much of this chapter is concerned with one play, *Friar Bacon and Friar Bungay*, that was not associated with the Admiral's Men until some time after Shakespeare wrote *A Midsummer Night's Dream*, and with two plays, *John of Bordeaux* and *A Knack to Know a Knave*, that were apparently not associated with them at all.[2] My justification for this is that in order to appreciate fully how Shakespeare's drama recycles elements of *Doctor Faustus* (a play that certainly was in the Admiral's repertory by 1594), we need to regard it alongside earlier plays that offered precedents for the comic treatment of magic, in some cases apparently drawing on Marlowe's tragedy. Furthermore, identifying these plays as a group with

---

[2] Philip Henslowe records a loan of five shillings to the Admiral's Man Thomas Downton on 14 December 1602 'to paye vnto mᵣ mydelton for a prologe & A epeloge for the playe of bacon for the corte'. *Henslowe's Diary*, ed. by R. A. Foakes [and R. T. Rickert], 2nd edn (Cambridge: Cambridge University Press, 2002), p. 207.

certain features in common gives us some basis for speculation about the likely content of the Admiral's play *The Wise Man of West Chester* if it was not, in fact, *John a Kent and John a Cumber*. Thus, while the current chapter departs slightly from the overall scheme of this book in looking in detail at non-Shakespearean plays outside the Admiral's repertory, it does so with the ultimate aim of locating Shakespeare's dramaturgical practice more clearly within the adult theatre of his time.

Christopher Marlowe and *A Midsummer Night's Dream*

Even more so than with *The Merchant of Venice*, discussion of Shakespeare's sources and influences for *A Midsummer Night's Dream* has not tended to devote much attention to the adult theatre. The play lacks an obvious dramatic antecedent such as can be found for some of Shakespeare's other plays of the mid-1590s, such as *King John* (*The Troublesome Reign of John, King of England*), *Richard II* (Marlowe's *Edward II*), *Henry IV* (*The Famous Victories of Henry V*), and indeed *The Merchant of Venice* (*The Jew of Malta*). Instead, it seems to draw on a bewildering array of largely non-dramatic texts, including Ovid's *Metamorphoses*, fairy lore, the chivalric romance *Huon of Bordeaux*, the story of Balaam's ass in Numbers 22, 'Seneca's *Hippolytus*, Plutarch's *Life of Theseus*, Apuleius' *Golden Ass*, Geoffrey Chaucer's dream-vision poems ... and his *Knight's Tale* and *Tale of Sir Thopas* ..., John Lyly's *Endymion* (1591), Spenser's *Faerie Queene* (1590–96) ... and more'.[3] As Helen Hackett's list suggests, the early modern dramatist most frequently mentioned in source studies is one associated not with the adult but with the children's theatre: John Lyly, whose *Sapho and Phao*, *Gallathea* and *Midas*, as well as *Endymion*, have been proposed as influences.[4] By the time of *A Midsummer Night's Dream*, the playhouse at St Paul's for which Lyly wrote had been closed for half a decade, and the children's theatre at Blackfriars for longer; however, Shakespeare could have consulted printed texts of *Endymion* (1591), *Midas* (1592) and *Gallathea* (1592). Nevertheless, to emphasise Lyly's works as Shakespeare's principal dramatic influence for *A Midsummer Night's Dream* means taking the play out of the commercial theatrical culture of the mid-1590s and associating it

---

[3] Helen Hackett, 'Introduction', in William Shakespeare, *A Midsummer Night's Dream*, ed. by Stanley Wells (London: Penguin, 2005), pp. xxxiii–xxxiv.

[4] See Leah Scragg, 'Shakespeare, Lyly and Ovid: The Influence of *Gallathea* on *A Midsummer Night's Dream*', *Shakespeare Survey*, 30 (1977), 125–34, and G. K. Hunter, *John Lyly: The Humanist as Courtier* (London: Routledge and Kegan Paul, 1962), pp. 298–340. See also *A Midsummer Night's Dream*, ed. Foakes, p. 5.

with a narrower, more socially exclusive one that would be in abeyance until the reopening of St Paul's and the Blackfriars at the end of the decade. Even if, as some critics have suggested, *A Midsummer Night's Dream* was written to be performed at an aristocratic wedding, perhaps that of Elizabeth Vere to William Stanley on 26 January 1595 or that of Elizabeth Carey to Thomas Berkeley on 19 February 1596, it was certainly intended also for the public theatre: the title page of the 1600 quarto advertises the play 'As it hath beene sundry times publickely acted, by the Right honourable, the Lord Chamberlaine his seruants'.[5] This fact is emphasised in the current chapter, which discusses Shakespeare's play in relation to the public theatre context that is often marginalised in discussions of its sources. My attempt to place *A Midsummer Night's Dream* within the theatrical culture of the mid-1590s begins with a play prominent in the Admiral's Men repertory during the period to which *A Midsummer Night's Dream* is usually assigned: Marlowe's *Doctor Faustus*, recorded as having been staged at the Rose twenty-four times between 30 September 1594 and 5 January 1597.[6]

In an essay published in 2010, Meredith Skura argues that *A Midsummer Night's Dream* displays 'extensive borrowing from Marlowe', in particular from the plays *Dido, Queen of Carthage* and *Doctor Faustus*.[7] The first of these should not be a surprise: *Dido*, co-written with Thomas Nashe and 'Played by the Children of her Maiesties Chappell', as the 1594 title page has it, belongs to the same child company milieu as the plays by John Lyly that are regularly cited as influences on *Dream*, and Shakespeare's depiction of individuals and their perceptions as helplessly enslaved to the promptings of love – which Skura legitimately sees as informed by *Dido* – also echoes plays like *Sapho and Phao* and *Gallathea*.[8] *Doctor Faustus*,

[5] At one extreme is the claim in William Shakespeare, *A Midsummer Night's Dream*, ed. by Harold E. Brooks (London: Methuen, 1979), p. liii, 'Most scholars are agreed that the *Dream* was designed to grace a wedding in a noble household'. At the other is that accusation in William Shakespeare, *A Midsummer Night's Dream*, ed. by Peter Holland (Oxford: Clarendon Press, 1994), p. 112, that the wedding theory appeals 'to those who wish to rescue the play from the clutches of the popular theatre audience'. For judicious surveys of the debate, see Helen Hackett, '*A Midsummer Night's Dream*', in *A Companion to Shakespeare's Works*, vol. III: *The Comedies*, ed. by Richard Dutton and Jean E. Howard (Malden: Blackwell, 2003), pp. 338–57, and *A Midsummer Night's Dream*, ed. Foakes, pp. 2–4. The text of the title page is given in Foakes, p. 143.
[6] *Henslowe's Diary*, pp. 24–8, 30–31, 34, 26, 47, 54–5.
[7] Meredith Skura, 'What Shakespeare Did to Marlowe in Private: Dido, Faustus, and Bottom', in *Christopher Marlowe the Craftsman: Lives, Stage, and Page*, ed. by Sarah Scott and Michael Stapleton (Aldershot: Ashgate, 2010), pp. 79–90 (p. 79).
[8] Christopher Marlowe and Thomas Nashe, *The Tragedie of Dido Queene of Carthage* (London, 1594; STC: 17441).

ostensibly so different from *A Midsummer Night's Dream* in genre, idiom and theme, might seem less likely as a source, but Skura finds interesting parallels at the level of 'scenic form' – she takes the term from Emrys Jones – between Lucifer's pageant of the Seven Deadly Sins in the seventh scene of *Faustus*, and the appearance of the fairies to Bottom in *Dream*, 3.1.[9] In both scenes, supernatural beings (Lucifer, Titania) assert their claims over mortals, and then bring in a troupe of other spirits (the Sins, the fairies) who introduce themselves in a pageant whose true implications the mortals are deaf to, instead falling further into captive delusion. As Skura points out, the genealogy Bottom ascribes Peaseblossom – 'commend me to Mistress Squash, your mother, and to Master Peascod, your father' (3.1.164–5) – recalls the lineage announced by each Sin when they introduce themselves: 'I am Envy, begotten of a chimney-sweeper and an oyster-wife', and so on (2.3.132–3).[10]

Skura's sense of the relationship between these two scenes, whose origins she finds in the calling-in of a medieval mummers' play, is primarily formal: she considers the structural relationships between the characters, their use of the stage, and their formulaic utterances rather than the details of what they say. When one attends to Shakespeare's language, however, further parallels become apparent that substantiate her argument:

> Out of this wood do not desire to go:
> Thou shalt remain here, whether thou wilt or no.
> I am a spirit of no common rate;
> The summer still doth tend upon my state,
> And I do love thee. Therefore go with me.
> I'll give thee fairies to attend on thee,
> And they shall fetch thee jewels from the deep,
> And sing, while thou on pressèd flowers dost sleep;
> And I will purge thy mortal grossness so
> That thou shalt like an airy spirit go. (3.1.126–35)

Titania's speech combines a number of Marlovian allusions. One is to the speech in the first part of *Tamburlaine* in which Tamburlaine asks his captive, 'Disdains Zenocrate to live with me?', and goes on to describe the riches and honours that will be hers:

---

[9] Skura, p. 88; Emrys Jones, *Scenic Form in Shakespeare* (Oxford: Clarendon Press, 1971).
[10] Christopher Marlowe, *Doctor Faustus: A- and B-texts (1604, 1616)*, ed. by David Bevington and Eric Rasmussen (Manchester: Manchester University Press, 1993), A-text. Subsequent references are to this edition.

> A hundred Tartars shall attend on thee,
> Mounted on steeds swifter than Pegasus;
> Thy garments shall be made of Median silk,
> Enchased with precious jewels of mine own.[11]

Tamburlaine's speech was by 1595 very well known and, as I shall show in Chapter 3, had been imitated by dramatists such as George Peele. Here, it gives Shakespeare not only the basic scenario of a speaker asserting dominance over another through promises of luxurious reward, but more specific verbal tags: if Bottom will 'go with me' (compare 'live with me') then fairies, instead of Tartars, will 'attend on thee'. The image of sleeping on pressed flowers recalls another Marlovian text in which the addressee is invited to 'live with me': 'The Passionate Shepherd to his Love', whose speaker promises to 'make thee beds of roses'.[12] The third Marlovian source Shakespeare is using here, however, is *Doctor Faustus*, whose protagonist's fantasies of power are burlesqued in Titania's speech to Bottom:

> Shall I make spirits fetch me what I please,
> Resolve me of all ambiguities,
> Perform what desperate enterprise I will?
> I'll have them fly to India for gold,
> Ransack the ocean for orient pearl,
> And search all corners of the new-found world
> For pleasant fruits and princely delicates. (1.1.81–7)

Titania seems to be answering Faustus's demonic prayer: her fairies will fetch Bottom 'jewels from the deep', and are told to

> Feed him with apricocks and dewberries,
> With purple grapes, green figs, and mulberries. (3.1.144–5)

It is noticeable that Titania describes herself not as a fairy, but as a 'spirit of no common rate'; and her promise to 'purge thy mortal grossness so / That thou shalt like an airy spirit go' echoes another of Faustus's demands, to 'be a spirit in form and substance' (2.1.97).

Though this episode is perhaps the clearest instance of Shakespeare borrowing from *Doctor Faustus* in *A Midsummer Night's Dream*, there may be others. Marlowe's play stages a spirit in the form of Helen of Troy, and Helen, as Laurie Maguire has emphasised, lies behind *Dream* in a number of respects:

---

[11] Christopher Marlowe, *Tamburlaine the Great*, ed. by J. S. Cunningham (Manchester: Manchester University Press, 1981), 1.2.82, 1.2.93–6.
[12] Christopher Marlowe, *The Complete Poems and Translations*, ed. by Stephen Orgel, 2nd edn (London: Penguin, 2007), p. 207.

she gives one character (Helena) her name, though not, Helena feels, her beauty ('I am as ugly as a bear', 2.2.94), while another character, Theseus, according to Plutarch took part in the rape of Helen, gesturing towards a theme of sexual consent that runs through the play.[13] Shakespeare did not need to know *Doctor Faustus* to know about Helen of Troy, of course, but there are moments when she is invoked in ways that bring the earlier play to mind. One is Lysander's rejection of Hermia once he has been bewitched by the love-juice:

> For, as a surfeit of the sweetest things
> The deepest loathing to the stomach brings,
> Or as the heresies that men do leave
> Are hated most of those they did deceive,
> So thou, my surfeit and my heresy,
> Of all be hated, but the most of me!
> And, all my powers, address your love and might
> To honour Helen, and to be her knight. (2.2.143–50)

Unlike Titania's, Lysander's speech is not modelled on any specific Marlovian passage, but the conjunction of heresy and surfeit recalls a linkage that is repeatedly made in *Faustus*, whose protagonist 'surfeits upon cursèd necromancy' (Prologue, 25) and upon 'deadly sin' (5.2.11). Faustus, like Lysander, wants to be Helen's knight:

> I will be Paris, and for love of thee
> Instead of Troy shall Wittenberg be sacked,
> And I will combat with weak Menelaus,
> And wear thy colours on my plumèd crest.
> Yea, I will wound Achilles in the heel
> And then return to Helen for a kiss. (5.1.98–103)

The association of Helen with the demonic is made again in Theseus's famous speech on imagination in Act 5, where the poet is compared to the lunatic and the lover:

> One sees more devils than vast hell can hold;
> That is the madman. The lover, all as frantic,
> Sees Helen's beauty in a brow of Egypt.
> The poet's eye, in a fine frenzy rolling,
> Doth glance from heaven to earth, from earth to heaven;
> And as imagination bodies forth
> The forms of things unknown, the poet's pen
> Turns them to shapes, and gives to airy nothing
> A local habitation and a name. (5.1.9–17)

---

[13] Laurie Maguire, *Shakespeare's Names* (Oxford: Oxford University Press, 2007), pp. 74–85.

Marlowe's play gives shapes both to devils and to Helen's beauty, which makes it tempting – if no more – to read Theseus's wry description of the ecstatic bard, his sublime vision extending beyond the earthly, as a double-edged tribute to Marlowe in terms that anticipate Drayton's in 1627:

> For that fine madness still he did retain,
> Which rightly should possess a Poet's brain.[14]

Attractive though it is, however, to read Theseus's lines as suggesting a personalised response to Marlowe on Shakespeare's part, it must be emphasised that there are more tangible reasons why *Doctor Faustus* – not in print, incidentally, until 1604 – might have been on Shakespeare's mind in the mid-1590s. As I have already noted, during that period it was a prominent staple in the repertory of the Admiral's Men, whose first known performance of the play (to his record of which Philip Henslowe did not add the note 'ne') was on 30 September 1594 when it garnered an impressive £3 12s. This was the company's most lucrative performance to date, although Henslowe had recorded higher takings by Lord Strange's Men after the premieres of *Harry VI* (£3 16s. 8d., 3 March 1591–2), *The Tanner of Denmark* (£3 13s. 6d., 23 May 1592) and *The Guise* – presumably *The Massacre at Paris* (£3 14s., 30 January 1592–3).[15] By 3 July 1596 Henslowe had recorded twenty performances of *Faustus*, a total equalled during that twenty-two month period only by *A Knack to Know an Honest Man* and surpassed only by *The Wise Man of West Chester* (performed an impressive twenty-nine times between 2 December 1594 and 7 July 1596). At the time when *A Midsummer Night's Dream* was being written, and when it first appeared, *Doctor Faustus* must have been a hard play to avoid for playwright and playgoers alike.

By that time, though, *Faustus* was very far from being a new play. The latest conceivable period of its writing is spring 1593, and while many twentieth-century critics followed W. W. Greg's 1950 edition of the play in assuming that it dated from the end of Marlowe's career, the balance of opinion now seems to have swung towards an early date, with David Bevington and Eric Rasmussen's 1993 edition providing strong arguments in favour of 1588–9 and Martin Wiggins's more recent

---

[14] Michael Drayton, 'Of Poets and Poesie', in *Marlowe: The Critical Heritage 1588–1896*, ed. by Millar MacLure (London: Routledge and Kegan Paul, 1979), p. 47.
[15] *Henslowe's Diary*, pp. 24, 16, 18, 20.

survey of Marlovian chronology reaching a similar conclusion.[16] By 1595, then, *Doctor Faustus* may have been as much as seven years old, and even a later dating allows it considerable time in which to exert an influence not only upon Shakespeare, but also upon other dramatists from whose example Shakespeare was able to learn. The sections that follow consider a number of plays in which this influence may be discerned.

Friar Bacon and Friar Bungay

The first play I will consider is the one whose relationship to *Faustus* is perhaps the most problematic: Robert Greene's *Friar Bacon and Friar Bungay*, a play that was certainly in existence by 19 February 1591–2, when Lord Strange's Men performed 'fryer bacvne' at the Rose, and which is conventionally dated to about 1590.[17] That the play has some sort of intertextual relationship with Marlowe's seems undeniable: the most obvious instance appears towards the end, where Friar Bacon renounces magic after two Oxford students persuade him to show them what their fathers are up to in distant Suffolk by means of his magic glass. The fathers have, in fact, arranged a combat over the hand of Margaret, the fair maid of

---

[16] Christopher Marlowe, *Doctor Faustus 1604–1616: Parallel Texts*, ed. by W. W. Greg (Oxford: Clarendon Press, 1950), pp. 1–10. Although the earliest known edition of the play's source, *The History of the Damnable Life and Deserved Death of Doctor John Faustus* (the so-called English Faust Book), did not appear until 1592, Bevington and Rasmussen cite evidence including apparent borrowings from Marlowe's play in the anonymous *The Taming of a Shrew* (whose latest date is 1593), *A Knack to Know a Knave* (performed 10 June 1592) and *A Looking Glass for London and England* (which dates from before August 1591), as well as an entry for a ballad about Faustus in the Stationers' Register on 28 February 1589 (ballads typically seeking 'to exploit a phenomenon that was sensational and widely known'). See *Doctor Faustus*, ed. Bevington and Rasmussen, pp. 1–3. Since 1993, John Henry Jones and R. J. Fehrenbach have separately offered evidence for an edition of the English Faust Book earlier than 1592, which, though it does not prove an early date for *Faustus*, at least questions the principal obstacle to such a date: see *The English Faust Book: A Critical Edition Based on the Text of 1592*, ed. by John Henry Jones (Cambridge: Cambridge University Press, 1994), pp. 52–72, and R. J. Fehrenbach, 'A Pre-1592 English Faust Book and the Date of Marlowe's *Doctor Faustus*', *The Library*, 2 (2001), 327–35. See also Martin Wiggins, 'Marlowe's Chronology and Canon', in *Christopher Marlowe in Context*, ed. by Emily C. Bartels and Emma Smith (Cambridge: Cambridge University Press, 2013), pp. 7–14.

[17] *Henslowe's Diary*, p. 16. Even if, as Lawrence Manley and Sally-Beth MacLean have recently argued, this record refers to the play's sequel, *John of Bordeaux*, that would in any case imply a terminal date of 1591 for the first play; see *Lord Strange's Men and Their Plays* (New Haven: Yale University Press, 2014), pp. 93–6. In his *Farewell to Folly*, Greene mocks lines from the play *Fair Em*, which may be indebted to *Friar Bacon*. See *Greenes Farewell to Folly* (London, 1591; STC 12241), sig. A3v; Robert Greene, *Friar Bacon and Friar Bungay*, ed. by Daniel Seltzer (London: Edward Arnold, 1964); p. ix; Robert Greene, *Friar Bacon and Friar Bungay*, ed. by J. A. Lavin (London: Ernest Benn, 1969), pp. xii–xiii. References to Greene's play use Lavin's edition.

Fressingfield; seeing them kill each other, the scholars fight and do likewise. Bacon breaks his glass and explains to Friar Bacon that all his efforts
in the art

> Are instances that Bacon must be damned
> For using devils to countervail his God.
> Yet, Bacon, cheer thee; drown not in despair.
> Sins have their salves. Repentance can do much.
> Think Mercy sits where Justice holds her seat,
> And from those wounds those bloody Jews did pierce,
> Which by thy magic oft did bleed afresh,
> From thence for thee the dew of mercy drops
> To wash the wrath of high Jehovah's ire,
> And make thee as a new-born babe from sin.
> Bungay, I'll spend the remnant of my life
> In pure devotion, praying to my God
> That he would save what Bacon vainly lost. (13.96–108)

It is difficult to avoid mentally contrasting Bacon with Faustus, whose
failure to repent – indeed, whose very capacity for repentance – is made
such a notorious crux of Marlowe's play. In the closing scenes, Faustus
excoriates himself, 'Damned art thou, Faustus, damned! Despair and die!'
(5.1.49); his tentative gesture towards redemption, 'I do repent, and yet
I do despair' (5.1.64) is met by Mephistopheles' threat to tear him in pieces,
and when he sees 'where Christ's blood streams in the firmament' it is all
too soon replaced by a God who 'Stretcheth out his arm and bends his
ireful brows' (5.2.78, 83). The language of damnation and repentance, and
the opposition of Christ's salvific blood to 'Jehovah's ire', are points of
contact between the plays, yet the outcomes could not be more different,
Greene offering Bacon a repentance that allows his play to conclude on a
much more optimistic note.

The appearance of intertextuality, however, generates the question of
priority: did the harrowing nature of Marlowe's tragedy impel Greene to
give his own magician play a less distressing ending? Or did Bacon's fuzzy
theology, where salvation is ascribed both to Christ's sacrifice and to a
repentance that 'can do much' yet seems to originate in the sinner, drive
Marlowe to a more searching exploration of Calvinist doctrine? Marlowe's
higher status than Greene within the canon might encourage the former
position; but this has not been the view of all commentators on the plays.
The editors of two significant modern editions of *Friar Bacon*, Daniel
Seltzer (Regents, 1964) and J. A. Lavin (New Mermaids, 1969) both give it
priority over *Faustus*, and critics such as Alexander Leggatt have followed

their lead.[18] However, Seltzer and Lavin base their arguments on Greg's late date for Marlowe's play – an orthodoxy, as we have seen, that has since fallen into question. By contrast, Bevington and Rasmussen, who incline towards an early date for *Faustus*, are of the opinion that Greene's play 'seems manifestly to have been written under the influence of Marlowe', and that furthermore, 'The possibility that Greene may have pioneered in bringing a famous magician on stage seems implausible in view of Greene's other blatant attempts to capitalise on Marlowe's success, as in *Alphonsus, King of Aragon* (1587–8) and its nearly parodic depiction of the overreacher Tamburlaine'.[19] In his edition of Marlowe's source, the English Faust Book, John Henry Jones makes an additional suggestion: that *The Most Famous History of the Learned Fryer Bacon*, published by Thomas Norris circa 1700, not only represents Greene's source for the play (rather than, as is usually supposed, whatever text lies behind *The Famous History of Fryer Bacon*, published by Francis Grove in 1627 or earlier); the source for *The Most Famous History* is itself the English Faust Book.[20] This would mean first, that a version of the English Faust Book was in circulation before *c*.1590, once again challenging the principal argument against an early date for *Faustus*, and second, that the plays share a common ultimate source, from which Marlowe's is at fewer removes than Greene's. Although I personally incline towards the view that *Faustus* appeared first, the question of priority cannot be regarded as settled beyond all doubt, so in order to avoid circularity of argument I attempt in the current chapter to treat the two plays as related, though divergent, ways of dealing with similar material. *Friar Bacon*, I shall argue, whether or not it was written in response to Marlowe's play, offered formal precedents that the writers of other plays that engaged with Faustian themes – including Greene himself – would find useful, and that would ultimately shape certain features of *A Midsummer Night's Dream*.

The most obvious point of difference between *Friar Bacon and Friar Bungay* and *Doctor Faustus* is the one implied by the contrasting fates of their protagonists: namely, where *Faustus* is a 'Tragical History' with significant morality play attributes, *Friar Bacon* is, broadly speaking, a comedy, albeit a comedy with casualties (most obviously the fathers and sons whose deaths lead Bacon to renounce magic). To give a comic

---

[18] *Friar Bacon and Friar Bungay*, ed. Seltzer, p. ix; *Friar Bacon and Friar Bungay*, ed. Lavin, p. xii; Alexander Leggatt, *An Introduction to English Renaissance Comedy* (Manchester: Manchester University Press, 1999), p. 38.
[19] *Doctor Faustus*, ed. Bevington and Rasmussen, p. 1.   [20] *English Faust Book*, pp. 55–7.

outcome to a plot about a man who deals with devils might seem to contravene the theology of *Doctor Faustus*, whose protagonist thinks he has 'incurred eternal death / By desp'rate thoughts against Jove's deity' (1.3.90–91) even before the formal pact with Lucifer. However, the possibility of an ending in which Faustus repents, like Philologus in one version of Nathaniel Woodes's *The Conflict of Conscience*, or is saved by divine mercy, as in medieval moralities like *Mankind* and *The Castle of Perseverance*, is one that hangs over the play, and our sense of the wrongness of the outcome is an important factor in its operation: witness William Empson's insistence, without much evidence to support it, that in Marlowe's original version Faustus cheated the devil.[21] Greene thus provides his audience with the very satisfaction that Marlowe denies his, and in doing so he sets the precedent for dramatic treatment of devil-raising in the late 1580s and 1590s: *John of Bordeaux*, *A Knack to Know a Knave* and *John a Kent and John a Cumber* all allow their leading magicians to escape punishment. (Although the dealings with devils of Joan de Pucelle in *1 Henry VI* and the Duchess of Gloucester in Part II have less happy results, John D. Cox points out that they are made secondary to the 'contention for political dominance' that drives the two plays.)[22]

This generic difference from *Faustus*, however, has important implications for *Friar Bacon*'s treatment of magic, devils and cosmology. If Bacon is to repent then the play needs to assume a fact that *Doctor Faustus* obfuscates: dealing with devils does not require one to give up one's soul. This theme is glanced at in a sequence that does not appear in Greene's putative source, *The Famous History of Fryer Bacon*, where Friar Bungay and the German scholar Jacques Vandermast dispute over 'whether the spirits of pyromancy or geomancy be most predominant in magic'. Arguing for the former, Vandermast explains:

> these earthly geomantic spirits
> Are dull and like the place where they remain;
> For, when proud Lucifer fell from the heavens,
> The spirits and angels that did sin with him
> Retained the local essence as their faults,

[21] William Empson, *Faustus and the Censor: The English Faust-book and Marlowe's 'Doctor Faustus'*, ed. by John Henry Jones (Oxford: Blackwell, 1987), p. 44. On *The Conflict of Conscience*, see David M. Bevington, *From 'Mankind' to Marlowe: Growth of Structure in the Popular Drama of Tudor England* (Cambridge, MA: Harvard University Press, 1962), pp. 246–7.
[22] John D. Cox, *The Devil and the Sacred in English Drama, 1350–1642* (Cambridge: Cambridge University Press, 2000), p. 141.

All subject under Luna's continent.
They which offended less hang in the fire,
And second faults did rest within the air;
But Lucifer and his proud-hearted fiends
Were thrown into the centre of the earth,
Having less understanding than the rest,
As having greater sin and lesser grace.
Therefore such gross and earthly spirits do serve
For jugglers, witches, and vild sorcerers. (9.56–69)

Vandermast's speech, like Bungay's which precedes it, bears some resemblance to the discussions of hell and the heavens in which Faustus and Mephistopheles engage, but it implies a radically different conception both of theology and of cosmology. In a sort of fusion of Heinrich Cornelius Agrippa's writings on elemental demons with Christian notions of the Fall, Vandermast describes a sliding scale of offence in which beings experience varying degrees of punishment, and inhabit different elements, depending on the extent of their sin, and in which Lucifer is not so much the enemy of mankind as the factotum of the less respectable sort of conjuror.[23] Given that Vandermast is ultimately defeated by Bacon, and given Bacon's eventual belief that he needs to repent, one cannot say that this view is unambiguously sanctioned by the play. However, the very existence of a substantial critical debate over the moral status of Bacon's magic would appear to suggest that the flat statement, 'Bacon must be damned / For using devils to countervail his God' does not satisfactorily encapsulate the play's position; and as will become apparent later in this chapter, other dramatists would find it convenient to allow themselves a degree of latitude when depicting the spiritual dangers of conjuring.[24]

Another important aspect of *Friar Bacon and Friar Bungay* that facilitates this more forgiving attitude towards magic is its setting. Chronologically speaking, the play is one that seems to inhabit different eras simultaneously. In some respects, it is very much a product of the 1580s: its depiction of a foreign conjuror, Vandermast, disputing about magic with Friar Bungay at Oxford recalls the visit of the Italian Neoplatonist Giordano Bruno to the University in 1583, and Bacon's repeated plan

---

[23] On Agrippa's demons, see Frances Yates, *Giordano Bruno and the Hermetic Tradition* (London: Routledge and Kegan Paul, 1964), p. 140.

[24] See, for example, Frank Towne, '"White Magic" in *Friar Bacon and Friar Bungay*?', *Modern Language Notes*, 67 (1952), 9–13; Albert Wertheim, 'The Presentation of Sin in *Friar Bacon and Friar Bungay*', *Criticism*, 16 (1974), 273–89.

'To compass English with a wall of brass' (2.29) suggests the invasion anxieties of that decade.[25] The fiction, though, is apparently set in the mid-thirteenth century, focusing on the historical individuals Roger Bacon (*c*.1214–1292?), Henry III (r.1216–1272) and Edward, Prince of Wales (1239–1307). Then again, the fact that a king named Henry retains a fool named Simnel who swaps identities with the Prince, in a play that also includes a character named Lambert, dimly suggests the era of Henry VII and the royal imposter Lambert Simnel, who was made to serve in the royal scullery after his capture, while the Skeltonic verses used by Bacon's subsizar Miles also connote the early Tudor period.[26]

This temporal instability serves to locate the play not so much in the thirteenth century as in a generalised pre-Reformation England, an effect that is emphasised by Greene's decision to base the love-plot in rural Suffolk, in his native East Anglia. He creates a distinctively English pastoral idiom of the kind that Shakespeare would go on to use in *The Winter's Tale*, all classical deities and dairy products, as in Prince Edward's description of Margaret of Fressingfield:

> Into the milkhouse went I with the maid,
> And there amongst the cream bowls she did shine
> As Pallas, mongst her princely huswifery. (1.74–6)

The idealised rusticity belongs not so much to the thirteenth century as to that mythical locale, Merry England, a concept that Greene himself surely wants to evoke with the rather overdone adjectives in such speeches as:

> Thou comest in post from merry Fressingfield,
> Fast-fancied to the keeper's bonny lass,
> To crave some succour of the jolly friar. (5.71–3)[27]

As Deanne Williams writes, 'Bringing together an idealised, bucolic world of milkmaids and country fairs, the grand pageantry of the royal court, and

---

[25] See also 2.57–60: 'And I will strengthen England by my skill, / That if ten Caesars lived and reigned in Rome, / With all the legions Europe doth contain, / They should not touch a grass of English ground'. On Giordano Bruno, see James Dow McCallum, 'Greene's *Friar Bacon and Friar Bungay*', *Modern Language Notes*, 35 (1920), 212–17.

[26] See Frank R. Ardolino, 'Robert Greene's Use of the Lambert Simnell Imposture in *Friar Bacon and Friar Bungay*', *American Notes and Queries*, 20 (1981), 37–9. On Miles's Skeltonics, see Deanne Williams, '*Friar Bacon and Friar Bungay* and the Rhetoric of Temporality', in *Reading the Medieval in Early Modern England*, ed. by David Matthews and Gordon McMullan (Cambridge: Cambridge University Press, 2007), pp. 31–48 (pp. 45–6).

[27] The term 'Merry England' had been in use for the best part of two centuries. See *OED*, 'Merry England', *n*.

the dank, dark lairs of magicians/scholars, the play presents a stereotypical, cardboard-cutout vision of the Middle Ages.'[28]

While critics often attribute the play's bucolic aspect to a nationalist agenda – 'the celebration of England', in Leggatt's phrase – it also helps to shape our response to the depiction of magic.[29] Firstly, Greene's medievalism connotes a 'world of romance' in which, as Kerstin Assarsson-Rizzi notes, a magician might be an enchanter like Merlin rather than a raiser of devils.[30] But secondly, as John D. Cox has argued, the hazily pre-Reformation setting evokes a 'more hopeful' England, one in which the magician's redemption is relatively unproblematic.[31] As we have already seen, Bacon worries that

> The hours I have spent in pyromantic spells,
> The fearful tossing in the latest night
> Of papers full of nigromantic charms,
> Conjuring and adjuring devils and fiends
> With stole and alb and strange pentaganon . . .
> Are instances that Bacon must be damned
> For using devils to countervail his God. (13.87–91, 96–7)

While Cox stresses the doctrinally '[t]raditional' elements that appear later in the same speech such as 'the invoking of Christ's passion as the effective antidote for evil' at ll. 101–5 (quoted earlier), Bacon's anxious scrutiny of his deeds for evidence that he may not be one of the elect is more characteristic of Elizabethan Protestantism. Greene anticipates the terms of Arthur Dent's *The Plaine Mans Path-way to Heauen* (1601), which lists 'nine verie cleare and manifest signes of a mans condemnation' and explains, 'hee that hath these signes vpon him, is in a most wofull case'. According to Calvinist orthodoxy, the fate of the damned, as well as that of the saved, is predestined: 'The scripture saith, they were of olde ordained to this condemnation.'[32] This means that such signs are not merely symptoms of spiritual ill-health, but indications that God has marked one out for hell – a view with which Bacon's interpretation of his actions as 'instances that Bacon must be damned' seems to correspond. And yet no sooner has Bacon expressed the problem than it vanishes and he repents. This could be understood as a sudden and unheralded conversion in the

---

[28] Williams, p. 31.   [29] Leggatt, p. 31.

[30] Kerstin Assarsson-Rizzi, '*Friar Bacon and Friar Bungay': A Structural and Thematic Analysis of Robert Greene's Play*, Lund Studies in English, 44 (Lund: C. W. K. Gleepup, 1972), p. 79, 81.

[31] Cox, p. 128.

[32] Arthur Dent, *The Plaine Mans Path-way to Heauen* (London, 1601; STC: 6626.5), pp. 33, 304.

manner of Paul, and indeed, Damascus is mentioned twice in the play (4.27, 8.113). But, following Cox, I would argue that Greene's decision to set his magician play before the Reformation also helps to make Bacon's repentance more dramatically plausible, in so far as it takes place in a context to which Protestant soteriology is alien. The obvious contrast is with *Doctor Faustus*, whose Wittenberg location makes the very same theological problems inescapable for the protagonist.

A final major way in which the broadly comic identity of *Friar Bacon and Friar Bungay* manifests itself is the incorporation of a love-plot involving Prince Edward's request that Ned Lacy, Earl of Lincoln, woo Margaret of Fressingfield on his behalf, with the predictable consequence that Lacy falls in love with her himself. Bacon expands considerably a chapter in *The Famous History of Fryer Bacon*, 'How Fryer *Bacon* did helpe a young man to his Sweetheart, which Fryer *Bungye* would haue married to another; and of the mirth that was at the wedding' (as well as changing the roles of the magicians), and it is worth noting that Greene's direction of travel here seems to contrast with that of Marlowe: the English Faust Book does include a description of 'How Doctor Faustus made a marriage between two lovers', but Marlowe omits it from his tragedy.[33] Rather than being subordinated to the magician plot that gives the play its name, the love-plot is substantial in its own right, leading Lavin to suggest that *Friar Bacon* is probably 'the first English play in which a true double-plot (as opposed to a comic sub-plot) was employed', although the paucity of romantic comedy surviving from the 1580s in fact makes it impossible to gauge Greene's originality with precision.[34] More than that: Greene has been praised both for the deftness with which he interweaves the two plots, and for their thematic interconnections, which as Empson observes represent the process of 'dramatizing a literary metaphor – "the power of beauty is like the power of magic"; both are individualist, dangerous, and outside the social order'.[35] Not only does the mutual attraction of Edward and Lacy sow enmity between them; Lambert and Serlsby fall out over Margaret with fatal results. The fact that it is Bacon's magic that enables their sons to see and emulate the combat neatly brings together the themes of magic and beauty that Empson identifies, and the fact that his repentance

---

[33] *The Famous History of Fryer Bacon* (London, 1629; STC: 1184), sig. F1r; *The English Faust Book*, p. 168.

[34] Robert Greene, *Friar Bacon and Friar Bungay*, ed. Lavin, p. xxi.

[35] William Empson, *Some Versions of Pastoral: A Study of the Pastoral Form in Literature* (London: Chatto and Windus, 1935; repr. Harmondsworth: Peregrine, 1966), p. 33. On the formal interweaving, see Assarsson-Rizzi, pp. 44–62.

is immediately followed by the scene of her preparing to become a nun emphasises the parallel.

The preceding paragraphs summarise significant divergences between Greene's treatment of magic and magicians in *Friar Bacon and Friar Bungay* and Marlowe's in *Doctor Faustus*. Unlike *Faustus*, *Friar Bacon* does not send its titular character to hell at the climax. The practice of dealing with devils is not treated as an insurmountable obstacle to salvation; indeed, the play gestures (very tentatively) towards an alternative cosmology that incorporates 'spirits' as well as devils such as Lucifer and company. This relatively accommodating treatment of magic is facilitated by the medieval setting, which distances the play from Calvinist theories of salvation as well as evoking the world of romance, and it reflects a generic preference for comedy that is also manifested in the incorporation of a substantial love-plot. This formula proved popular: while *Doctor Faustus* has become the more canonical text, it was *Friar Bacon and Friar Bungay*, I shall argue, that set the pattern that other plays on similar themes would follow over next few years.

John of Bordeaux and *A Knack to Know a Knave*

John of Bordeaux, the sequel to *Friar Bacon and Friar Bungay*, was not printed in the early modern period: W. L. Renwick's Malone Society edition of 1936 is derived from a manuscript in the library of the Duke of Northumberland at Alnwick Castle.[36] Although the play's authorship is not stated on the manuscript, Waldo McNeir in 1949 offered substantial reasons for supposing it to be the work of Greene. These include points of style and rhetoric and the appearance of themes and motifs common in Greene's other work, but also a combination of a 'close and suggestive' dependency of *John of Bordeaux* upon *Friar Bacon* in several particulars, and a willingness to develop the material in ways that seem to be anticipated in the original drama. Rather than the playwright simply reprising *Friar Bacon*, 'In the sequel Bacon is no longer the "jolly friar" of the earlier play. He is older, more staid, and more religious-minded.' This allows *John of Bordeaux* to incorporate entertaining depictions of magic without totally invalidating Bacon's repudiation of it at the end of the first play. The 'coherent development' that McNeir identifies led Paul Dean to argue that

---

[36] *John of Bordeaux; or, The Second Part of Friar Bacon*, ed. by William Lindsay Renwick (Oxford: Malone Society, 1936), p. v. References to the play use this edition. Speech prefixes have been regularised. For ease of reading, I have speculatively inserted line-breaks, using the symbol '[/]'.

we should see *Friar Bacon/John of Bordeaux* as a two-part drama in the manner of *Tamburlaine* or *Henry IV*, one in which the second part repeats elements of the first but in a different, more sombre key.[37] On the other hand, Lawrence Manley and Sally-Beth MacLean have recently argued that the second play offers not simply a development, but 'an opposing approach to the problem of magic' to that in *Friar Bacon*, in keeping with the different company auspices that they propose for the two plays (as well as implicitly rejecting Greene's authorship): 'so far has Bacon forgotten his earlier renunciation that he now . . . masters the power of the devil in order to defend persecuted virtue'.[38] Although, in the paragraphs below, I argue that *John of Bordeaux* is entirely compatible with *Friar Bacon* given the limitations Greene creates at the end of the first play, the uncertainties of authorship and company attribution that Manley and MacLean highlight need to be borne in mind when constructing narratives about the two plays' relationship.

As McNeir indicates, *John of Bordeaux* indicates from the outset that the protagonist is not what he was. Told by the Emperor Frederick – whose court Bacon is visiting – to 'be meri' (l. 38), he explains that 'Bacon is ould and age can not be blith [/] fo^r many yeares must meditat on sin' (ll. 43–4), recalling his determination in the first play to 'spend the remnant of my life / In pure devotion' (13.106–7). Although Bacon continues to use magic, he does so in a way that is much less morally dubious, for example in helping to protect John of Bordeaux's wife Rossalin from the predatory attentions of the Emperor's son Ferdinand (in a reversal of the first play, where he abetted Prince Edward in hindering the true love of Lacy and Margaret). In a scene where Bacon, imprisoned with Rossalin, attempts to loosen his chains by magic, Greene makes it unambiguously clear that he has not given away his soul. When the magic fails, Bacon summons devils:

> [ASTEROTH] Quid petes Bacon
> BACON Quid petes why stubbern hellhound[es] what[es] the case
>   this rusti Iorne hang[es] vpon my narme
>   why shakes not of theas Chaynes when as I charme
>   heaven yearth and hell why quak[es] not all yor poures
> ASTEROTH no Bacon no it goes not with the as twas wont
>   the hellish sperrit[es] ar no mor at thy commaund

[37] Waldo F. McNeir, 'Robert Greene and *John of Bordeaux*', *PMLA* 64 (1949), 781–801 (pp. 782, 798); Paul Dean, *Friar Bacon and Friar Bungay* and *John of Bordeaux*: A Dramatic Diptych', *English Language Notes*, 28 (1980–81), 262–6.
[38] Manley and MacLean, pp. 197–8; on the play's company auspices, see pp. 93–6.

thy tyme prefickst thy pour hath a nend
and thow art ours both bodie and soull ho ho ho
BACON away presuming speright away thow hast no
    pouer over a Cristian fayth willt thow do what
    I commaund the do [/]
DEVIL no Bacon no
BACON no Seleno frater hecatis vnbrarum pater
    et trux erinis nube tenarivm nemvs
    flintisqui frodis horida mici teges it nox Cleno
    qui flctis manv negra et retortes luna pernox
    cornibus ha desta [/]
ASTEROTH stay Bacon I will do
    what so ever thou commandst me do (ll. 1135–52)

The devils' claims that Bacon's body and soul are theirs are revealed to be
no more than threats, presumably uttered with the intention of making
him despair. By contrast, Bacon's spells appear to have actual power over
devils, in a reversal of Protestant orthodoxy which held that devils merely
pretended that this was so in order to entrap the conjuror.[39]

While Bacon is spared both the moral dubiousness and the spiritual
danger that are attached to magic in the first play, these qualities do not
disappear altogether from *John of Bordeaux*: instead they are displaced onto
the German conjuror Vandermast, whose role as antagonist is more
substantial than in *Friar Bacon and Friar Bungay* (perhaps in a recollection
of the prose *Famous History*, where Vandermast tries to have Bacon killed).
Here, Vandermast aids Ferdinand in his attempts to seduce Rossalin,
deludes the Emperor into thinking John of Bordeaux has betrayed him,
and then persuades him to have Bacon and Rossalin arrested for treason.
Bacon eventually punishes Vandermast by having him struck mad, 'and
whilst he lives this spiret shall wait on him' (l. 1283):

> BACON blush ferdenaund and tremble at the sigh
>   of my reveng, se how the partener of
>   thy practies is plaged with feweris
>   how his conshince stinges
>   gerasles repent and thow shallt
>   yet find grace
> VANDERMAST grace I grace is a pretie wench I know her well
>   com hether phelossopher what[es] hell
>   tell me how manie drope of blud ther

[39] See Genevieve Guenther, 'Why Devils Came when Faustus Called for Them', *Modern Philology*, 109 (2011), 46–70 (pp. 52–3).

is in the sea or thow diest non place tibe domene
ther is no grace fo^r me com awea to hell (ll. 1289–99)

While the relationship of *Friar Bacon and Friar Bungay* to *Doctor Faustus* may be disputable, Vandermast's deranged inability to respond to Bacon's exhortation that he repent, his questioning of his attendant devil about the nature of hell, and the echoes of specific lines from *Faustus* such as 'Away, to hell, to hell' (2.3.164) and 'I charge thee wait upon me whilst I live' (1.3.37) strongly suggest that *John of Bordeaux*, at least, came after Marlowe's play. It is quite conceivable that Marlowe would take Bacon's repentance in the first play and subversively re-imagine it, but it is difficult to see why he would want to reinvest Vandermast as we see him here with tragic dignity, recasting his pathetic outbursts as serious intellectual inquiry.

   If one reason for Vandermast's prominence in the second play is the need to provide a focus for the more disreputable aspects of magic that Friar Bacon has left behind, a second reason is dictated by structural considerations. In the first part Bacon is, in a sense, his own enemy, as well as that of other sympathetic characters: he himself obstructs the nuptials of Margaret and Lacy, and following the deaths of the Suffolk farmers and their sons he comes to understand that the practice of magic is something that imperils his soul. In *John of Bordeaux*, however, he uses magic to intervene on the side of good and there is no indication that he should regret doing so; but the advantage that magic gives him over others means that as a meaningful antagonist he requires another magician – namely Vandermast, who uses spirits to produce a counterfeit letter incriminating John of Bordeaux and to bring Rossalin in her nightgown to Ferdinand, as well as magically enabling the Emperor to see Bacon conferring with the interdicted Rossalin. The defeat of Vandermast appears towards the end of *John of Bordeaux* – part of the manuscript is lost, but the general shape of the ending can be inferred – and it would surely have been problematic for Greene to develop the Friar Bacon material beyond this point.[40] As Barbara Howard Traister says of magicians in romance, 'the entrance ... of a powerful good magician requires some magical competition just to keep the plot alive': in the drama, an individual whose magical powers give him mastery over others, but whose reformed character means he need not fear death, is not conducive to

---

[40] For a conjectural ending, see Waldo McNeir, 'Reconstructing the Conclusion of *John of Bordeaux*', *PMLA*, 66 (1951), 540–43.

dramatic tension.[41] This impasse is one to which other plays featuring magicians can be seen to respond.

John of Bordeaux, logically enough, shares the medieval setting of *Friar Bacon and Friar Bungay*, although in the sequel Greene deserts his English pastoral idyll for the world of chivalric romance: John fights to defend Ravenna against the Turks, and announces in the first scene that 'Huan of Burdiox was myn Awnsester' (ll. 14–15) – alluding to the hero of the medieval *chanson de geste, Huon de Bordeaux*, translated from the French by Lord Berners during the reign of Henry VIII (and, incidentally, featuring a fairy king called Oberon).[42] As was noted in the discussion of *Friar Bacon*, the romance idiom is one in which a positive treatment of a magician may be appropriate. While the next magician play I shall consider, *A Knack to Know a Knave* (first performed by Lord Strange's Men at the Rose on 10 June 1592), cannot be called a romance, it does retain a medieval setting, this time in the tenth-century England of King Edgar.[43]

As Arthur Freeman notes, *A Knack to Know a Knave* is 'an extremely allusive play', including references to texts by contemporary dramatists such as Greene, Lodge, Marlowe and Peele.[44] Its depiction of a dying usurer who utters the words 'My heart is hardened, I cannot repent' (l. 369) before being carried away by a devil seems to place it in the ranks of plays influenced by *Doctor Faustus*, whose protagonist finds that 'My heart's so hardened I cannot repent' (2.3.18).[45] The romantic plot strand in which King Edgar sends Ethenwald to woo the fair Alfrida on his behalf only for Ethenwald to marry her himself is in fact derived from historical sources: the narrative appears in Holinshed, albeit with a less happy outcome for Ethelwold/Ethenwald.[46] However, the recent appearance of a very similar plot in *Friar Bacon and Friar Bungay* may well have been the immediate stimulus to its use in *A Knack to Know a Knave*.

The magician in *A Knack to Know a Knave* is Saint Dunstan, the ninth-century Abbot of Glastonbury and subsequently Archbishop of Canterbury.

---

[41] Barbara Howard Traister, *Heavenly Necromancers: The Magician in English Renaissance Drama* (Columbia: University of Missouri Press, 1984), p. 24.

[42] The first edition may date from as early as 1515, but the date is not given. See James P. Carley, 'Bourchier, John, second Baron Berners (c.1467–1533)', *Oxford Dictionary of National Biography* (Oxford: Oxford University Press, 2004); online edn www.oxforddnb.com/view/article/2990 (accessed 30 July 2015). On Oberon, see Hackett, 'Introduction', p. xxxiii.

[43] *Henslowe's Diary*, p. 19.

[44] Arthur Freeman, 'Two Notes on *A Knack to Know a Knave*', *Notes and Queries*, 207 (1962), 326–7.

[45] *A Knack to Know a Knave*, ed. by G. R. Proudfoot (Oxford: Malone Society, 1964). References to the play use this edition, with regularised speech prefixes.

[46] Raphael Holinshed et al., *The First and Second Volumes of Chronicles* (London, 1587; STC: 13569), vol. II, p. 160.

According to Holinshed's *Chronicles*, 'Of this Dunstane manie things are recorded by writers, that he should be of such holinesse and vertue, that God wrought manie miracles by him, both whilest he liued heere on earth, and also after his decease.' The main text records (amongst other things) Dunstan's visions of devils, his premonitions of royal deaths, his banishment 'for rebuking king Edwin for his vnlawfull lust and lewd life', and his recall by King Edgar, whom he puts to penance for unchastity, although it passes over as 'friuolous' such matters as 'The common tale of his plucking the diuell by the nose with a paire of pinsors, for tempting him with women, while he was making a chalice'. However, the printed marginalia are positively cynical about 'the deep hypocrisie of Dunstane', who is accused of making up a story about an angel in order to conceal his misappropriation of royal funds.[47] More extremely, in *The Actes of Englysh Votaryes* John Bale offers a violently anti-Catholic reading of the historical record, casting Dunstan as a sorcerer who 'founde the meanes to augment and enryche the monasteryes of monkes and nonnes euerye where whithin Englande, not withstandynge he had oft tymes moche a do with deuyls and with women'. This Dunstan manipulates kings such as Edward, 'whom by hys necromancye he brought to the poynte, inuysysyblye [*sic*] to haue bene torne in peces', and is particularly reprehensible for his actions against married priests.[48]

While a variety of images of Dunstan were available to Elizabethan dramatists, ranging from the saintly to the almost satanic, the playwright (or playwrights) responsible for *A Knack to Know a Knave* apparently chose the frivolous version discarded in the chronicles: an upright man who is on terms with devils, while firmly retaining both the upper hand and his spiritual integrity. This is evident when Dunstan seeks to discover what King Edgar has in store for Ethenwald (Dunstan's nephew) following his illicit marriage:

> DUNSTAN *Asmoroth ascende, veni Asmoroth, Asmoroth veni.*
> *Enaer [sic] the Deuill.*
> DEVIL What wilt thou?
> DUNSTAN Tell me what means the King?
> DEVIL I will not tell thee.
> DUNSTAN I charge thee by the eternall liuing God,

---

[47] Holinshed et al., pp. 165, 158, 161.
[48] John Bale, *The Actes of Englysh Votaryes* (Antwerp, 1546 (false imprint); STC: 1270), fols 54v–55r, 61r–62r.

That keeps the Prince of darknes bound in chaines,
And by that Sun, that thou wouldst gladly see,
By heauen and earth, and euery liuing thing,
Tel me that which I did demand of thee.
DEVIL Then thus, the king doth mean to murther *Ethenwald*
DUNSTAN But where is the king?
DEVIL Seeking for *Ethenwald*.
DUNSTAN But Ile preuent him, follow me inuuisible.
DEVIL I wil. (ll. 1582–96)

In a later episode, the precise nature of which the stage direction leaves unclear, the Devil brings in 'Alfrida disguised' (l. 1717) in a manner that causes Edgar to pardon Ethenwald.

It would be wrong to see Dunstan as idealised in *A Knack to Know a Knave*. While he does attempt to offer Edgar wise counsel, for example in telling him he must marry Alfrida rather than making her his concubine (ll. 188–9), he is ultimately something of a yes-man, quoting with approval Hephaestion's words 'When *Alexander* wan rich *Macedone*': 'That what so ere the King himselfe thought meete, / He would in dutifull obedience yield vnto' (ll. 124–6). This is hardly the Dunstan who 'kepeth the Kynges of Englande vndre', as Bale has it.[49] However, he is sufficiently good for the playwright to encounter in him the problem made apparent at the end of *John of Bordeaux*: namely, what to do with a character who combines moral probity with supernatural power, and therefore lacks meaningful obstacles. The answer, in this play, is to make him a relatively marginal figure. He hardly participates in the love-plot until forced to intervene in order to save his nephew, and not at all in the play's other main plot strand, in which Honesty lays bare the villainies of the Priest, the Conycatcher, the Courtier and the Farmer. The representative misdeeds of the various social estates are ills too profound even for a magician-saint to meddle in.

While *John of Bordeaux* and *A Knack to Know a Knave* are apparently influenced by *Doctor Faustus* both generally (in depicting magicians who conjure devils) and in more specific verbal parallels, the two plays treat their material in a way much closer to *Friar Bacon and Friar Bungay*. Their magicians do not seem to be headed for damnation, an impression that is reinforced by the use of medieval settings in which the positive depiction of magic is appropriate; and the broadly comic nature of the plays is reflected in the incorporation of love-plots in which the magicians

---

[49] Bale, fol. 57r.

intervene. These tendencies are particularly in evidence in the final magician play I shall consider before going on to examine *A Midsummer Night's Dream*: Anthony Munday's *John a Kent and John a Cumber*.

John a Kent and John a Cumber

John a Kent and John a Cumber presents two substantial problems to the literary historian. The first concerns the text '. . . Decembris 159[-]' that appears at the end of the manuscript in which the play is preserved. In the Malone Society edition of the play, Muriel St.Clare Byrne gives the digit after the 9 as a 6, correcting John Payne Collier who read it as a 5.[50] This ostensibly provides a terminal date for the writing of the play, although its precise significance is unclear (not least because the script is in a different hand from that which produced the text of the play proper, which is signed 'Anthony Mundy'). However, in a *Shakespeare Survey* article of 1955, I. A. Shapiro printed enlarged images of the manuscript that, he argued, showed that the date was in fact 1590 – a reading that was generally accepted over the decades that followed.[51] More recently, though, Grace Ioppolo has asserted that 'the flourish still visible at the top of the last number in this date in the manuscript . . . makes clear that it is a 5, not a 0', while MacDonald P. Jackson has found other examples of sixes (but not of noughts) being formed as they are on the *John a Kent* manuscript, concluding 'that the old *terminus ad quem* of December 1596 should be reinstated.'[52]

The question of whether 1590, 1595 or 1596 should be regarded as the play's terminal date is important for several reasons. It has implications for the dating of the play *Sir Thomas More*, a manuscript largely in Munday's hand that includes additions many think to be Shakespeare's. It has a bearing on the question of whether an allusion in *The Protestation of*

---

[50] *John a Kent and John a Cumber*, ed. by Muriel St.Clare Byrne (Oxford: Malone Society, 1923), l. 1707 and n. Subsequent references to the play use this edition.

[51] I. A. Shapiro, 'The Significance of a Date', *Shakespeare Survey*, 8 (1955), 100–5. E. A. J. Honigmann questions 'the assumption that a date added at the end of a torn manuscript, for purposes unknown and apparently *not* in Mundy's hand, must have been added in December 1590 rather than at a later date'; however, he does not question the reading of the date as 1590, and his essay argues that 1590 is in fact the date of the play. '*John a Kent* and Marprelate', *Yearbook of English Studies*, 13 (1983), 288–93 (p. 288).

[52] Grace Ioppolo, *Dramatists and Their Manuscripts in the Age of Shakespeare, Jonson, Middleton and Heywood: Authorship, Authority and the Playhouse* (Abingdon: Routledge, 2006), p. 209 n3; MacDonald P. Jackson, 'Deciphering a Date and Determining a Date: Anthony Munday's *John a Kent and John a Cumber* and the Original Version of *Sir Thomas More*', *Early Modern Literary Studies* 15.3 (2011): 2, paragraph 8.

Martin Marprelate (September 1589) to 'John a Cant his hobby-horse' as one of the 'rimers and stage-players' suborned to write against the Marprelate pamphlets may refer to Munday and to this drama.[53] And finally, it is inextricably related to the second substantial problem offered by this play: its possible position in the Admiral's Men repertory. Some commentators, such as W. W. Greg, have argued that the *John a Kent* manuscript preserves the play that in references from 2 December 1594 onward Henslowe calls 'the wise man of chester', 'the wissman of weschester', and variations thereon; as Jackson succinctly puts it, *'John a Kent* is set in Chester and its hero is a "wise man" or magician'.[54] However, in an article of 1984 Roslyn L. Knutson forcefully argues the reverse, pointing out that recent scholarship in theatre history has shown how 'the duplication of other troupes' plays with similar but original texts of one's own' was 'a regular feature of competition among the professional companies'. Accordingly, we should be wary of assuming that 'two plays were identical merely because they shared titles and/or leading characters'.[55] Furthermore, if we want to identify *John a Kent* with *The Wise Man of West Chester* then a 1590 date for the earlier play requires us to accept that in 1594 the Admiral's Men revived (as 'ne') a play written four years ago for another company and went on to play it very profitably under a different name for another three years. In fact, Knutson argues, it makes much more sense to see *John a Kent* as a magician play written around 1590 to capitalise on the success of *Friar Bacon and Friar Bungay* and its sequel (and perhaps *Doctor Faustus*), and *The Wise Man of West Chester* as a new play written to accompany *Faustus* in the repertory from 1594 onwards.[56] However, while Knutson's statement that we should not assume that two plays were identical just because they apparently featured similar characters is indisputable, her demolition of Greg's argument takes it as given that the date on the *John a Kent* manuscript is 1590: if the date is in fact 1595 or 1596, then (as Jackson and Douglas H. Arrell have both pointed out) Greg's position is much less problematic, and requires only that Anthony Munday

---

[53] See Shapiro; *The Martin Marprelate Tracts: A Modernized and Annotated Edition*, ed. by Joseph L. Black (Cambridge: Cambridge University Press, 2008), p. 204.

[54] *Henslowe's Diary*, ed. Foakes and Rickert, p. 26; Walter W. Greg, *Henslowe's Diary*, 2 vols (London: A. H. Bullen, 1904–8), vol. II, p.172; Jackson, 'Deciphering a Date', paragraph 9.

[55] Roslyn L. Knutson, 'Play Identifications: *The Wise Man of West Chester* and *John a Kent and John a Cumber; Longshanks* and *Edward I*', *Huntington Library Quarterly*, 47 (1984), 1–11 (pp. 3–4).

[56] Knutson, pp. 4–5, 7. A further detail of Knutson's dispute with Greg concerns Greg's identification of 'Kentes woden leage' in an inventory dating from 1598 as a property connected with this play (which does not require a wooden leg), although 'Kent' seems sufficiently generic as a name for this complication to be left out of the picture.

produced a manuscript some time before December 1596 of a play that was in existence in 1594.[57] This does not diminish the force of her caveat about play identifications: we certainly cannot assume that the two plays are identical, but given that Henslowe apparently gives several plays different titles to those they survive under elsewhere, nor can we assume that they were different.[58]

The argument that will be made over the following paragraphs, which identifies points of similarity between *John a Kent* and *A Midsummer Night's Dream*, therefore has two alternative sets of implications. If we take the date on the *John a Kent* manuscript as 1595 or 1596, which permits us to view the play as *The Wise Man of West Chester* under a different name, then it means that Shakespeare was influenced by a play that, like *Doctor Faustus* (and unlike the Friar Bacon plays or *A Knack to Know a Knave*), was in the Admiral's repertory at the time when he was writing *A Midsummer Night's Dream*. If we accept the date as 1590, however, then it reduces the likelihood that *John a Kent* is *The Wise Man of West Chester*. That would indicate that Shakespeare knew the play by some other means – perhaps as a member of the company that first acted it – but that in the mid-1590s it remained sufficiently memorable for the Admiral's to want to stage a different play whose title recalled it; thus, *John a Kent and John a Cumber* was kept alive in the memory of playwrights and playgoers alike, perhaps encouraging Shakespeare to write another play that drew upon Munday's original. This would place *The Wise Man of West Chester* along with 'palamon & a'sett' and 'the greasyon comedy' as a group of lost plays whose titles suggest a dramatic environment in which *A Midsummer Night's Dream* was an appropriate offering: a magician play in the *Friar Bacon* mould, a play derived from Chaucer's 'Knight's Tale' and a comedy set in Greece, all playing alongside *Doctor Faustus*.[59] The readers may choose between these two positions depending on their interpretation of the evidence set out above.

---

[57] Jackson, 'Deciphering a Date', n. 15; Douglas H. Arrell, 'John a Kent, the Wise Man of Westchester', *Early Theatre* 17.1 (2014), 75–92. I do not, however, follow Arrell in reading *John a Kent* as an imitation of *A Midsummer Night's Dream*.

[58] Possible examples are 'Jeronymo' (*Henslowe's Diary*, p. 17), typically identified with *The Spanish Tragedy*, and 'the comodey of vmers' (p. 58), typically identified with *An Humorous Day's Mirth*. One instance where the titles are similar enough to indicate that the same play is being referred to is the 'seconde parte of the downefall of earlle huntyngton surnamed Roben Hoode', also known as 'the seconde pte of Roben Hoode' (p. 87) but published as *The Death of Robert, Earle of Huntington* (see Chapter 5).

[59] For 'palamon & a'sett', see *Henslowe's Diary*, p. 24 (17 September 1594). For 'the greasyon comody', see p. 25 (23 November 1594).

Like *John of Bordeaux* and *A Knack to Know a Knave*, *John a Kent and John a Cumber* seems in some respects to be indebted to *Doctor Faustus*. Its magic-working protagonist is 'deeply seene, / [i]n secret artes' (ll. 106–7), an epithet that recalls Cornelius's requirement for the would-be magician to be 'well seen in minerals' (1.1.141). When John a Kent is asked,

> Canst thou my freend, from foorth the vaultes beneathe,
> call vp the ghostes of those long since deceast?
> Or from the vpper region of the ayre:
> fetche swifte wingde spirits to effect thy will? (ll. 108–11)

Munday seems to be combining Emperor Charles V's request that Faustus raise Alexander the Great and his paramour 'from hollow vaults below' (4.1.36), Faustus's caveat that he cannot present 'the true substantial bodies of those two deceased princes, which long since are consumed to dust' (4.1.48–50), and Faustus's earlier plan to 'make spirits fetch me what I please' and 'Perform what desperate enterprise I will' (1.1.81, 83).[60] John a Kent is reputed to be able to 'make a man a Munkey in lesse then halfe a minute of an houre' (ll. 1037–8), a trick we see performed in Act 3, Scene 2 of Marlowe's play. And a supernatural presence is experienced as 'a voice [that] buzzeth comfort in mine eare' (l. 1126): compare *Faustus* 2.3.14, where the Evil Angel 'buzzeth in mine ears'.

However, Munday's treatment of his magician also conforms to the pattern that has been identified in the Friar Bacon plays and *A Knack to Know a Knave*. Like Bacon and Dunstan, John a Kent takes part in a romantic intrigue, helping Sir Griffin Meriddock and Lord Geoffrey Powis marry Sidanen and Marian, whose fathers Llwellen, Prince of North Wales and Ranulph, Earl of Chester have arranged for them to marry the Earl of Morton and the Earl of Pembroke. This ostensibly situates the play in the time of Ranulf de Blundeville, Earl of Chester (1170–1232), the subject of a number of ballads and tales.[61] However, in so far as the titular character has a historical source it seems to be Siôn Cent, a Welsh poet active in the early fifteenth century, who, as his *ODNB* biographer puts it, 'was later confused with several other figures of similar name and became a popular character in the folklore of the Welsh marches, famed as a trickster and wizard'.[62] Thus, as in *Friar Bacon and Friar Bungay*, an air of generic

---

[60] For 'region of the air', see *1 Tamburlaine*, 4.2.30 and 5.1.250.

[61] See J. W. Ashton, '"Rymes of . . . Randolf, Erl of Chestre"', *ELH*, 5 (1938), 195–206.

[62] Dafydd Johnston, 'Siôn Cent [John Kent] (*fl.* 1400–1430)', *Oxford Dictionary of National Biography* (Oxford: Oxford University Press, 2004); online edn www.oxforddnb.com/view/article/15419 (accessed 30 July 2015).

medievalism is created by the combination of multiple historical specificities. And as in *John of Bordeaux*, the rival lovers are assisted by a rival magician, John a Cumber.

As a basis for a central character, Sîon Cent/John a Kent has points of affinity both with Faustus and with Bacon. The historical Sîon Cent may have studied at Oxford, as of course Bacon did, 'where he would have been influenced by the empirical philosophy of *scientia experimentalis*, which may have provided a basis for his attack on the Platonic ideals of the Welsh bards'.[63] The folklore John a Kent is harder to trace: since Munday's play is his first appearance in the literary record, it is possible that the tales with which he is associated grew up after or even in response to his dramatic manifestation. (One unexpected literary appearance is in the writings of Titus Oates, fabricator of the Popish Plot, who uses both John a Kent and John a Cumber as bywords for familiarity with the devil.)[64] At any rate, Ella Mary Leather's researches in oral and printed sources in the early twentieth century found that 'Jack o' Kent'

> was a wizard in league with the Devil, and when still a boy he sold his body and soul to the 'old un' in exchange for supernatural power in this world, whether he was buried in the church or out of the church, that was the bargain. He was therefore buried at Kentchurch, or some may say at Grosmont, in the wall of the church, so that he should be 'neither in nor out.'[65]

Not only does the motif of selling one's soul link Jack o' Kent to Faustus: the trick with the church wall was presumably attached at some point to the story of Friar Bacon, explaining his otherwise unrationalised decision at the end of *The Famous History* to have 'made in the Church wall a Cell, where he locked himselfe in, and there remained till his death'.[66]

As he is imagined in the play, though, John a Kent is fundamentally different from Faustus, Bacon and Dunstan in the degree of control he has over the action. Rather than being simply a participant, Kent seems to feel a 'sense of responsibility for plot complication', as Traister puts it, that

---

[63] Johnston, 'Sîon Cent'.

[64] Titus Oates, Εικων Βασιλικη Τριτη; or, The Picture of the Late King James Further Drawn to the Life (London, 1697), p. 98: 'old *Nick* and *John of Kent*'; Εικων Βασιλικη Τεταρτη; or, The Picture of the Late King James Further Drawn to the Life (London, 1697), p. 3: 'what game he is playing, the Dee'l and *John a Cumber* knows best'.

[65] Ella Mary Leather, *The Folk-lore of Herefordshire Collected from Oral and Printed Sources* (Hereford: Jakeman and Carver; London: Sidgwick & Jackson, 1912; repr. Hereford: Lapridge Publications, 1992), p. 163.

[66] *The Famous History of Fryer Bacon*, sig. G3v.

anticipates Shakespeare's Prospero.[67] Asked by Meriddock and Powis to help them obtain their loves, he soliloquises on his reasons for accepting the task:

> since so good a subiect they present,
> vppon these loouers practise thou thy wit.
> help, hinder, giue, take back, turne, ouerturne,
> deceiue, bestowe, breed pleasure, discontent.
> yet comickly conclude, like Iohn a Kent. (ll. 132–6)

Rather than simply being deserving recipients of his help, the lovers are material on which John a Kent can exercise his wit, alternately helping and hindering them in a manner that creates the plot twists of the play and ultimately leads to a comic conclusion. The metadramatic language reappears once Kent has first conveyed Marian and Sidanen to their true loves:

> Heer's looue and looue, Good Lord, was nere the lyke,
> but must these ioyes so quickly be concluded?
> Must the first Scene make absolute a play?
> no crosse? no chaunge? what? no varietie? (ll. 528–31)

He laments the loss of entertainment that results from the curtailment of this 'play', wishing that 'some other lyke my selfe' were here 'to driue me to sound pollicyes indeed' (ll. 541–2), and names 'one in Scotland, tearmed Iohn a Cumber, / that ouerreachte the deuill by his skill' (ll. 543–4) as a suitable candidate. 'But since my selfe must pastime wth my selfe' (l. 547), as he puts it, he sends his attendant spirit Shrimp to wake the other set of bridegrooms and create further mischief. Not only does Kent here exemplify the recurrent topos of the magician as the dramatist's 'surrogate', to use Andrew V. Ettin's term; he makes explicit in theatrical terms the problem referred to earlier in relation to the end of *John of Bordeaux*, namely the loss of dramatic tension in a play where a broadly benevolent character is given powers that elevate him above the rest.[68] In *A Knack to Know a Knave*, it is resolved only by placing Dunstan at the margins of the action; Munday deals with it by giving Kent a worthy adversary, John a Cumber (who, it turns out, is alerted by Kent naming him in his thoughts, ll. 909–14), and also by giving Kent himself a ludic streak that disinclines him from easy solutions.

---

[67] Traister, p. 44.
[68] Andrew V. Ettin, 'Magic into Art: The Magician's Renunciation of Magic in English Renaissance Drama', *Texas Studies in Literature and Language*, 19 (1977), 268–93 (p. 284).

The theatrical self-consciousness that is manifested in Kent's speeches is, in fact, characteristic of *John a Kent and John a Cumber*, in that drama and disguise are used by both magicians as a way of achieving their designs. Having made himself look like John a Kent, Cumber uses a masque in which the brides' fathers and the rival grooms, each in the guise of a singing antic, gain access to the castle where the young women are held. Cumber seeks to rub Kent's nose in his failure by staging a play ostensibly featuring the lovers but really performed by 'shaddowes' (l. 1015), which will culminate in the real Kent being insulted by local rustics who have a grudge against him. However, Kent replaces the shadows with their substances, and (it seems) reverses the appearances of himself and John a Cumber, so that it is Cumber who is abused by lovers and rustics alike. The dramatic theme is embodied by Munday in a troupe of amateur actors led by Turnop, one of the Earl of Chester's household servants, who reappear several times in the action. Early on, they waylay the Earl's favoured suitors and treat them to a rather woeful pageant which Chester's son excuses with less than Thesean magnanimity by saying 'my fathers tennants after their homely guise, / welcome ye with their countrey merriment, / How bad so ere, yet must ye needes accept it' (ll. 389–91).[69] Later, they sing at the bridegrooms' window a song that Shrimp transforms to 'a Song of the Brydes losse' (581–2) to alert the grooms to their brides' absconding. Finally, they are the ones whom John a Cumber invites to abuse John a Kent, which they do by making him (really Cumber) the fool in their morris dance.

The playful atmosphere that is achieved through giving John a Kent a degree of control over the action corresponds with a diminution of the spiritual threat that was evident in the comedies discussed earlier. Bacon repudiates magic, fearing damnation, in his first play, and is menaced by a devil in *John of Bordeaux*; Vandermast goes mad; Dunstan's devil is initially disobedient; and the usurer in *A Knack to Know a Knave* is carried away to hell (as is Miles in *Friar Bacon*, although he goes voluntarily). By contrast, Kent never seems especially concerned that magic will put his soul in danger, although Donna B. Hamilton has read the ending of *John a Kent* (which does not survive in its entirety) as a rejection of disguise in so far as Kent apparently succeeds in getting Meriddock and Powis married to Sidanen and Marian without transforming their appearance.[70]

---

[69] Compare *A Midsummer Night's Dream*, 5.1.82–3: 'For never anything can be amiss / When simpleness and duty tender it.'
[70] Donna B. Hamilton, *Anthony Munday and the Catholics, 1580–1633* (Aldershot: Ashgate, 2005), pp. 114–18.

Nevertheless, while Hugh the Sexton (one of Turnop's associates) affirms that Kent 'neuer goes abroad with out a bushell of deuilles about him, that if one speak but an ill woord of him, he knowes it by and by' (ll. 1041–3), the only spirit we see is Shrimp, 'a boy' (l. 549), who transforms the clowns' music, enters Sir Gosselen Denville's castle through the keyhole to listen in on John a Cumber's plans (l. 983), charms asleep the men guarding Sidanen and Marian, and on their waking leads them on 'a merrie walke' (l. 1185) that culminates in their being forced to dance in a ring around a tree. Though mischievous, Shrimp never seems likely to demand John a Kent's soul, or anyone else's, and the audience may in any case have known that Kent would ultimately outwit the devil. For his part, Kent is not presented as theologically preoccupied, unlike the doctor Faustus, the friar Bacon, or the bishop Dunstan. When he appears 'like an aged Hermit' (l. 214), it is merely a disguise, and Powis is surprised to see that he has 'turnd greene to ffryers gray' (l. 304). This refers to Kent's first appearance, when he bid Powis and Meriddock 'stand' and demanded 'Such coyne you haue' (ll. 69, 71). This green-clad trickster is closer to Robin Hood than to Faustus or Bacon.

Indeed, Kent's Robin Hood overtones exemplify the final aspect of *John a Kent and John a Cumber* that I will discuss, one that it shares with the other magician comedies described above: namely, its studied medievalism. Munday achieves this, not only through the obvious device of incorporating historical or pseudo-historical figures, but through a recurrent reference to practices that, by the late Elizabethan period, were becoming associated with a pre-Reformation past. As Paul Whitfield White notes, Robin Hood plays and games were 'an integral part of the religious culture, even the spiritual life, of parish communities in many parts of England' right up to the Reformation, used by parish religious guilds as a means of fund-raising on holidays.[71] One feature of these games was sometimes mock-robbery (for charitable purposes), such as we see at the start of *John a Kent*.[72] Another was morris dancing, often featuring Maid Marian, Friar Tuck and other characters, which is the means Turnop and the others use to revenge themselves upon Kent (really Cumber). After letting 'mayde Marian haue the f[irst] flurt at him', and then presumably

---

[71] Paul Whitfield White, 'Holy Robin Hood! Carnival, Parish Guilds, and the Outlaw Tradition', in *Tudor Drama Before Shakespeare, 1485–1590: New Directions for Research, Criticism, and Pedagogy*, ed. by Lloyd Edward Kermode, Jason Scott-Warren and Martine van Elk (Basingstoke: Palgrave Macmillan, 2004), pp. 67–89 (p. 67).

[72] John Forrest, *The History of Morris Dancing 1458–1750* (Cambridge: James Clark, 1990) *passim*, but for example pp. 147, 152–3.

offering some physical abuse themselves, they put the fool's coat on him and 'ierk it ouer the greene, seeing we haue got such a goodly foole as M^r. Iohn a Kent' (ll. 1364–5, 1386–7). Though the morris was still practised in the 1590s, it was opposed (as John Forrest argues) both by puritans who regarded it as a pagan and Romish relic, and by an ecclesiastical hierarchy who wanted to drive it off Church property in the interests of order and conformity of worship. Forrest notes that the Visitation Articles for Chester (1581) enquire 'Whether . . . your said church, chapel or church-yard be abused or prophaned by any unlawful or unseemly act, game, or exercise, as by Lords of Misrule, Summer lords or ladies, pipers, rush-bearers, Morris dancers, pedlars, bearwards, and such like', and that, perhaps relatedly, the Chester borough accounts stop recording payments to morris dancers at the time of the midsummer watch after 1593.[73] If, as Manley and MacLean have argued, the immersion of *John a Kent and John a Cumber* in 'the landscape of Chester, Flintshire, and Holywell Priory' is evidence for its originally having belonged to Lord Strange's Men, who toured that region and whose patron was a local magnate, perhaps its incorporation of morris dancing was some kind of comment on Chester's local politics.[74] The play has also been taken as alluding to another feature of Chester's ritual calendar: the route from the castle to St John's church that the Earl of Chester expects Morton and Pembroke to take with their brides apparently echoes that of medieval religious cycle plays, which were finally suppressed in Chester during the 1570s.[75] Whatever the significance of these local references, the fact that certain practices had become contro-versial is explicitly (and anachronistically) flagged up in the play by Marian's mother when Kent, disguised as a hermit, tells the young ladies they must wash at St Winifred's spring before they marry: her husband, she says, 'condemnes these auncient rules, / religiously obserued in these partes' (ll. 271–2).

A number of possible motives for and effects of these allusions to festive and religious practices might be identified. Forrest sees the play's incorpor-ation of morris dancing as motivated by commercial considerations: in an era when the morris was becoming 'predominantly a rural sport', play-wrights included it in their drama to bring 'an authentic rustic air', appealing both as a spectacle in its own right and as part of the fiction.[76]

---

[73] Forrest, p. 117.   [74] Manley and MacLean, p. 125.

[75] Hamilton, p. 116. On the suppression of religious plays in Chester, see *English Professional Theatre, 1530–1660*, ed. by Glynne Wickham, Herbert Berry and William Ingram (Cambridge: Cambridge University Press, 2000), pp. 65–8.

[76] Forrest, p. 217.

The theatrical meanings of morris dancing may have been more complex than this, however. Mary Ellen Lamb has suggested that Spenser, Shakespeare and Jonson used it, along with other figures such as St George and the hobby horse, as 'signs of a degraded aesthetic through and against which these authors were fashioning their own forms of professionalism', distancing themselves from cultural forms they deemed popular even as they harnessed their energies.[77] In *John a Kent and John a Cumber*, a similar ambivalence may be reflected in the fact that the dance itself is performed by clownish amateur actors whose incompetent performance earlier on presumably contrasts with that of the real-life playing company.[78] On a very different tack, Hamilton's reading of the play's references to pre-Reformation culture is informed by her view that Munday was secretly Catholic, and certainly one does not need to share her biographical assumptions to find sectarian overtones in other aspects of the play – for example, its thematic concern with the relationship between shadows and substances, a binary that 'belongs to the Catholic and anti-Catholic rhetoric that had its roots in arguments over the Eucharist'.[79] The fact that all the magician comedies discussed so far are set in pre-Reformation times may be connected to views that some Protestants held about Catholicism in general and transubstantiation in particular: Kurt Tetzeli von Rosador notes William Perkins' words, 'if a man will but take a view of all poperie, he shall easily see, that the most part is meere Magique'.[80] However, as I have suggested throughout this chapter, another effect of the choice of setting is to distance the action from a Protestant orthodoxy that would tend to see the practice of magic not only as grounded on 'a league or couenant made betweene the Witch and the Deuill: wherein they doe mutually bind themselues each to other', but as a sign of reprobation.[81] By situating his play in a world of holy wells, Robin Hood, morris dancing and Corpus Christi plays, Munday evokes a cultural context where such anxieties seem less relevant.

---

[77] Mary Ellen Lamb, *The Popular Culture of Shakespeare, Spenser, and Jonson* (London: Routledge, 2006), p. 64.

[78] See Tom Rutter, *Work and Play on the Shakespearean Stage* (Cambridge: Cambridge University Press, 2008), pp. 45–7.

[79] Hamilton, pp. 117–18.

[80] William Perkins, *A Golden Chaine: or, The Description of Theologie Containing the Order of the Causes of Salvation and Damnation, According to Gods Word* (Cambridge, 1600; STC: 19646), p. 51. See Kurt Tetzeli von Rosador, 'The Sacralizing Sign: Religion and Magic in Bale, Greene, and the Early Shakespeare', *Yearbook of English Studies*, 23 (1993), 30–45 (p. 32).

[81] William Perkins, *A Discourse of the Damned Art of Witchcraft* (Cambridge, 1610; STC: 19698), pp. 41–2.

The decision to place *John a Kent and John a Cumber* at the end of my discussion of comic responses to *Doctor Faustus* inevitably makes it look like the culmination of a series, so that its incorporation of pre-Reformation cultural forms and its minimising both of the risks attendant on magic and of the physical size of John a Kent's attendant spirit appear to be the final stages of a trend already visible in the earlier plays. This may well be wrong: if we knew for a fact that the play dated from 1590 or earlier, then these attributes would instead have to be seen as representing paths that other plays did not follow so enthusiastically. More securely, it can be said that *John a Kent* graphically exemplifies features identifiable in other dramatic responses to *Doctor Faustus* that take their cue from *Friar Bacon and Friar Bungay*. These are: a preference for comedy over tragedy; the involvement of magicians in the plays' love-plots; an insistence that, *contra* William Perkins, the practice of magic does not necessitate the surrender of one's soul; and a pre-Reformation setting. The last two are taken to extremes in Munday's play, which omits stage devils entirely and includes several references to medieval religious practices as well as staging a morris dance and a mock-robbery à la Robin Hood. In these respects it is the closest of the plays I have discussed to Shakespeare's magician play of the mid-1590s, *A Midsummer Night's Dream*.

A Midsummer Night's Dream

This book is not the first to suggest that *John a Kent and John a Cumber* is a source for *A Midsummer Night's Dream*. When I. A. Shapiro first proposed a 1590 date for the former, he pointed out that this would refute the findings of previous critics who had assumed that Munday was Shakespeare's debtor, and in a later article he summarised the main points of resemblance: the use of magic to bring pairs of lovers together; the likeness of Bottom and company to the theatrical clowns in *John a Kent*; and the similarity between Puck and Shrimp.[82] Soon afterwards, Nevill Coghill undertook a more sustained comparison between the two plays, arguing that Shakespeare found in Munday's 'shallow but pleasing play' structural elements that 'could be put to better use'.[83] He expanded on the points made by Shapiro, noting for example the way Shrimp, like Puck, disrupts

---

[82] Shapiro, 'The Significance of a Date', p. 103; 'Shakespeare and Mundy', *Shakespeare Survey*, 14 (1961), 25–33 (p. 28).

[83] Nevill Coghill, *Shakespeare's Professional Skills* (Cambridge: Cambridge University Press, 1964), pp. 42, 45.

the activities of the amateur entertainers in transforming the song they sing to wake the bridegrooms; Shrimp's Puckish enjoyment of the chaos he causes, exulting 'in the height of his brauery, / that he may execute some part of his maisters knauery' (ll. 577–8); and the way he invisibly leads the brides' guards until they fall asleep, as Puck does Lysander and Demetrius. At the same time, Coghill emphasised the ways in which Shakespeare enriches the material he takes from Munday, for example in giving his sprite, as Puck/Robin Goodfellow, a considerably expanded back-story; in personalising the relationships and conflicts between the lovers to the extent that one pair of suitors and a rival magician can be left out of the picture; and in drawing on other writers such as Chaucer and Plutarch.[84] Coghill's arguments were given additional circulation through Brooks's 1979 edition of the play.[85]

It would be otiose simply to rehearse at length the arguments already made by Shapiro and Coghill. Instead, I would like to suggest that once we identify *John a Kent and John a Cumber* as one of a number of responses to *Doctor Faustus* in the manner of *Friar Bacon and Friar Bungay*, several features that *A Midsummer Night's Dream* shares with some or all of those plays become apparent. Most obviously: it is a romantic comedy in which a character who is not one of the principal lovers intervenes in the love-plot using magical means. Oberon uses his knowledge about the erotogenic properties of love-in-idleness not only to achieve his principal aim of humiliating Titania but to make the 'disdainful youth' Demetrius fall in love with the 'sweet Athenian lady' Helena (2.1.260–61), and employs another herb as an antidote when the first one is mistakenly administered to Lysander. Though he is a fairy rather than a human magician, Oberon shares this structural role with Bacon, Dunstan and the two Johns; and as Bacon uses a devil to prevent Bungay from marrying Lacy to Margaret, Dunstan uses a devil to make Edgar spare Ethenwald, and John a Kent uses Shrimp to free Sidanen and Marian from their captors, so Oberon makes Puck fetch the flower, use it on Lysander (and later Demetrius), and lead the lovers a merry dance until they fall unconscious.

That Puck occupies a role in *A Midsummer Night's Dream* analogous to that of the devils in earlier plays is entirely appropriate, given the writings of a number of critics of the play who have emphasised that character's affinities with the demonic. As K. M. Briggs notes, Robin Goodfellow is equivocally referred to by Samuel Rowlands in *More Knaves Yet* (1613?) as 'a good fellow devil, / So called in kindness, cause he did no evill', while

---

[84] Coghill, pp. 42–60. [85] *A Midsummer Night's Dream*, ed. Brooks, pp. lxiv–lxvi.

Mary Ellen Lamb describes Robin as he appears on the title page of the 1628 pamphlet *Robin Good-fellow, His Mad Prankes and Merry Iests* as 'a rough and hairy devil figure or satyr with cloven hoofs, erect penis, horns, and animal ears'.[86] He also carries a broom, as does Shakespeare's Puck in the final scene ('To sweep the dust behind the door', 5.1.368), and Lamb suggests that in *A Midsummer Night's Dream* the prop evokes the little devil in mumming plays who 'steps out before the audience at the end . . . to sweep up money thrown by the crowd'.[87] A further devilish feature of Puck is his laugh of 'Ho, ho, ho!' at 3.2.421: according to Briggs this is a traditional attribute of Robin Goodfellow, but it is more generally the noise a stage devil or vice makes, as in the anonymous play *The Trial of Treasure* and in Robert Ingeland's *The Disobedient Child*. More pertinently, as we have seen, Asteroth laughs in this way in *John of Bordeaux* when claiming Bacon's soul.[88] And in *Friar Bacon and Friar Bungay*, Miles uses another of Puck's names when he is alarmed by the 'great noise' that precedes the long-awaited moment when the brazen head 'by the enchanting forces of the devil / Shall tell out strange and uncouth aphorisms' (11.18–19): 'here's some of your master's hobgoblins abroad' (11.51–2).

And yet, as Oberon is at pains to point out, he and Puck are 'spirits of another sort' from the 'ghosts wandering here and there' who, as dawn approaches,

> Troop home to churchyards. Damned spirits all,
> That in crossways and floods have burial,
> Already to their wormy beds are gone. (3.2.381–4)

Admittedly, this is not a categorical denial that Oberon and Puck are devils (as opposed to ghosts). But at least superficially it serves to distance the fairies in *A Midsummer Night's Dream* from the scarier supernatural characters who populated the Friar Bacon plays and *A Knack to Know a Knave*. In this respect, as in others, Puck has affinities with Munday's Shrimp: not unambiguously *not* a devil, given that the clowns say that John a Kent carries devils around with him, but not the kind of spirit who carries one

[86] K. M. Briggs, *The Anatomy of Puck: An Examination of Fairy Beliefs among Shakespeare's Contemporaries and Successors* (London: Routledge and Kegan Paul, 1959), p. 72; Mary Ellen Lamb, 'Taken by the Fairies: Fairy Practices and the Production of Popular Culture in *A Midsummer Night's Dream*', *Shakespeare Quarterly*, 51 (2000), 277–312 (p. 298).

[87] Lamb, *Popular Culture*, p. 123. On the devil in mummers' plays, see Alan Brody, *The English Mummers and Their Plays* (London: Routledge and Kegan Paul, n. d.), pp. 11, 60.

[88] Briggs, p. 41; *A New and Mery Enterlude, Called the Triall of Treasure* (London, 1567; STC: 24271), sig. E2r; Robert Ingeland, *A Pretie and Mery New Enterlude: Called the Disobedient Child* (London, 1570; STC: 14085), sig. F3r.

off to hell either. His and Oberon's interventions in mortal affairs are motivated not by the need to ensnare human souls, but by a somewhat mischievous desire to pair off human lovers: Oberon wants to make Demetrius not as fond as Helena, but 'More fond on her than she upon her love' (2.1.261), while Puck positively enjoys the chaos that ensues from his mistake, since 'those things do best please me, / That befall prepost'rously' (3.2.120–21). Much the nearest equivalent to this playfulness in the dramas discussed earlier in the chapter is John a Kent devising plot complications for their own sake, and Shrimp delighting in bringing them about.

As in the other magician comedies, a significant factor in defusing the threat of magic is location: as has frequently been remarked, while *A Midsummer Night's Dream* is notionally set in ancient Athens, the forest scenes appear rather to be set in rural England.[89] The dialogue between Puck and the Fairy in Act 2, Scene 1, for example, evokes a world of milkmaids and gossips in which the spiritual danger of being led astray by the devil is less worrying than the material danger resulting from Robin's propensity to 'mislead night-wanderers, laughing at their harm' (2.1.39). Rather than dragging souls down to hell, this spirit sends grave aunts tumbling to the floor when they sit down to tell stories (2.1.51–7). *Friar Bacon and Friar Bungay* is surely an important influence on the play's creation of a rustic ambience, as Norman Sanders recognises when he compares the binary Shakespeare sets up between Athens and the forest with the way Greene's play shifts between the worlds of Oxford, the court and rural Suffolk.[90] Alexander Leggatt makes a comparable point, albeit with a different emphasis, when he writes that in Titania's description of how 'The fold stands empty in the drowned field, / And crows are fatted with the murrion flock' (2.1.96–7) because of her and Oberon's disharmony, we see the 'lush England of *Friar Bacon and Friar Bungay* ... in ruins'.[91] However, contrary to Leggatt's reference to this England's 'agricultural wealth and its country pastimes', Greene does not appear particularly interested in the festive or recreational side of popular culture (barring a brief allusion to Prince Edward becoming 'love's morris-dance', 2.163). This is certainly important in *A Midsummer Night's Dream*, a play that takes its title from one festival (St John's Eve) and that refers to two more,

---

[89] See for example *A Midsummer Night's Dream*, ed. Foakes, p. 33.
[90] Norman Sanders, 'The Comedy of Greene and Shakespeare', *Early Shakespeare*, Stratford-upon-Avon Studies, 3, ed. by John Russell Brown and Bernard Harris (London: Edward Arnold, 1961), pp. 34–53 (p. 41).
[91] Leggatt, p. 51.

May Day (at 1.1.167) and St Valentine's Day (at 4.1.136). Shakespeare's drama also alludes to forms of popular merriment such as the 'nine men's morris' and 'quaint mazes' in Titania's speech (2.1.98–9), while aspects of the mechanicals plot – Bottom's ass-head, his revival at the end of 'Pyramus and Thisbe' – have been compared to mummers' plays.[92] But in this respect it is, once again, closest to *John a Kent and John a Cumber* out of all the plays discussed in this chapter. That play, too, mentions Midsummer's Day, during the Earl of Chester's speech telling Morton and Pembroke that they are to be married at St John's Church: 'ffor to that Churche, *Edgar*, once Englands King, / was by eight Kinges, conquerd by him in warres: / rowed royally on S[t]. Iohn Baptist day' (ll. 163–5). Perhaps this is meant to point to the festive resonances of Sidanen and Marian's moonlit journey to wash their hands in St Winifred's well: although maidens' nocturnal walks from town to country were more a feature of May Eve than Midsummer Eve, Shakespeare's play, for one, confuses the two.[93] Furthermore, as we have seen, Munday's play stages cultural forms – Robin Hood games, morris dancing – that were practised on festive occasions, Midsummer in particular, and glances (conceivably) at the Chester mystery cycle. There is no explicit reference to morris dancing in *A Midsummer Night's Dream*: 'the nine men's morris' is a competitive game, not a dance. However, the mechanicals do perform a Bergomask dance at the end of 'Pyramus and Thisbe', a prospect that Theseus seems to greet with rather more enthusiasm than he does the play itself ('come, your Bergomask', 5.1.340). It is difficult to be sure what this dance consisted of, given that the *OED* is able to cite only Shakespeare's play in support of its definition ('Bergamask', *n.*, 1), 'a rustic dance, framed in imitation of the people of Bergamo ..., ridiculed as clownish in their manners and dialect'; but in view of the fact that morrises had been regularly performed at aristocratic weddings in the earlier Tudor period, perhaps it was a morris dance.[94]

Repeatedly in this chapter I have suggested that the medieval settings of the Friar Bacon plays, *A Knack to Know a Knave*, and *John a Kent and John a Cumber* were in keeping with their fundamentally comic depiction of

---

[92] *A Midsummer Night's Dream*, ed. Holland, pp. 78–9; Meredith Anne Skura, *Shakespeare the Actor and the Purposes of Playing* (Chicago: University of Chicago Press, 1993), p. 112.

[93] Forrest, pp. 128–9; on the confusion of May Day and Midsummer, see François Laroque, *Shakespeare's Festive World: Elizabethan Seasonal Entertainment and the Professional Stage* (Cambridge: Cambridge University Press, 1991), p. 217.

[94] Forrest, pp. 67–8, 54 notes references to 'morisks' at the wedding of Prince Arthur (1501) and the proxy marriages of Princess Margaret (1502) and Princess Mary (1508).

magic as something that need not lead to the damnation of the practitioner. In the same way, I would suggest, the evocation in *A Midsummer Night's Dream* of an idealised rural culture along with festive customs that were no longer dominant in Shakespeare's London, and indeed were seen by the godly as tainted with paganism and Catholicism, helps to situate the action in a pre-Reformation past in order to defuse anxieties about the moral and religious status of magic in the play.[95] The remarks of Reginald Scot in his epistle to the reader at the beginning of *The Discouerie of Witchcraft* (1584), a text that is frequently linked to *A Midsummer Night's Dream*, are suggestive in this respect.[96] Scot accepts that if he were to ask 'parciall readers' to read impartially his debunking of magic as fraud, he should 'no more preuaile herein, than if a hundred yeares since I should haue intreated your predecessors to beleeue, that Robin goodfellowe, that great and ancient bulbegger, had been but a cousening merchant, and no diuell indeed', or if he were to ask a papist to believe his arguments about the impiety and ridiculousness of 'popish charmes'. But, he continues, 'Robin goodfellowe ceaseth now to be much feared, and poperie is sufficientlie discouered. Neuertheles, witches charms, and coniurors cousenages are yet thought effectuall.'[97] Not only do these statements indicate the ongoing currency of magical beliefs in the 1580s; they also suggest firstly that Robin Goodfellow was seen as a thing of the past, and secondly that he was seen as sharing that past with 'poperie'. It may be that belief in fairies has always been to some extent residual, constituting (as Wendy Wall puts it) 'a belief system held reverently until *just recently*'; and there is no doubt a degree of wishful thinking and anxiety behind Scot's consignment of Catholicism to the past.[98] Nevertheless, I would suggest that Scot's rhetorical strategy here illuminates Shakespeare's practice in *A Midsummer Night's Dream*. In an era when Perkins was insisting that witches really could 'worke wonders' with satanic help and should therefore be put to death, and when the King of Scotland could write a book assuming the reality and efficacy of witchcraft, it made sense to locate non-tragic depictions of witchcraft firmly in the pre-Reformation past.[99]

---

[95] For a nuanced discussion of Catholic and Reformed attitudes towards popular festivity, see Phebe Jensen, *Religion and Festivity in Shakespeare's Festive World* (Cambridge: Cambridge University Press, 2008), pp. 26–38.

[96] See *A Midsummer Night's Dream*, ed. Foakes, p. 7.

[97] Reginald Scot, *The Discouerie of Witchcraft* (London, 1584; STC: 21864), sigs. B2r-Brv.

[98] Wendy Wall, *Staging Domesticity: Household Work and English Identity in Early Modern Drama* (Cambridge: Cambridge University Press, 2002), p. 96.

[99] Perkins, *A Discourse of the Damned Art of Witchcraft*, sig. ¶6r.

Shakespeare, like Munday, invokes cultural forms such as morris dancing, mumming and May games that, while undeniably still in existence in sixteenth-century England, were embattled due to being 'perceived as idolatrous Catholic practices'.[100]

*

In the first section of this chapter, I expanded upon Meredith Skura's observations regarding similarities in scenic form between *A Midsummer Night's Dream* and *Doctor Faustus*, pointing to the use of Marlovian language in Titania's speeches to Bottom. In subsequent sections I discussed plays that, following the pattern of *Friar Bacon and Friar Bungay*, anticipated *A Midsummer Night's Dream* in reshaping into comedy the tragic materials of *Faustus*, incorporating love-plots, reducing the spiritual dangers of magic and using medieval and/or rural settings to distance the action from the religious context of the present. When Shakespeare's play is read alongside these comedies, the structural homology of Oberon and Puck to earlier magicians and devils becomes apparent, while Munday's deployment of morris dancing and Robin Hood games in *John a Kent and John a Cumber* seems to resemble the festive quality that C. L. Barber influentially identified in Shakespeare, his plays' 'participation in native saturnalian traditions of the popular theatre and the popular holidays'.[101] *A Midsummer Night's Dream* thus responds to a play by Marlowe current in the Admiral's repertory in a manner informed by other comedies that had appeared in the intervening years, one of which, *John a Kent and John a Cumber*, may itself have been the highly popular Admiral's play *The Wise Man of West Chester*.

By way of conclusion, I want to point out two aspects of Shakespeare's play where these intertextual relationships seem particularly in evidence. The first is its thematic interest in Helen of Troy. As has already been noted, this is a point of contact with *Doctor Faustus*; but it is also something that the play shares with *Friar Bacon and Friar Bungay*. In Greene's play Prince Edward uses formulaic, if onomastically appropriate, comparisons with Helen to praise his destined bride Eleanor of Castile (12.6–12), but there is no doubt that the real Helen is Margaret of Fressingfield, 'Suffolk's fair Helen and rich England's star' (10.35), who laments after Serlsby has accepted Lambert's challenge:

---

[100] Jensen, p. 32.
[101] C. L. Barber, *Shakespeare's Festive Comedy: A Study of Dramatic Form and its Relation to Social Custom* (Princeton: Princeton University Press, 1959), p. 3.

Shall I be Helen in my froward fates,
As I am Helen in my matchless hue,
And set rich Suffolk with my face afire? (10.93–5)

As in *Doctor Faustus*, Helen is used to figure both the summit of female beauty and the disasters that ensue when men compete over it: rather than burning 'the topless towers of Ilium' (5.1.92), Margaret's face sets Suffolk aflame. In Marlowe's play the summoning of Helen is Faustus's culminating act of magic, and 'Her lips sucks forth' his soul in a literalisation of his earlier line, ''Tis magic, magic that hath ravished me' (5.1.94, 1.1.112). In Greene's play the relationship is purely metaphorical: to return to Empson's formulation, the power of beauty is *like* the power of magic. In *A Midsummer Night's Dream*, however, rather than being summoned by magic or being magical in its power, Helena's beauty requires the assistance of magic in order to work its effects on Lysander and Demetrius. All three plays, then, participate in a tendency to link the themes of beauty, magic and Helen of Troy.

The second feature of *A Midsummer Night's Dream* I want to highlight is the moment in Act 4 when Theseus and his hunting party encounter the sleeping lovers:

THESEUS Go, bid the huntsmen wake them with their horns.
        Shout within; wind horns; [the lovers] all start up.
  Good morrow, friends. Saint Valentine is past;
  Begin these woodbirds but to couple now?
        [The lovers kneel.]
LYSANDER Pardon, my lord.
THESEUS I pray you all, stand up.
  I know you two are rival enemies:
  How comes this gentle concord in the world,
  That hatred is so far from jealousy
  To sleep by hate, and fear no enmity? (4.1.135–42)

The stage direction, 'winde his horn' appears also in *John a Kent and John a Cumber* when Kent, having conveyed Marian, Sidanen and the Countess of Chester out of the town in his disguise as a hermit, blows his horn to summon their waiting lovers. The similarity would be unremarkable were it not for Kent's speech beforehand: 'And for my woordes may yeeld but dallying hope, / see what is doone in twinckling of an eye' (ll. 468–9). The phrase 'in twinckling of an eye' is one that Munday's play shares with *Doctor Faustus*, and though Marlowe's editors note the phrase as 'a familiar expression' (5.1.90n) its resonances are suggestive given the context in which it appears. Faustus, having confirmed his vow to Lucifer and having asked Mephistopheles to torment the Old Man, requests

> That I might have unto my paramour
> That heavenly Helen which I saw of late,
> Whose sweet embracings may extinguish clean
> These thoughts that do dissuade me from my vow,
> And keep mine oath I made to Lucifer.
> MEPHISTOPHELES Faustus, this, or what else thou shalt desire,
> Shall be performed in twinkling of an eye. (5.1.84–90).

Mephistopheles then brings Helen onto the stage, prompting Faustus's famous speech. Faustus's anxiety about his own impending death, and his craving to see a dead woman brought back to life, suggest that the echo of 1 Corinthians: 15 is not coincidental:

> Beholde, I shewe you a secret thing, We shal not all slepe but we shal all be changed,
>   In a moment, in the twinkling of an eye at the last trumpet: for the trumpet shall blowe, and the dead shal be raised vp incorruptible and we shalbe changed. (Geneva version)

The fact that this 'paramour' is indeed, as Flute later puts it in *A Midsummer Night's Dream*, 'a thing of naught' (4.2.10–11), a disguised spirit rather than a dead woman raised up, makes Marlowe's evocation of St Paul's account of the resurrection deeply ironic. These layers of irony are missing from Munday's play, but the use of the phrase 'in twinckling of an eye' immediately before the winding of a horn (if not actually a trumpet) suggests that Munday, too, was sensitive to its Pauline overtones. So when Shakespeare's Theseus asks for a horn to be sounded and the lovers rise up from sleep, the rivals changed from enemies to friends amid a 'gentle concord in the world', the episode gains a symbolic charge from its resemblance both to a well-known biblical passage and to earlier theatrical moments in which that passage had been echoed. The likeness of Bottom's words when he wakes up later in the same scene to the second chapter of 1 Corinthians is regularly noted by editors and critics; reading this earlier instance in the light of other magician plays of the late 1580s and early 1590s brings its allusiveness, too, to light.[102]

---

[102] See for example *A Midsummer Night's Dream*, ed. Foakes, 4.1.205–7n.

CHAPTER 3

'I speak of Africa and golden joys'
Henry IV and the Stukeley Plays

In the last two chapters, I have attempted to situate plays that Shakespeare wrote for the Lord Chamberlain's Men in 1595–6 within their immediate commercial environment. During this period, as we know from Henslowe's diary, the Admiral's Men staged revivals of old plays such as *The Jew of Malta* and *Doctor Faustus*, whose influence can be discerned in *The Merchant of Venice* and *A Midsummer Night's Dream* respectively. However, they also staged new plays including *A Knack to Know an Honest Man*, which significantly informed Shakespeare's reshaping of Marlovian materials in *The Merchant of Venice*, and *The Wise Man of West Chester*, which – if it was Munday's *John a Kent and John a Cumber* under a different name – did likewise for *A Midsummer Night's Dream*. If *The Wise Man* is not *John a Kent*, then this lost play, presumably featuring the same legendary magician of the Welsh borders, joins others such as *The Venetian Comedy*, *Palamon and Arcite*, and *The Grecian Comedy* as a play whose title suggests the background against which Shakespeare wrote his own Grecian, Chaucerian comedy of magic, and his own Venetian comedy.

The current chapter switches genre to consider Shakespeare's highly successful *History of Henry the Fourth*, to give it the title by which it appeared in 1598 in the first of seven quartos before 1623, and its sequel, *The Second Part of Henry the Fourth*, which appeared in quarto in 1600 and then in the 1623 Folio (subsequent references will be to *1 Henry IV* and *2 Henry IV*). Much as *The Merchant of Venice* can be (and has been) viewed as a rewriting of *The Jew of Malta*, so the two parts of *Henry IV*, along with *Henry V*, are often read in relation to the anonymous play *The Famous Victories of Henry the Fifth*, which similarly presents the protagonist's life as a progression from dissolute youth through to heroic kingship.[1] However, when *The Famous Victories* was printed in 1598, it was ascribed to a company – the Queen's Men – that, while still very much in evidence as a touring outfit, had apparently slipped from the position of prominence in London that it had enjoyed during the 1580s.[2] *The Famous Victories* was an old play, entered in the Stationers' Register on 14 May 1594, and its publication in 1598 may well have been an attempt 'to capitalize on the popularity of *1 Henry IV*'; its title-page attribution to the Queen's Men makes it less likely that this was the 'harey the v' that Henslowe first recorded (as 'ne') on 28 November 1595, and which was performed a further twelve times by the Admiral's Men between then and 15 July 1596.[3]

However, the Admiral's Men *Harry V* should give us pause for another reason. It shows us that, as with *The Merchant of Venice* and *A Midsummer Night's Dream*, Shakespeare in *1 Henry IV* (conventionally dated to 1596–7) was once again writing a play about a topic that the Admiral's had recently made current, namely the life of Prince Hal, the future Henry V.[4] Furthermore, while the Admiral's Men *Harry V* is apparently lost, other surviving plays that the company performed during the mid-1590s suggest that in *Henry IV*, Shakespeare was drawing on ways of understanding and staging historical subject matter that were already in evidence in the London theatre. One is *The Battle of Alcazar*, a play from the late 1580s usually attributed to George Peele.[5] It is very possible that this play was still being performed, under the title of *Mahomet*, by the Admiral's between August 1594 and February 1595, and its influence on *Henry IV* is more significant than its notorious parodying in one of Pistol's lines from Part II might suggest. The other is *Captain Thomas Stukeley*, which exists in a

[1] See, for example, William Shakespeare, *Henry IV Part One*, ed. by David Bevington (Oxford: Clarendon Press, 1987), pp. 17–24; *King Henry IV Part 1*, ed. by David Scott Kastan (London: Arden Shakespeare, 2002), p. 342; Janet Clare, *Shakespeare's Stage Traffic: Imitation, Borrowing and Competition in Renaissance Theatre* (Cambridge: Cambridge University Press, 2014), pp. 144–64.

[2] Scott McMillin and Sally-Beth MacLean, *The Queen's Men and Their Plays* (Cambridge: Cambridge University Press, 1998), pp. 49–55.

[3] *The Famous Victories of Henry the Fifth*, ed. by Chiaki Hanabusa (Oxford: Malone Society, 2007), pp. v, xxiii, 1; *Henslowe's Diary*, ed. by R. A. Foakes [and R. T. Rickert], 2nd edn (Cambridge: Cambridge University Press, 2002), pp. 33–4, 36–7, 47–8.

[4] On the dating of *1 Henry IV*, see William Shakespeare, *The First Part of King Henry IV*, ed. by Herbert Weil and Judith Weil (Cambridge: Cambridge University Press, 1997), pp. 4–6, as well as the editions by Bevington, pp. 1–10, and Kastan, p. 76. Weil and Weil and Kastan suggest 1597; Bevington thinks the play may date from 1596, probably after the re-opening of the theatres in late October. References to *1 Henry IV* use Weil and Weil.

[5] *The Stukeley Plays: 'The Battle of Alcazar' by George Peele; 'The Famous History of the Life and Death of Captain Thomas Stukeley'*, ed. by Charles Edelman (Manchester: Manchester University Press, 2005), pp. 16–19. References to *The Battle of Alcazar* and *Captain Thomas Stukeley* use this edition.

quarto dating from 1605 but which may be the same as the 'stewtley' premiered by the Admiral's on 11 December 1596. Linguistic, scenic and thematic resemblances between this play and *1 Henry IV* suggest either that Shakespeare's play needs to be dated somewhat earlier than is usually thought, namely in the first half of 1596; or that Shakespeare drew on *Captain Thomas Stukeley* when writing it.

The Battle of Alcazar and *Captain Thomas Stukeley* have a great deal in common, most obviously their shared interest in the 1578 battle of El-Ksar El-Kebir which saw the deaths of the Moroccan King Abd al-Malek, his nephew Muly Mahammad, who was fighting to regain the throne from which Abd al-Malek had deposed him, and King Sebastian of Portugal, who hoped to obtain African territories through his support of Muly Mahammad. (Henceforth this chapter follows the spelling of Edelman's edition: Alcazar, Abdelmelec, Muly Mahamet.) The plays also share an interest in the English adventurer Thomas Stukeley, who met his end fighting for Sebastian. Stylistically, they both make use of high-flown verse clearly modelled on that of *Tamburlaine*, and indeed, the view of *Alcazar* as an inferior rehash of Marlowe's play has been a recurrent critical theme. As I will shortly argue, this is a rather unjust estimation of a play that is a more intelligent response to Marlowe than is usually supposed, and which was apparently popular enough to merit several revivals by the Admiral's Men. Indeed, both it and *Stukeley* engage creatively with *Tamburlaine* – both parts of which were revived by the Admiral's in 1594 and went on to be performed repeatedly until November 1595 – in ways that can be seen as informing Shakespeare's own two-part drama.

The Battle of Alcazar and the Sons of Tamburlaine

In the final scene of *2 Tamburlaine*, the dying warrior reviews his conquests with his surviving sons, Amyras and Celebinus, exhorting them to complete what death has prevented him from achieving. Although he is confident that his 'flesh, divided in your precious shapes, / Shall still retain my spirit though I die, / And live in all your seeds immortally' (5.3.172–4), the hesitancy with which Amyras ascends Tamburlaine's chariot leaves the audience in some doubt as to the son's ability to guide it 'with thy father's hand' (5.3.229).[6] Having already killed one of his three sons for cowardice,

---

[6] Christopher Marlowe, *Tamburlaine the Great*, ed. by J. S. Cunningham (Manchester: Manchester University Press, 1981). Subsequent references are to this edition.

Tamburlaine in this scene talks of his fragmenting body imparting its 'impressions / By equal portions' into the breasts of the other two (5.3.170-1): the implication is that neither Amyras nor Celebinus can be the sole inheritor of his greatness, which must instead suffer a splitting and a diminution.

Several critics of the drama of the late 1580s and early 1590s have been drawn to the image of Tamburlaine and his sons as a way of talking about the dramatic influence of Marlowe's play. Felix E. Schelling wrote in 1925 that the tragedy 'begot a numerous progeny of imitation'; G. K. Hunter's 1997 survey of these plays refers to them as the 'sons of Tamburlaine'; and Peter Berek's 1982 article on 'Imitation as Interpretation Before 1593' is entitled '*Tamburlaine*'s Weak Sons'.[7] Berek's title makes clear what is implicit in Schelling and Hunter: just as the conqueror's heroic *virtù* cannot be fully reproduced in his descendants, so the moral complexity and ideological subversiveness of Marlowe's two plays is not passed on to his theatrical heirs, superficially similar though their plays might seem. Berek writes of the authors of plays like *The Wounds of Civil War, Alphonsus, King of Aragon, The Battle of Alcazar* and *Selimus*,

> these immediate inheritors seem to have felt that the best way to capitalize on the success of *Tamburlaine* was by mediating between that play and their audience's perhaps uneasy, but fundamentally conservative tastes. Not only did Lodge, Greene, Peele, and their peers 'applaud the fortunes' of Marlowe's heroic play by trying to emulate its popular and financial success, but they invited their audience to applaud the fortunes of their stage heroes 'as they pleased' – that is, in a manner which tempered thrills with reassurances, and allowed the pleasures of style without many dangers of substance.[8]

As Roslyn Knutson has pointed out, there are grounds for thinking this strategy successful. The fact that the plays were printed implies a degree of popularity, while *The Battle of Alcazar* may have been revived by the Admiral's (under the title of *Mahomet*) between 14 August 1594 and 5 February 1595, and the surviving 'plot' of *Alcazar* seems to indicate

---

[7] Felix E. Schelling, *Elizabethan Playwrights: A Short History of the English Drama from Mediaeval Times to the Closing of the Theaters in 1642* (New York: Harper, 1925, repr. New York: Blom, 1965), p. 85; G. K. Hunter, *English Drama 1586–1642: The Age of Shakespeare*, Oxford History of English Literature, vol. VI (Oxford: Clarendon Press, 1997), p. 49; Peter Berek, '*Tamburlaine*'s Weak Sons: Imitation as Interpretation Before 1593', *Renaissance Drama*, 13 (1982), 55–82.

[8] Berek, p. 82.

another revival, probably around 1600–1601.[9] The play thus remained a worthwhile commercial proposition over a decade after its first appearance. However, as a critical judgement on this group of plays, Berek's argument is open to debate. While this chapter lacks the space to discuss all of the plays Berek refers to, a case can be made that *The Battle of Alcazar*, at least, is more than a watered-down imitation.

A productive starting point for consideration of *The Battle of Alcazar* may be David Riggs's identification of a group of 'heroic histories' that attempted to respond to a particular aspect of the *Tamburlaine* plays: their depiction of a naturally noble 'Herculean hero' (to use Eugene Waith's term) whom Marlowe strives 'to insulate ... from conventional moral judgements'.[10] They did so by placing the warrior hero in specific cultural contexts, generally closer to home than Tamburlaine's Asia, against which he could be evaluated.[11] In some instances, such as Robert Greene's *Alphonsus, King of Aragon*, this generated plays that apparently espoused the orthodoxy of hereditary rule; in others, such as the Shakespearean *Henry VI*, it placed the chivalric ethos and competing claims to the throne under greater scrutiny.

Although Riggs does not discuss *The Battle of Alcazar* in detail, he does count it as one of the heroic histories, and when some of its undeniably Marlovian aspects are examined in detail, they do look less like the politically reassuring imitations that Berek suggests and more like intelligent engagements with Marlowe's play. To begin with what is probably the play's best-known scene – best-known because most frequently parodied – the King of Morocco, Muly Mahamet, has been forced to flee to the desert with his family by the arrival of his uncle Abdelmelec, whose brother Muly Mahamet Sheikh cut him out of the succession in favour of Muly Mahamet, in alliance with the Ottoman Sultan. When the exiles begin to starve, Mahamet leaves the stage in search of food and reappears, bringing on his sword raw flesh he stole from a lioness – or as he puts it in a combination of paronomasia and antimetabole that Muriel

---

[9] Roslyn L. Knutson, 'Strength Training for Tamburlaine's Weak Sons Through Repertorial Commerce', unpublished paper, Modern Language Association annual convention (2011). On the dating of the 'plot', see Martin Wiggins, 'A Choice of Impossible Things: Dating the Revival of The *Battle of Alcazar*', in *Shakespeare et ses Contemporains*, ed. by Patricia Dorval and Jean-Marie Maguin (Paris: Société Français Shakespeare, 2002), pp. 185–202.

[10] David Riggs, *Shakespeare's Heroical Histories: 'Henry VI' and its Literary Tradition* (Cambridge, MA: Harvard University Press, 1971), p. 18; Eugene M. Waith, *The Herculean Hero in Marlowe, Chapman, Shakespeare and Dryden* (New York: Columbia University Press, 1962).

[11] Riggs, p. 20.

Bradbrook could only describe as 'lamentable', 'Meat of a princess, for a princess meet' (2.3.72).[12] He invites his wife,

> Feed then and faint not fair Calipolis,
> For rather than fierce famine shall prevail
> To gnaw thy entrails with her thorny teeth,
> The conquering lioness shall attend on thee
> And lay huge heaps of slaughtered carcasses
> As bulwarks in her way to keep her back.
> I will provide thee of a princely osprey,
> That as she flieth over fish in pools,
> The fish shall turn their glistering bellies up
> And thou shalt take thy liberal choice of all.
> Jove's stately bird with wide commanding wings
> Shall hover still about thy princely head
> And beat down fowl by shoals into thy lap.
> Feed then and faint not, fair Calipolis. (2.3.81–94)

The inclusion of 'Then feed and be fat, my fair Calipolis' among Ancient Pistol's ranting speeches in *2 Henry IV*, 2.4, which are partly made up of garbled fragments from old plays, suggests that by the late 1590s the potential for passages like this to look dated and bombastic was all too apparent.[13] However, another of Pistol's (mis)quotations, 'hollow pampered jades of Asia, / Which cannot go but thirty miles a day' (2.4.131–2) is, of course, from the second part of *Tamburlaine*, and the affinity that this implies between the quoted texts is borne out by the fact that Mahamet's lines are plainly modelled on the same speech by Tamburlaine to Zenocrate as those of Titania to Bottom discussed in Chapter 2:

> A hundred Tartars shall attend on thee,
> Mounted on steeds swifter than Pegasus;
> Thy garments shall be made of Median silk,
> Enchased with precious jewels of mine own,
> More rich and valurous than Zenocrate's;
> With milk-white harts upon an ivory sled
> Thou shalt be drawn amidst the frozen pools
> And scale the icy mountains' lofty tops,
> Which with thy beauty will be soon resolved;

---

[12] M. C. Bradbrook, *Themes and Conventions of Elizabethan Tragedy*, 2nd edn (Cambridge: Cambridge University Press, 1980), p. 93.
[13] William Shakespeare, *The Second Part of King Henry IV*, ed. by Giorgio Melchiori (Cambridge: Cambridge University Press, 1989), 2.4.143. Subsequent references are to this edition.

> My martial prizes, with five hundred men,
> Won on the fifty-headed Volga's waves,
> Shall all we offer to Zenocrate,
> And then myself to fair Zenocrate. (Part I, 1.2.93–105)

The similarity is evident in details of diction and imagery, but more generally in overall mood and syntax. The assertive male speaker promises the 'fair' female addressee eye-catching servants – 'A hundred Tartars', 'The conquering lioness' – that 'shall attend on thee', as well as animal helpers in the form of 'milk-white harts', 'a princely osprey' and 'Jove's stately bird'; offerings will be made, whether of food or of 'martial prizes'; and the confidence with which the speaker makes these assurances is reinforced by the use of the phrase 'thou shalt'. There are no ifs or buts: as Marlowe's hero elsewhere puts it, '"will" and "shall" best fitteth Tamburlaine' (3.3.41).

In an essay published elsewhere I have made the argument that Peele's echo of Marlowe here is not simply imitative but an 'act of emulation' by a competitive fellow dramatist.[14] I still hold that opinion, but in view of the context in which the lines are delivered one can also discern a considerable irony at Mahamet's expense. In the second scene of Marlowe's play, Tamburlaine is the coming man: he may not yet have acquired the kingship for which he longs, but he has captured the Sultan's daughter along with her entourage and treasure, and is about to persuade a Persian captain to defect to his side before going on to defeat the King of Persia in battle. The erstwhile King of Morocco, by contrast, is destitute and starving, and though he will later persuade Sebastian to uphold his cause, for the moment he looks a lot more like the fallen Bajazeth, offered meat by Tamburlaine 'from my sword's point' (4.4.40), than he does the Scythian conqueror. His promises that regal beasts will provide Calipolis with food, though strangely beautiful in their lurid savagery, come across as bravado and bluster. In Mahamet's speech, Peele is thus able to have it both ways: he has the chance to demonstrate mastery of a Marlovian idiom, but he also shows how the idiom and the speaker are alike diminished when the prevailing situation does not measure up to the grandeur of the rhetoric.

Although it is Muly Mahamet who advertises most explicitly the intertextual relationship between *The Battle of Alcazar* and *Tamburlaine*, greeting news of the alliance between Abdelmelec and the Turkish Amurath with the defiant words 'Tamburlaine, triumph not, for thou must die' (1.2.37), he is not the only character to be given Marlovian language and

---

[14] Tom Rutter, 'Marlovian Echoes in the Admiral's Men Repertory: Alcazar, Stukeley, Patient Grissil', *Shakespeare Bulletin*, 27 (2009), 27–38 (p. 30).

attitudes ironically at odds with his actual situation. The scene in which Sebastian of Portugal first encounters Thomas Stukeley and tries to dissuade him from his intended course to Ireland echoes the first meeting between Tamburlaine and Theridamas in which Tamburlaine comments on 'With what a majesty he rears his looks' and invites him, 'Forsake thy king, and do but join with me', leading Theridamas to confess himself 'Won with thy words and conquered with thy looks' (1.2.165, 172, 228). Sebastian greets Stukeley as 'a man of gallant personage, / Proud in thy looks, and famous every way', and asks him to 'Frankly tell me, wilt thou go with me?' (2.4.90–92). Sebastian proves less persuasive than Tamburlaine: Stukeley continues to insist that he cannot swerve from the mission given him by the Pope, forcing Sebastian to point out that as the weather has driven Stukeley to Portugal he and his men are now 'captives to our royal will' (2.4.158).

It is Stukeley himself, though, who along with Mahamet seems most obviously designed to evoke the Marlovian hero. The historical Thomas Stukeley enjoyed a highly colourful career. Born into a gentle Devonshire family, he served as a volunteer in various European armies before marrying an English heiress and seeking to augment his wealth as a privateer (which led to his imprisonment under suspicion of piracy). He took part in an embassy to Shane O'Neill in 1566, and subsequently attempted to acquire land and offices in Ireland, only to be imprisoned again over the dubious means he employed before finally departing for Spain in 1570. He was hospitably received at the Spanish court, and over the following years, as well as fighting the Turks at Lepanto, he repeatedly attempted to involve Philip II in an invasion of Ireland; he was persuaded to join Sebastian of Portugal's African expedition after the ill-equipped fleet with which he had been dispatched to Ireland by the Pope put in at Lisbon.[15]

Thomas Fuller's account of Stukeley in *The History of the Worthies of England* presents him as a man with designs of kingship:

> Having prodigally mis-spent his Patrimony, he entred on several projects (the *issue general* of all decaied estates) and first pitched on the peopleing of *Florida,* then newly found out in the *West Indies.* So confident his ambition, that he blushed not to tell *Queen Elizabeth,* that *he preferred rather to be Soveraign of a Mole-hill, than the highest Subject to the greatest King in Christendome;* adding moreover, that, *he was assured he should be a Prince*

---

[15] Peter Holmes, 'Stucley, Thomas (c.1520–1578)', *Oxford Dictionary of National Biography* (Oxford: Oxford University Press, 2004); online edn www.oxforddnb.com/view/article/26741 (accessed 23 August 2015).

before his death: I hope (said Queen Elizabeth) *I shall hear from you, when you are stated in your Principality: I will write unto you* (quoth Stukely.) *In what Language?* (said the Queen) He returned, *In the Stile of Princes; To our dear Sister.*[16]

It seems unlikely, to say the least, that the Queen would really have countenanced any project that could have led to one of her subjects acquiring quasi-regal authority, and Stukeley's *ODNB* biographer thinks that the alleged destination of Florida 'was probably no more than a cover for the real intention which was to prey on French shipping'.[17] It is also unclear whether Stukeley actually thought he could become King of Ireland, be that with the aid of Philip II, Pope Gregory XIII, or Sebastian. However, Peele's play unambiguously depicts Stukeley as a man ambitious for monarchy. When we first encounter him he responds to the Governor of Lisbon's comment that as an Englishman he should not be participating in an invasion of Ireland with a radical statement of freedom from national ties:

> I am Stukeley so resolved in all
> To follow rule, honour and empery,
> Not to be bent so strictly to the place
> Wherein at first I blew the fire of life,
> But that I may at liberty make choice
> Of all the continents that bounds the world. (2.2.28–33)

Although the Irish Bishop emphasises that they are 'Conquering the land for his Holiness' so as to 'restore it to the Roman faith' (2.2.15–16), in his soliloquy at the end of the scene Stukeley makes his own agenda clear:

> There shall no action pass my hand or sword
> That cannot make a step to gain a crown,
> No word shall pass the office of my tongue
> That sounds not of affection to a crown,
> No thought have being in my lordly breast
> That works not every way to win a crown. (2.2.69–74)

Peele's use of epistrophe here, whereby lines repeatedly end with the word 'crown', the object of Stukeley's desire, is surely meant to recall

---

[16] Thomas Fuller, *The History of the Worthies of England* (London, 1662), p. 258.

[17] Holmes. Richard Simpson cites a letter from William Cecil in the Queen's name to the Earl of Sussex, Lord Deputy of Ireland, requiring that if it should 'so happen that for lack of favourable winds he may be diverted from his direct voyage', any French ships Stukeley might bring in to port in Ireland should be received and inventoried. *The School of Shakespere*, ed. by Richard Simpson, 2 vols (London: Chatto and Windus, 1878), vol. I, pp. 33–4.

Tamburlaine's speech over the dying Cosroe in which he says that 'The thirst of reign and sweetness of a crown / . . . Moved me to manage arms against thy state' (Part 1, 2.6.52, 56) and proceeds to explain that Nature impels us to strive for 'That perfect bliss and sole felicity, / The sweet fruition of an earthly crown' (2.6.69).[18] Stukeley goes on to utter the soundbite that Fuller would associate with him:

> King of a mole-hill had I rather be
> Than the richest subject of a monarchy.
> Huff it, brave mind, and never cease t'aspire,
> Before thou reign sole king of thy desire. (2.2.81–4)

The penultimate line clinches the allusion to *Tamburlaine*, recalling the protagonist's assertion in the speech referred to above that Nature 'Doth teach us all to have aspiring minds' (2.6.60).

However, as Stukeley's encounter with Sebastian two scenes later graphically demonstrates, these Tamburlaine-like ambitions are wildly disproportionate to his actual room for manoeuvre. His invasion of Ireland requires papal sanction and resources, and he and his party are anyway forced to disregard the vows they have made to the Pope when, weather-beaten into Lisbon, they are co-opted by Sebastian into his Moroccan adventure. In fact, Stukeley's vulnerability is but one example of the play's repeated tendency to depict vaunting would-be heroes buffeted around by greater political forces. Muly Mahamet's invocation of Tamburlaine as Abdelmelec and the Turks advance upon Morocco, and his promise to make 'Such slaughter with my weapon . . . / As through the stream and bloody channels deep, / Our Moors shall sail in ships and pinnaces' (2.2.57–9), is immediately followed by his ignominious flight. Sebastian, who is consistently shown to be motivated by 'Honour, the spur that pricks the princely mind' (1.Prol.1) and by the desire to 'enlarge the bounds of Christendom' (3.4.16) in a 'rightful war, that Christians' God will bless' (3.4.76), is himself less in control of events than he thinks. He is manipulated by Mahamet, who is entirely happy to 'set these Portugals awork / To hew a way for me unto the crown' (4.2.70–71), and hung out to dry by Philip of Spain, whose ambassadors promise Sebastian 'men, munition, and supply of war' (3.1.14) when in reality 'nothing less than King Sebastian's good / He means' (3.Prol.16–17) and supplies are withheld at the last minute. As G. K. Hunter puts it, Sebastian and Stukeley 'are bought and sold before ever they set foot in Barbary'.[19]

---

[18] The similarity to *Tamburlaine* is noted by Berek, p. 66.
[19] Hunter, *English Drama 1586–1642*, p. 80.

One way of seeing the failures of (in particular) Mahamet and Stukeley in *The Battle of Alcazar* might be as an example of the unwillingness of Marlowe's imitators to accept the moral vertiginousness of *Tamburlaine*, whose protagonist's violent disregard of orthodoxy apparently goes unpunished. For Berek, 'Peele was trying, not altogether successfully, to combine Marlowe's new hero with traditional strategies for directing the audience's sympathies in ways *Tamburlaine* doesn't attempt'; 'Peele wants to exploit new sensations while clinging to an undisturbing moral vision'.[20] However, the play might more charitably be seen as demonstrating the limited viability of *Tamburlaine*'s political vision within any recognisable political context. In its world of uncertain alliances, inadequately prepared armies, and deluded monarchs who ignore sensible advice (as Sebastian does in Act 4, Scene 2), neither impressive rhetoric nor Herculean courage count for that much. The fact that both Philip II and Amurath (Murad) III, the Ottoman Emperor, are kept offstage throughout the play contributes to a sense that real power resides elsewhere than with the three unfortunate kings who meet their demise at Alcazar. The emptiness of these figureheads is perhaps epitomised by the decision of Abdelmelec's brother Muly Mahamet Seth to keep Abdelmelec's death secret for fear of discouraging the army: instead, 'in this apparel as he died / My noble brother will we here advance, / And set him in his chair with cunning props' (5.1.49–51). It is difficult to be sure whether to see this as an example of El Cid-style leadership from beyond the grave, or a demystification of political authority as reliant more on 'cunning props' than on martial heroism.

Though printed in 1594, *The Battle of Alcazar* is conventionally dated to about 1588, partly on the basis of Peele's exhortation in his 1589 'Farewell' to generals departing to fight the Spanish to 'Bid Theaters and proude Tragaedians, / ... King Charlemaine, Tom Stukeley and the rest / Adiewe'.[21] However, it is often also identified either with the 'mvlamvlluco' (i.e. 'Muly Molocco', a variant spelling of Abdelmelec) played at the Rose by Lord Strange's Men between February 1592 and January 1593, or with the 'mahomett' played by the Admiral's Men between August 1594 and February 1595.[22] The play's most recent editor, Charles Edelman, supports the former, partly because he sees Abdelmelec as 'the play's central character' and partly because of similarities between stage directions

[20] Berek, p. 68.
[21] George Peele, *A Farewell. Entituled to the Famous and Fortunate Generalls of Our English Forces* (London, 1589; STC: 19537), sig. A3r.
[22] *Henslowe's Diary*, pp. 16–19, 23–7.

in the quarto and those in other plays possibly written for Strange's Men.[23] However, the quarto's title page offers the play 'As it was sundrie times plaid by the Lord high Admirall his seruants', not Strange's, and in the 'plot' of *The Battle of Alcazar* created for a revival of the play it is the role of Muly Mahamet, not Abdelmelec, that is assigned to the star actor Edward Alleyn. In my view this makes it more likely that 'mahomett', of the two plays, represents *The Battle of Alcazar*, as does the fact that (as Martin Wiggins notes) Henslowe on 4 August 1601 records a payment of fifty shillings by the Admiral's Men 'for mackynge of crown[es] & other thing [es] for mahewmet'.[24] *The Battle of Alcazar*, with its multiple kings and dumb-show of crowns at the start of Act 5, is particularly 'demanding' of these properties, supporting both an identification of 'mahewmet' with Peele's play and Wiggins's argument that the plot dates from 1601.[25] Another possibility is that both 'mvlamvlluco' and 'mahomett' represent *Alcazar* under different titles, as Lawrence Manley and Sally-Beth MacLean have recently suggested, although it is also salutary to bear in mind John Yoklavich's observation that 'both the quarto and the playhouse document called the "plot" bear the title *The Battle of Alcazar*, and there is no evidence that the play was known by a nickname'.[26]

The question of play identification is significant because of the bearing it has on *The Battle of Alcazar's* currency in the mid-1590s theatre: was it a forgotten relic of the 1580s, or a play that, like *Tamburlaine*, *Faustus* and *The Jew of Malta*, survived in the Admiral's repertory? That Shakespeare, for one, remembered it in other contexts than the parodic one of *2 Henry IV* is suggested by the possible echo of the doomed Muly Mahamet's demand in battle for 'A horse, a horse, villain, a horse' (5.1.96) in *Richard III*.[27] However, I am inclined to avoid discussion of whether *Alcazar* influenced the *Henry VI* plays, partly because they predate Shakespeare's time with the Lord Chamberlain's Men, but also because the persistent question of whether Shakespeare was their sole author makes it difficult to know whether to interpret any points of resemblance as evidence of influence or of joint authorship with Peele.[28] Instead, the following section focuses on

[23] *The Stukeley Plays*, pp. 23–4.   [24] *Henslowe's Diary*, p. 178.

[25] Wiggins, 'A Choice of Impossible Things', p. 198.

[26] Lawrence Manley and Sally-Beth MacLean, *Lord Strange's Men and Their Plays* (New Haven: Yale University Press, 2014), p. 77; *The Dramatic Works of George Peele*, gen. ed. Charles Tyler Prouty, 3 vols (New Haven: Yale University Press, 1952–70), vol. II, p. 223.

[27] Maurice Pope, 'My Kingdom for a Horse', *Notes and Queries*, 41 (1994), 472–7.

[28] Most obviously, Richard of Gloucester's soliloquy in *3 Henry VI* 3.3 resembles Stukeley's of 2.2 in its repeated deployment of 'crown' at the ends of lines, and his image of himself seeking the crown in a

Henry IV, the first part of which Shakespeare probably wrote a year or so after *Mahomet* ended its run in 1595.

Henry IV and *The Battle of Alcazar*

In James Shapiro's book *Rival Playwrights*, which explores the creative relationship between Marlowe, Shakespeare and Ben Jonson, early dramatic responses to Marlowe such as *The Battle of Alcazar* do not fare very well. Shapiro's view of Peele, Greene and Lodge resembles that of Berek: 'Attempting to imitate and capitalize on Marlowe's success, their imitative encounters rendered them vulnerable to those aspects of Marlowe's work that resisted such acts of containment.' In the second part of *Tamburlaine*, for example, the way Marlowe gestures towards the possibility that the protagonist's death might be divine retribution only to leave the matter ambiguous pre-emptively undermines later dramas that would place similar heroes in more morally orthodox contexts. To the critic, such plays 'serve as instructive foils to Shakespeare's and Jonson's subsequent and far more successful efforts to appropriate Marlowe's work', while the two dramatists' own parodies (in *2 Henry IV* and Jonson's *Poetaster*) suggest that they were 'attentive to how and why these imitations failed, and learned from their mistakes'. Although Shapiro does not focus on *The Battle of Alcazar*, he does find evidence for his argument in Greene's *Alphonsus, King of Aragon*, whose hero is a legitimate monarch rather than a usurper, and Lodge's *The Wounds of Civil War*, in which Scilla ultimately resigns the tyrannical power he has acquired.[29] However, as I have argued over the preceding paragraphs, to view *The Battle of Alcazar* as a poor imitation of *Tamburlaine* is to criticise it for failing to achieve something it does not attempt: instead, it ironises Marlovian language and attitudes while claiming to unveil the workings of European *realpolitik*. Peele's play, perhaps remaining in the Admiral's repertory as *Mahomet* and still commercially viable at the end of the decade, represented not a dramatic dead end but rather a dramatic model that, I will argue, informed Shakespeare's treatment of historical materials in *Henry IV*.

A number of readers of Shakespeare's histories – particularly the second tetralogy – have found one of their distinctive features to be their secular

---

thorny wood from which he will 'hew my way out with a bloody axe' recalls Muly Mahamet using the Portuguese 'To hew a way for me unto the crown', 4.2.71.

[29] James Shapiro, *Rival Playwrights: Marlowe, Jonson, Shakespeare* (New York: Columbia University Press, 1991), pp. 29, 32–6.

understanding of historical causation. Phyllis Rackin, for example, sees Shakespeare as influenced partly by a religious interpretation of history that discerned in it the unfolding of God's Providence, but also by a school of thought associated with Italians such as Guicciardini and Machiavelli that stressed human agency. While *Richard III* completes the first tetralogy by 'retroactively imposing a providential order' on the events of the *Henry VI* plays, the second tetralogy exhibits 'an increasingly self-conscious and sceptical attitude'.[30] Paola Pugliatti similarly argues that 'in Shake-speare's plays second causes tend to prevail over the workings of provi-dence' (although she finds this tendency in the first as well as the second tetralogy), while Hugh Grady writes that from 1595 onwards, Shakespeare's histories 'seem to take for granted a secular, realpolitik understanding of political power' that the playwright may have derived from Machiavelli, from Marlowe, or from the Tacitean historians associated with the Earl of Essex's circle.[31] Readings like these typically focus on such features of the plays as the way a sacramental view of monarchical authority is held up to scrutiny in *Richard II*; Prince Hal's plan in *1 Henry IV* to stage his own moral reformation as a public relations exercise; and, in the sequel, Henry IV's deathbed advice to his son to use foreign war as a distraction from domestic quarrels.

As Grady points out, one likely source for Shakespeare in this respect may have been the work of Marlowe, not least the *Tamburlaine* plays, which had been in print since 1590 and which the Admiral's continued to stage from late 1594 through to November 1595. Although it is the plays' possible influence on *Henry V* that has garnered the most critical attention (as, for example, from Shapiro, Marjorie Garber, Robert Logan and Sara Munson Deats), as a two-part history play they created an obvious prece-dent for *Henry IV*.[32] G. K. Hunter has argued that the two pairs of plays achieve artistic unity through similar methods: 'a parallel setting-out of the incidents' rather than a simple 'picking-up of all the threads of Part One'.[33]

---

[30] Phyllis Rackin, *Stages of History: Shakespeare's English Chronicles* (London: Routledge, 1990), pp. 65, 60.

[31] Paola Pugliatti, *Shakespeare the Historian* (Basingstoke: Macmillan, 1996), p. 50; Hugh Grady, *Shakespeare, Machiavelli, and Montaigne: Power and Subjectivity from 'Richard II' to 'Hamlet'* (Oxford: Oxford University Press, 2002), p. 26.

[32] Shapiro, pp. 81–5, 97–101; Marjorie Garber, 'Marlovian Vision/Shakespearean Revision', *Research Opportunities in Renaissance Drama*, 22 (1979), 3–9; Robert A. Logan, *Shakespeare's Marlowe: The Influence of Christopher Marlowe on Shakespeare's Artistry* (Aldershot: Ashgate, 2007), pp. 143–67; Sara Munson Deats, 'Mars or Gorgon? Tamburlaine and Henry V', *Marlowe Studies: An Annual*, 1 (2011), 99–124.

[33] G. K. Hunter, '*Henry IV* and the Elizabethan Two-Part Play', *Review of English Studies*, n.s., 5 (1954), 236–48 (p. 243).

An example from *Tamburlaine* is the way the protagonist's destruction of Babylon at the end of Part II mirrors that of Damascus at the end of Part I; from *1 and 2 Henry IV*, the second-act Eastcheap scenes that both culminate in an irruption from the wider world. In both sequels, the sense of repetition generates an atmosphere of decay: the pervasive 'images of sickness and disease' that Giorgio Melchiori finds in *2 Henry IV* are also to be discerned in *2 Tamburlaine*, where the death of Zenocrate supplies an intimation of the mortality which will ultimately claim the protagonist. To note one perhaps trivial detail, Falstaff's first line in *2 Henry IV*, in which he asks 'what says the doctor to my water' (2.1.1), revisits a topic on which the Physician gives a detailed account in the final scene of *2 Tamburlaine* (5.3.82–99).[34]

It is surely the case that *Tamburlaine* supplied Shakespeare with an invaluable model for how to write a sequel to a successful play, as well as suggesting individual themes such as the question of whether kings are divinely ordained and the legitimacy of oath-breaking, or at least tactical equivocation, between military adversaries. However, Marlowe's work is far from being the only available precedent for Shakespeare's secular treatment of politics in *Henry IV*. Although *The Battle of Alcazar* emphasises, in Sebastian's lengthy speech to Stukeley, that invasion of Ireland is both pointless and wrong because 'heavens and destinies / Attend and wait upon her majesty' Queen Elizabeth and protect her realm (2.4.107–8), and the Duke of Avero seems to anticipate the Armada in predicting that heaven will punish Philip II for his oath-breaking, the actual incidents depicted in the play appear to take place in a fallen political world. Here, military outcomes are determined not by Providence but by the support, or lack of it, of continental superpowers (Spain, the Ottoman Empire); the deceitful behaviour of monarchs (Philip, Mahamet); and the wisdom of political leaders and the preparedness of their armies, both of which are conspicuously lacking amongst the Portuguese. Encumbered with 'Horse-boys, laundresses and courtesans / And fifteen hundred waggons full of stuff / For noble men brought up in delicate' (4.1.11–13), 'Their payment in the camp is passing slow, / And victuals scarce, that many faint and die' (4.1.18–19). Certainly, the rival Kings of Morocco make use of providentialist language to bolster their views of themselves as divinely ordained monarchs: Abdelmelec insists that 'The gods shall pour down showers of sharp revenge' upon the usurper (1.1.88), while Mahamet defies those who seek 'To chastise and to menace lawful kings' (1.2.36).

---

[34] *2 Henry IV*, ed. Melchiori, p. 29.

Both monarchs, however, are dead by the end of Act 5. Although the play's sympathies lie more with Abdelmelec than with Mahamet, reflecting (as Matthew Dimmock argues) England's strategic alliances of the time, Peele offers not 'crude nationalism' but 'a precisely fictionalized consider-ation of the causes and consequences of Sebastian's Barbary campaigns'.[35]

This insistence on the practical considerations that determine political and military outcomes is similarly in evidence in the *Henry IV* plays. In Part I, rather than presenting the King's victory at Shrewsbury as divinely sanctioned, Shakespeare makes clear that the Earl of Northum-berland, Owen Glendower, and Lord Mortimer all failed to turn up in support of Hotspur's party (4.1.18–85, 124–7, 5.1.23), and in Part II, he depicts Prince John's misleading assurance to the rebels that 'these griefs shall be with speed redressed' (4.1.287) as the immediate cause of their downfall. Both plays emphasise King Henry's lack of political legitimacy: in Part II, Hotspur recalls how his father and uncle 'Did gage them both in an unjust behalf' (1.3.171) in aiding him to the throne, and Northumberland asserts that he was present when King Richard named Mortimer his heir (1.3.155), while in Part II the dying King is all too aware of 'By what by-paths and indirect crooked ways / I met this crown' (4.2.312–13). None of this prevents Henry from dying in his bed and passing on the crown unproblematically to his son.

It is, admittedly, undeniable that *Tamburlaine* is a more significant dramatic source for this aspect of *Henry IV* than is *The Battle of Alcazar*. What *The Battle of Alcazar* adds to *Tamburlaine*, however, is, as we have seen, a recurrent tendency to undercut Marlovian rhetoric by emphasising its inadequacy both in representing and in shaping the actual state of things, as well as a profound scepticism about the claims of honour and about the Herculean heroes who espouse it. In *1 Henry IV*, the value of honour is comically deconstructed in Falstaff's soliloquy of Act 5, Scene 1, which includes a phrase – 'honour pricks me on' (5.1.130) – that recalls *Alcazar*'s opening invocation of 'Honour, the spur that pricks the princely mind' (1.Prol.1). However, the character whose treatment by Shakespeare most resembles Peele's ironic depiction of Mahamet, Sebastian and Stukeley is surely Hotspur. Roberta Barker has shown how Hotspur's critical and theatrical fortunes have varied over the centuries: regarded as a tragic hero and leading role in the Romantic period, he was dismissed by E. M. W. Tillyard as an example of 'provincial boorishness' who 'verges

---

[35] Matthew Dimmock, *New Turkes: Dramatizing Islam and the Ottomans in Early Modern England* (Aldershot: Ashgate, 2005), pp. 121, 114.

on the ridiculous', and has been seen by some more recent historicist
critics as the anachronistic embodiment of a residual chivalric mindset,
a casualty of Lancastrian policy.[36] A focal point of debate is his speech in
Act 1, Scene 3:

> By heaven, methinks it were an easy leap
> To pluck bright honour from the pale-faced moon,
> Or dive into the bottom of the deep,
> Where fathom-line could never touch the ground,
> And pluck up drownèd honour by the locks,
> So he that doth redeem her thence might wear
> Without corrival all her dignities. (3.1.199–205)

As Barker demonstrates, this speech has variously been read as dazzling
rhetoric, as absurd bombast and as an example of Hotspur's outdated
attitudes.[37] There is ample evidence for all of these views, which are by no
means incompatible, but I would add that in the context of the play they
express an ethic of individual heroism that is simply deluded. We do not
need Falstaff's cynicism to tell us that honour is inadequate when the
rebels' reinforcements do not arrive. Moreover, Hotspur's valorisation of
honour above other considerations leads him to voice the strategically
unconvincing opinion that the absence of Northumberland 'lends a lustre
and more great opinion, / A larger dare to our great enterprise' (4.1.77–8);
it is but a small step to the heroic but disheartening 'Doomsday is near.
Die all, die merrily' (4.1.134). Finally, his one-track mind makes him
vulnerable to manipulation by Worcester, who knows how to lead him
on with talk of 'matter deep and dangerous', 'full of peril and adventurous
spirit' (1.3.188–9), but betrays him in refusing to pass on the King's offer of
clemency (5.2.1–25). All of these qualities are shared with Sebastian in
The Battle of Alcazar, of whom the Act 4 Prologue unambiguously states,
'Let fame of him no wrongful censure sound, / Honour was object of his
thoughts, ambition was his ground' (4.Prol.12–13). His counsellors' advice
to pause before advancing on Alcazar sounds to him like cowardice:
'We come to fight, and fighting vow to die, / Or else to win the thing

---

[36] E. M. W. Tillyard, *Shakespeare's History Plays* (London: Chatto and Windus, 1944), pp. 280, 283.
[37] Roberta Barker, 'Tragical-Comical-Historical Hotspur', *Shakespeare Quarterly*, 54 (2003), 288–307
    (p. 298). Barker cites Herschel Baker's introduction to the play in *The Riverside Shakespeare*, ed. by
    G. Blakemore Evans (Boston: Houghton Mifflin, 1974), pp. 842–6; C.W.R.D. Moseley,
    Shakespeare's History Plays: 'Richard II' to 'Henry V': The Making of a King (London: Penguin,
    1988), p. 134; Alexander Leggatt, *Shakespeare's Political Drama: The History Plays and the Roman Plays*
    (London: Routledge, 1988), p. 85; Graham Holderness, *Shakespeare: The Histories* (London:
    Macmillan, 2000), p. 162.

for which we came' (4.2.8–9). Avero's comment that magnanimity needs to be joined with 'advice and prudent foresight' (4.2.26) goes unregarded. And, of course, Philip treats Sebastian as a mere pawn in his attempt to gain control of the Iberian peninsula.

Of equal importance to Hotspur's attitude towards honour is the language he uses to express it. In Part II, Lady Percy recalls him 'speaking thick' (2.3.24), and in Part I this quality is most emphatically (and comically) exemplified in the third scene, where his father and uncle repeatedly have to manage his rhapsodic interruptions – as Maurice Charney puts it, 'as if he were a headstrong adolescent'.[38] Barker finds in him 'a parody of a Marlovian overreacher', and notes that his 'By heaven' speech is (inaccurately) quoted in Francis Beaumont's *The Knight of the Burning Pestle* (c.1608) when the Citizen's Wife asks Rafe the prentice to 'speak a huffing part' (Induction, 3) to demonstrate his histrionic ability.[39] While the episode in Beaumont can be read as satirising the speech as bombast, or the citizens for reading it uncritically, it evidently responds to the way Hotspur's style teeters on the boundary between the impressive and the overblown. This characteristic, I would argue, is another that Shakespeare could have drawn from *The Battle of Alcazar*, where the vaunting speeches of Stukeley, in particular, seem intended to verge on the ludicrous. There is a degree of incongruity in the penultimate line of his soliloquy in Act 2, Scene 2, 'Huff it, brave mind, and never cease t'aspire' (2.2.83): he, or Peele, seems to recognise himself as speaking 'a huffing part' in a way that Tamburlaine never does. When he is finally stabbed by resentful Italian soldiers, the Second Italian's comment 'Why suffer we this English man to live?' comes across as an admission that killing Stukeley may be the only way of getting him to shut up; and yet even then, Stukeley manages a dying speech of almost fifty lines in which he narrates his life story, very much like Rafe at the end of *The Knight of the Burning Pestle*. There is a pleasing parallel between Beaumont's comic recycling of a heroic speech from *1 Henry IV* in that play, and the way Shakespeare draws on *The Battle of Alcazar* for Pistol's bar-room idiolect in *2 Henry IV*, perhaps reflecting the slightly excessive quality that Hotspur's language sometimes shares with that of Peele's drama. And indeed, even after the stage direction in *1 Henry IV* indicates

---

[38] Maurice Charney, 'The Voice of Marlowe's Tamburlaine in Early Shakespeare', *Comparative Drama*, 31 (1997), 213–23 (p. 220).

[39] Francis Beaumont, *The Knight of the Burning Pestle*, ed. by Michael Hattaway (London: Ernest Benn, 1969).

that 'The Prince killeth Percy' (5.4.75s.d.), Hotspur manages over nine lines of dialogue that end mid-sentence, emphasising the volubility to which death puts an end:

> HOTSPUR ... O, I could prophesy,
>   But that the earthy and cold hand of death
>   Lies on my tongue. No, Percy, thou art dust,
>   And food for –
> PRINCE For worms, brave Percy. (5.4.82–6, modern editors' stage
>   direction omitted)

At the Battle of Shrewsbury, Hotspur's histrionic self-assertiveness contrasts with the theatricality of a different sort that is practised by King Henry, who as Hotspur explains to Douglas 'hath many marching in his coats' (5.3.25). Drawing on Holinshed, who writes that Douglas killed 'sir Walter Blunt, and three other, apparelled in the kings sute and clothing', Shakespeare has both Blunt and the Lord of Stafford meet their deaths as decoys for the King.[40] As Kastan points out, while this stratagem ostensibly sets up a dichotomy between the real monarch and the fakes, this distinction is undermined by the fact that 'the King cannot be distinguished from his representations'.[41] The subversive insinuation that 'Henry's majesty can be effectively mimed' recalls the climactic moments of *The Battle of Alcazar*, where Abdelmelec's propped-up corpse is just as effective a rallying point for his troops as his living body.

It is important to retain a sense of perspective when discussing the relationship between *The Battle of Alcazar* and the *Henry IV* plays. Shakespeare's drama differs fundamentally from Peele's in a number of respects: it possesses a self-consciousness about the writing of history, and its own role in that process, that *Alcazar* (which admittedly records much more recent events) does not.[42] The dominant historical narrative is undercut by a various elements, including the comic history tradition, the carnivalesque element embodied in Falstaff, the voices of female characters and the use of metadrama, that do not figure significantly in Peele's play.[43] However, *The Battle of Alcazar*, which was available in print from 1594 and was very

---

[40] *The First Part of King Henry IV*, ed. Weil and Weil, 5.3.7–9n.; Raphael Honlinshed et al., *The Third Volume of Chronicles* (London, 1587; STC: 13569), p. 523.

[41] David Scott Kastan, "'The King Hath Many Marching in His Coats," or, What Did You Do in the War, Daddy?', in *Shakespeare, Left and Right*, ed. by Ivo Kamps (New York: Routledge, 1991), pp. 241–58, p. 253.

[42] See for example Rackin; also Graham Holderness, *Shakespeare's History* (Dublin: Gill and Macmillan; New York: St. Martin's Press, 1985).

[43] See for example Grady, pp. 127–79; Barbara Hodgdon, *The End Crowns All: Closure and Contradiction in Shakespeare's History* (Princeton: Princeton University Press, 1991), pp. 155–61;

possibly still being staged in 1594–5, represented an ironic response to Marlovian rhetoric and concepts on which Shakespeare was able to draw in *1* and *2 Henry IV*, while more generally its continued popularity (along with *1* and *2 Tamburlaine*) may have encouraged Shakespeare to write a play that combined a vaunting hero with a clear-eyed view of politics and war. Shakespeare's parodies of *The Battle of Alcazar* and *Tamburlaine* in *2 Henry IV* can be viewed as testimony to the by now old-fashioned nature of those plays; but the impulse to parody may also have stemmed from a desire to distance his drama from others to which it was more indebted than he cared to admit.

Captain Thomas Stukeley

The ongoing appeal of *The Battle of Alcazar* in the mid-1590s is suggested not just by its possible revival as *Mahomet* and by the influence it exerted over *Henry IV*, but by the appearance of at least one other play featuring the same battle, this time as part of a depiction of major events in the life of its best-known English participant. *The Famous Historye of the Life and Death of Captaine Thomas Stukeley* (hereafter *Captain Thomas Stukeley*) did not appear in print until 1605, without attribution to a dramatist or acting company.[44] However, it had apparently been in existence at least since August 1600, when it was entered in the Stationers' Register, and there has been a good deal of critical discussion over the extent of its similarity to the 'stewtley' first performed by the Admiral's Men on 11 December 1596 and staged a further nine times over the following seven months.[45] A complicating factor is the problematic nature of the quarto: amongst other things, it contains two versions of the same scene, apparently refers to an episode in Rome that is absent from the printed text, and culminates in a series of scenes where events that have not yet been depicted are spoken of as if they had. This led the Victorian editor Richard Simpson to conclude that while 'The three first acts are finished parts of a whole', the remainder of the play interweaves material from one lost play about the claim of Don Antonio to the Portuguese throne, and from yet another lost play ('in a more archaic style, like that of Peele or Greene') about the battle of Alcazar, with incoherent

---

Jean E. Howard and Phyllis Rackin, *Engendering a Nation: A Feminist Account of Shakespeare's English Histories* (London: Routledge, 1997), pp. 160–85.

[44] *The Famous Historye of the Life and Death of Captaine Thomas Stukeley* (London, 1605; STC: 23405).

[45] *The Stukeley Plays*, p. 34; *Henslowe's Diary*, pp. 55–9.

results.[46] Although subsequent editors and commentators followed Simpson in assuming that the quarto includes material derived from more than one play, Martin Wiggins has argued that *Stukeley*'s stylistic and other inconsistencies are more convincingly explained by multiple authorship, a practice common among dramatists writing for the Admiral's Men.[47] In this he is followed by Edelman and by the current author.[48] Edelman also addresses the question of authorship, joining Joseph Quincy Adams, Jr 'in attributing much of the first half of the play to Thomas Heywood' on the basis of style, characterisation and versification.[49] While arguments of this type are never wholly immune from the charges of selectivity and subjectivity, I am inclined to agree with Edelman and Adams on the basis both of general points of similarity between *Stukeley*'s opening London scenes and plays such as *If You Know Not Me You Know Nobody* (especially the way Alderman Curtis's verbal mannerisms resemble those of Hobson in Part II of that play), and of more specific phrases that recall other works by Heywood – notably 'To call back yesterday' (13.91), which reappears in one of the playwright's most famous speeches.[50] Both Adams and Edelman note that at some point after 14 October 1596 Henslowe lent the Admiral's Men 30 shillings 'for hawodes bocke', and that 'stewtley' was first performed on 11 December; the sum of 30 shillings, which is less than was typically paid for a whole play, is in keeping with the assumption that Heywood was only one of two or more playwrights who contributed to *Captain Thomas Stukeley*.[51]

Neither Adams nor Edelman, however, discusses another feature of *Captain Thomas Stukeley* that would support a 1596 dating: its several points of similarity to *A Midsummer Night's Dream* and *Richard II*, both

---

[46] *The School of Shakespere*, vol. I, pp. 140–1.

[47] See for example Irving Ribner, *The English History Play in the Age of Shakespeare* (Princeton: Princeton University Press, 1957), p. 195; *The Famous History of Captain Thomas Stukeley*, ed. by Judith C. Levinson (Oxford: Malone Society, 1975), pp. v–viii; Joseph Candido, 'Captain Thomas Stukeley: The Man, the Theatrical Record, and the Origins of Tudor "Biographical" Drama', *Anglia*, 105 (1987), 50–68 (p. 58). Wiggins surveys the debate in 'Things That Go Bump in the Text: Captain Thomas Stukeley', *Proceedings of the Bibliographical Society of America*, 98 (2001), 5–20.

[48] *The Stukeley Plays*, pp. 34–8.

[49] *The Stukeley Plays*, pp. 38–42; Joseph Quincy Adams, Jr., 'Captaine Thomas Stukeley', *Journal of English and Germanic Philology*, 15 (1916), 107–29.

[50] Thomas Heywood, *A Woman Killed With Kindness*, ed. by Brian Scobie (London: A. & C. Black, 1985), 13.53–4: 'O God, O God, that it were possible / To undo things done, to call back yesterday.'

[51] Adams, p. 114; *The Stukeley Plays*, pp. 41–2; *Henslowe's Diary*, p. 50. The usual price for a play by the late 1590s was about 6 pounds: see G. E. Bentley, *The Profession of Dramatist in Shakespeare's Time 1590–1642* (Princeton: Princeton University Press, 1971), p. 98.

of which are usually dated to 1595–6.[52] Like *A Midsummer Night's Dream*, which pits Hermia's beloved Lysander against her father's choice Demetrius, the play opens with a scene in which we are shown two suitors for the hand of the same young woman, Nell Curtis: Vernon, who has the support of Nell's parents, and Stukeley, who is favoured by Nell. As Stukeley insists,

> I am a gentleman and well derived,
> Equal, I may say, in all true respects,
> With higher fortune than I aim at now. (1.72–4).

Given the parallel between the situation and that at the start of *A Midsummer Night's Dream*, it seems reasonable to conclude that Heywood (if it be he) is recalling the words of Lysander:

> I am, my lord, as well-derived as he,
> As well-possessed: my love is more than his,
> My fortunes every way as fairly ranked,
> If not with vantage, as Demetrius'. (1.1.99–102)

Heywood's innovation, however, is to have Vernon voluntarily relinquish his claim to Nell knowing that another has her heart. In Stukeley's words, 'my dear friend to me hath yielded up / What right he might prefer to your fair child / In true regard of our so mutual love' (1.77–9) – again echoing the language of Shakespeare's play, where Demetrius asks Lysander to 'yield / Thy crazèd title to my certain right' (1.1.91–2).[53] The conflict that in Shakespeare generates the action of the play is in Heywood instantly resolved, perhaps reflecting a belief on the part of the playwright that marriage (even of heiresses) should be voluntarily entered into by both parties, but also indicating the generic gap between *Captain Thomas Stukeley* and *A Midsummer Night's Dream*. The play opens, rather than ending, with a marriage, offering a harmonious beginning that will be overturned with Stukeley's squandering of his wife's inheritance, her early death, and his ultimate demise at Alcazar. As for *Richard II*: Edelman compares the enquiry of Stukeley's father, 'When saw you that unthrifty boy, Tom Stukeley?' (2.30), to that of Bullingbrook, 'Can no man tell me of my unthrifty son?' (5.3.1); he does not note, however, that just as Bullingbrook acknowledges that he sees 'some sparks of better hope' in

---

[52] On *A Midsummer Night's Dream*, see previous chapter. See also William Shakespeare, *King Richard II*, edn. by Andrew Gurr, updated edn. (Cambridge: Cambridge University Press, 2003), pp. 1–3.
[53] William Shakespeare, *A Midsummer Night's Dream*, ed. by R. A. Foakes, updated edn. (Cambridge: Cambridge University Press, 2003).

Hal despite his dissolute behaviour (5.3.21), so Old Stukeley hopes that in consorting with gallants his son 'Shows the true sparks of honourable worth / And rightly shows in this he is mine own' (2.60–61).[54] Just as Heywood takes the opening situation in *Stukeley* from that of *A Midsummer Night's Dream*, so he derives from *Richard II* a dynamic of concerned father and unthrifty son; and while there was obviously nothing to prevent him from echoing lines from Shakespeare years after their first appearance, the fact that not one but two plays from about 1595 seem to be recalled in *Stukeley* is an argument for identifying it with the play premiered in December 1596.

At this point, however, things become problematic, because other moments in the opening scenes of *Captain Thomas Stukeley* unmistakeably resemble ones from *1 Henry IV* – a play, as we have seen, usually dated to 1597 or late in 1596. For example, the anxious aside with which Stukeley's Page responds to Old Stukeley's enquiries about his son's legal studies takes the form of a construction repeatedly used in the Falstaff scenes:

> If he have e'er a book there, but old hacked swords, as foxes, bilboes and horn-bucklers, I am an infidel. (2.91–2)

Compare *1 Henry IV*, 3.3.130–33: 'if there were anything in thy pocket but tavern-reckonings, memorandums of bawdy-houses, and one poor pennyworth of sugar to make thee long-winded . . ., I am a villain.' Or 2.4.108–9: 'If manhood, good manhood, be not forgot upon the face of the earth, then am I a shotten herring.' Or 2.4.157–8: 'if I fought not with fifty of them I am a bunch of radish.'[55] Heywood, too, likes this kind of conditional sentence well enough to use it more than once, making Old Stukeley comment on the bareness of his son's study: 'If he have so much as a candlestick, I am a traitor, but an old hilt of a broken sword to set his light in' (2.116–17). As with Prince Hal's inventory of the contents of Falstaff's pocket, physical objects – hacked swords, old hilts – are invoked, humorously adding a sense of concrete reality to the fictional world.

Given that this chapter has just interpreted the parallels between *Stukeley* and *A Midsummer Night's Dream* and *Richard II* as instances of indebtedness on Heywood's part that can be used to date the play to 1596, it would be perverse and inconsistent to assume that parallels between the same play and *1 Henry IV* – both those noted above and

---

[54] *The Stukeley Plays*, 2.30n.
[55] On the use of conditional sentences in *1 Henry IV*, see Dolores M. Burton, *Shakespeare's Grammatical Style: A Computer-Assisted Analysis of 'Richard II' and 'Antony and Cleopatra'* (Austin: University of Texas Press, 1973), pp. 22–5.

others that will be discussed later – are examples of Heywood's influence on Shakespeare. However, before taking the play as an instance of Falstaff's boast, 'I am not only witty in myself, but the cause that wit is in other men' (Part 2, 1.2.6–7), it is worth noting that if *Captain Thomas Stukeley* was performed in December 1596, then in order to have been influenced by *1 Henry IV* Heywood would have to have seen it staged before late July of that year, when the theatres closed (due to plague) until late October.[56] This would place Shakespeare's play in the first half of 1596, earlier than the Cambridge, Oxford and Arden editors are inclined to date it (although James M. Gibson has recently argued for just such an early date).[57] Furthermore, while the formative influence that Shakespeare exerted over Heywood in works such as *Oenone and Paris* is not in doubt, some Shakespeare plays have been identified as responses to the success of dramas by Heywood: *A Woman Killed with Kindness* in the case of *Measure for Measure*, *The Rape of Lucrece* in the case of *Coriolanus*.[58] Moreover, Shakespeare's willingness to take his cue from the successes of the contemporary stage has been repeatedly demonstrated in the course of this study. We should not, therefore, reject out of hand the possibility that *Captain Thomas Stukeley* may have had priority over *1 Henry IV* simply because it troubles our assumptions about who ought to be influencing whom. If we do reject it, on the reasonable grounds that Shakespeare's influence is evident elsewhere in the play, then the date of composition of *1 Henry IV* needs to be revised accordingly. Rather than closing down further discussion of the question by opting for one alternative rather than the other, the current chapter attempts to retain an open mind, as with *Doctor Faustus* and *Friar Bacon and Friar Bungay* in the previous chapter: points of contact between the plays are regarded as roughly contemporaneous attempts to deal with similar themes and material.

Captain Thomas Stukeley is clearly the work of dramatists familiar with *The Battle of Alcazar*. Not only does it contain several of the same

---

[56] See Shakespeare, *Henry IV, Part 1*, ed. Bevington, p. 9.

[57] See note 4 and also James M. Gibson, 'Shakespeare and the Cobham Controversy: The Oldcastle/Falstaff and Brooke/Broome Revision', *Medieval and Renaissance Drama in England*, 25 (2012), 94–132.

[58] '*Oenone and Paris' by T. H.: Reprinted from the Unique Copy in the Folger Shakespeare Library*, ed. by Joseph Quincy Adams (Washington DC: Folger Shakespeare Library, 1943), p. ix; Clare Smout, 'Actor, Poet, Playwright, Sharer ... Rival? Shakespeare and Heywood, 1603–4', *Early Theatre*, 13.2 (December 2010), 175–89; Tom Rutter, 'Adult Playing Companies, 1603–1613', in *The Oxford Handbook of Early Modern Theatre*, ed. by Richard Dutton (Oxford: Oxford University Press, 2009), pp. 72–87 (pp. 85–6).

characters, including Stukeley, Abdelmelec, Muly Mahamet and Calipolis, and incidents, including Sebastian's disregard of his counsellors' military advice, the concealment of Abdelmelec's death, the killing of Stukeley by Italian soldiers and the stuffing of Mahomet's skin with straw: in a number of details of style and characterisation it remembers Peele's play. Once again, Stukeley is given speeches that recall the idiom of Tamburlaine, as when he justifies his use of the money he has acquired through marriage to pay off his substantial debts:

> It is mine own, and Stukeley of his own
> Will be as frank as shall the emperor.
> I scorn this trash, betrayer of men's souls;
> I'll spurn it with my foot, and with my hand
> Rain showers of plenty on this barren land.
> Were it my fortune could exceed the clouds,
> Yet would I bear a mind surmounting that. (5.113–9)

As in *The Battle of Alcazar*, the image of Stukeley's mind ascending above the clouds recycles Tamburlaine's 'aspiring minds' speech, while that of raining showers of plenty echoes his observation of how Jove 'rains down heaps of gold in showers / As if he meant to give my soldiers pay' (Part 1, 1.2.182–3). This multiple intertextuality of the *Stukelely* dramatists remembering Peele remembering Marlowe is also in evidence when Calipolis welcomes Sebastian to Morocco, her name seemingly acting as the trigger for a set-piece speech that in its extravagant promises, classical deities and animal imagery recalls Muly Mahamet's famous address to her in *Alcazar*:

> All welcome that Calipolis can give
> To the renownèd mighty Portuguese.
> Here sit, sweet prince, and rest thee after toil.
> I'll wipe thy brows with leaves more sweet and soft
> Than is the down of Cytherea's doves,
> I'll fan thy face with the delicious plumes
> Of that sweet wonder of Arabia.
> With precious waters I'll refresh thy curls,
> Whose very savour shall make panthers wild
> And lonely smell of those delicious sweets,
> And with such glorious liquors please thy taste
> As Helen's goblet never did contain,
> Nor never graced the banquets of the gods. (21.34–46)

However, as its title suggests, *Captain Thomas Stukeley* is wholly different in its focus from Peele's play. Richard Simpson called it a 'biographical drama', a term that subsequent commentators have also adopted, and this reflects the way it derives its unity from the presentation of a sequence of episodes in Stukeley's life: his marriage to Nell Curtis in London; his military service in Ireland; his arrival in Cadiz and subsequent employment by Philip II; and his participation in Sebastian's African campaign.[59] As in *Alcazar*, there is a strong sense of the wider political context in which Stukeley fights and dies: more explicitly than in the earlier play, we see Philip advised by his counsellors to offer support to Sebastian and then betray him (14.89–136). But Stukeley's service for Sebastian is only the last phase in an eventful life. As Joseph Candido writes, the play creates our sense of its hero's character through a process of 'accretion' in which 'the dramatist reveals to us, by the simple accumulation of incidents, a noteworthy facet of his subject's personality that can appear either charming or cruel, ingratiating or satiric'.[60] Over the opening scenes we see Stukeley alternately as the true lover of Nell Curtis; a law student turned prodigal; a vaunting Marlovian hero; and a cynical gold-digger who goes off to fight in Ireland leaving his wife penniless. He is the scourge of Irish rebels who draws his sword on the governor of the town he is supposed to be defending; he charms the wife of the Governor of Cadiz only to be thoroughly manipulated by the King of Spain. This kaleidoscopic presentation reflects the fundamentally conflicted nature of Stukeley as a historical figure: on the one hand the quintessential Elizabethan action-man, present at some of the defining military encounters of the age, engaging in privateering and contemplating colonial projects; on the other the traitor who defects to the court of Philip II and agrees to win back Ireland for the Pope.

The profound ambivalence of Stukeley as a character has been commented on by several critics of the play. In particular, the scenes set in Ireland have been read as blurring the boundaries between Stukeley and the rebels he is supposed to be fighting: Stukeley with his men slays 'Two hundred Irish' (11.44) but revives an old quarrel with Harbert, the governor of Dundalk, ignores the order to retreat, and is consequently shut out of the town overnight in a gesture that as Jean E. Howard puts it marks him out as 'unfit for the civil and civilized enclosure represented by the garrison' and leaves him out in the fields with his enemies.[61] Claire Jowitt similarly notes that Stukeley is 'represented as a more serious threat

---

[59] *The School of Shakespere*, vol. I, p. 139; Ribner, p. 195; Candido, p. 50.   [60] Candido, pp. 59, 62.
[61] Jean E. Howard, 'Gender on the Periphery', in *Shakespeare and the Mediterranean: The Selected Proceedings of the International Shakespeare Association World Congress, Valencia, 2001*, ed. by Tom Clayton, Susan Brock and Vicente Forés (Newark: University of Delaware Press, 2004), pp. 344–62, p. 351.

to the integrity of the English forces than the rebellious Irish', and argues that in him 'the play documents the evolution of a rebel ... from greed and aggression to treason'.[62] Stukeley's shift from combating a Gaelic enemy through to deserting the monarch he originally fought for is one of several ways in which (as in *Alcazar*) his representation resembles that of Shakespeare's Hotspur, who at the outset of *1 Henry IV* has recently defeated the Scottish army at Holmedon but will fall out with Henry over the rights to the ransom of his prisoners. Hotspur is an ambivalent figure for similar reasons to Stukeley: Pugliatti regards him as a 'noble and courageous' character and notes various ways in which Shakespeare directs our sympathies towards him, but Rackin points out that his honour code is compromised 'not only by the slightly comical enthusiasm with which he embraces it but also by the fact that it inspires him to rebel against the king'.[63] As Holderness observes, even King Henry is unable to make up his mind about Hotspur, variously envying 'that my Lord Northumberland / Should be the father to so blest a son' (1.1.78–9), admonishing him and his father for the 'indignities' they inflict in withholding their prisoners (1.3.2), and identifying with him ('even as I was then is Percy now') during his interview with Prince Hal (3.2.96).[64] Beyond these general points of similarity, there are more specific details that seem to indicate either that Shakespeare was familiar with *Stukeley*, or that the *Stukeley* dramatists knew *1 Henry IV*.

The first of these is the two characters' manner of speech. The fact that Stukeley, as in *The Battle of Alcazar*, is given lines that echo *Tamburlaine* has already been remarked upon; but just as one characteristic of Hotspur's speech is its propensity towards 'overt shifts between ... two registers, legendary and earthly', so Stukeley's Marlovian flights alternate with more earthy utterances.[65] A pertinent example appears when Stukeley, newly arrived at Cadiz, refuses to surrender to the governor a toll of the horses he captured from the Irish:

> STUKELEY Had I known thus much, Governor, I would have burnt my ships in the haven before thy face, and have fed haddocks with my horses.
> GOVERNOR Is thou and all thou hast at my dispose, and dost deny me upon courtesy, what I may take whether thou wilt or no? Stukeley, if thou be called so, I'll make thee know a governor of Cales.

---

[62] Claire Jowitt, *Voyage Drama and Gender Politics 1589–1642: Real and Imagined Worlds* (Manchester: Manchester University Press, 2003), pp. 90, 82.
[63] Pugliatti, p. 49; Rackin, p. 77.   [64] Holderness, *Shakespeare: The Histories*, pp. 160, 165.
[65] Barker, p. 304.

STUKELEY Governor, will nothing but five of my horses serve your turn?
Sirrah, thou gets not one of them, and a hair would save thy life.
If I had as many horses as there be stones in this island, thou shouldst
not have one of them. (13.1–10)

Stukeley uses an idiom also employed by Hotspur in the scene where he is
insisting to his uncle that he will not give up his prisoners to King Henry:
'he shall not have a scot of them, / No, if a Scot would save his soul he shall
not' (1.3.212–13). This verbal parallel would be insignificant in itself were it
not for the fact that it reflects a broader parallel between the situations of
Stukeley and Hotspur: each is refusing to give up the spoils of war to the
relevant authority. The twofold resemblance, in action and in language,
makes it less likely that the similarity is merely coincidental.

Another scenic parallel between *1 Henry IV* and *Captain Thomas Stukeley* relates to the way both Hotspur and Stukeley are characterised in terms
of their marital relationships. Various critics have stressed the importance
of Lady Percy in representing a domestic space in contrast to which Hotspur fashions himself, whether that space is understood as a threatening
distraction (as Grady and Howard and Rackin see it), whether the presence
of a wife defuses the homoerotic tension that might otherwise be present
in Hotspur's relationships with his allies and enemies (as Hodgdon suggests), or whether the emphasis is on the contrast between Hotspur's
resistance to his wife and Mortimer's subjection to his own, as in the view
of J. L. Simmons.[66] This process is worked out in two scenes: 2.3, where
Hotspur announces that he must leave Lady Percy 'within these two
hours' (2.3.30), eliciting a long speech in which she requests an explanation for his odd behaviour recently, and 3.1, in which the couple squabble
over the Welsh song Lady Mortimer sings her new husband. There is also
the speech in which Prince Hal humorously imagines a conversation
between the Percies (2.4.88–95), and Lady Percy's continued presence
in Part II, where she delivers a substantial elegy on her late husband
(2.3.9–45).

The authors of *Captain Thomas Stukeley*, too, go to great lengths to
emphasise Stukeley's role as husband. While Stukeley's first appearance in
The Battle of Alcazar is at the court of Sebastian, the later play, as we have
seen, opens with scenes that (fictionally, as far as is known) present him as
a prodigal law student competing with Vernon for the hand of Nell Curtis.

---

[66] Grady, p. 166; Howard and Rackin, p. 163; Hodgdon, p. 155; J. L. Simmons, 'Masculine Negotiations
in Shakespeare's History Plays: Hal, Hotspur, and "the foolish Mortimer"', *Shakespeare Quarterly*, 44
(1993), 440–63.

They are no sooner married than London's tradesmen are queuing up in the hope that Stukeley will settle his accounts with them, and the tradesmen are no sooner paid than Stukeley has announced to his wife his intention to leave for Ireland. His subsequent allusions to her display a casual cruelty that Hotspur lacks: he boasts that he has sold all her possessions 'And all the clothes belonging to her back, / Save one poor gown' (9.62–3), and when he hears of her death and those of her parents he is concerned only about whether his father-in-law bequeathed him anything (17.7). However, like *1 Henry IV* the play offers a farewell scene in which the wife remonstrates with the husband – in Shakespeare's play over his refusal to tell her where he is going, here over the fact that he is going at all. As Lady Percy asks 'For what offence have I this fortnight been / A banished woman from my Harry's bed?' (2.3.32–3), so Nell complains that 'We scarce are warm within our nuptial bed, / And you forsake me there to freeze alone' (6.33–4). In both plays the men present themselves as rejecting a world that is characterised as idle and emasculating. Hotspur does so half-teasingly:

> I care not for thee, Kate; this is no world
> To play with mammets, and to tilt with lips.
> We must have bloody noses, and cracked crowns,
> And pass them current too. God's me! My horse! (2.3.85–8)

Stukeley does so in another Tamburlaine-like flight of fancy:

> It is not chambering,
> Now I have beauty to be dallying with,
> Nor pampering of my self with belly cheer,
> Now I have got a little worldly pelf,
> That is the end or levels of my thought.
> I must have honour, honour is the thing
> Stukeley doth thirst for, and to climb the mount
> Where she is seated, gold shall be my footstool. (6.43–50)

Not only does the image of climbing on a footstool recall Tamburlaine's treatment of the deposed Emperor Bajazeth in Part I, 4.2; Stukeley's description of honour parallels that in Hotspur's celebrated speech of *1 Henry IV*, 1.3. Stukeley imagines honour seated on high, as Hotspur talks of leaping 'To pluck bright honour from the pale-faced moon' (1.3.200), and he personifies honour as a woman, as Hotspur does when he talks of diving to 'pluck up drownèd honour by the locks' so as to wear 'Without corrival all her dignities' (1.3.203, 205). Both men, in effect, are leaving a real woman to go off in pursuit of a symbolic one.

In defining themselves against values they associate with their wives, though, Hotspur and Stukeley are not merely identifying themselves as males: they are identifying themselves as gentlemen. When he takes exception to Lady Percy's use of the phrase 'in good sooth' (3.1.240), Hotspur complains that she swears 'like a comfit-maker's wife' (3.1.241–2),

> And givest such sarcenet surety for thy oaths
> As if thou never walk'st further than Finsbury.
> Swear me, Kate, like a lady as thou art,
> A good mouth-filling oath, and leave 'In sooth',
> And such protest of pepper-gingerbread,
> To velvet-guards, and Sunday citizens. (2.3.244–9)

His wife's alleged primness is associated with citizen values that Hotspur, who sees himself as adhering to an aristocratic honour code, utterly rejects. Hotspur's self-definition against an urban middle class is paralleled in *Captain Thomas Stukeley*, where the citizen comedy idiom of scenes one to six serves as the counterpoint to the protagonist's heroic self-image. Stephen O'Neill is right to argue that these scenes offer 'a delineation of the emotional and personal costs of war as seen through the protestations of Stukeley's wife, father and father-in-law': it is not just that 'Stukeley's abandonment of Nell casts a shadow over his pursuit of honour', it is also that Old Stukeley and Sir Thomas Curtis articulate values of diligence and thrift incompatible with Stukeley's heroic ambitions.[67] The former is aghast to find his son 'so lewd and prodigal a spendthrift' (3.185), while the latter complains at seeing his new son-in-law paying off his debts for clothes, wine, weapons, tennis, fencing and affray 'with my money' (5.112):

> Would you e'er have thought
> That taverns, fencers, bailiffs and such like,
> Should by the fruits of my late sitting up
> And early rising have maintained their state? (5.131–4)

The hard work valued by the citizen is transformed into the conspicuous consumption and display of the prodigal gentlemen who wants to 'be as frank as shall the emperor' and scorns wealth as 'trash' (5.114–15). Given the fact that the play moves beyond these London scenes to consider other episodes in Stukeley's life, it cannot be said that it wholeheartedly shares Curtis's insistence on regarding heroic aspirations in material terms. However, Heywood's innovation in holding up a would-be Herculean

---

[67] Stephen O'Neill, *Staging Ireland: Representations in Shakespeare and Renaissance Drama* (Dublin: Four Courts Press, 2007), p. 124.

hero to the scrutiny of Hotspur's 'velvet-guards, and Sunday citizens' engineers a clash of personal outlooks and dramatic genres that complicates from the outset the play's depiction of its protagonist. Perhaps Shakespeare remembered Curtis's lines on 'late sitting up / And early rising' when he made the dying Henry IV complain of his son's prematurely seizing the crown,

> For this the foolish over-careful fathers
> Have broke their sleep with thoughts,
> Their brains with care, their bones with industry;
> For this they have engrossèd and pilled up
> The cankered heaps of strange-achievèd gold. (Part 2, 4.2.197–201)

Rather incongruously, the King imagines himself as an acquisitive merchant toiling to amass riches for an ungrateful child. In *Captain Thomas Stukeley*, Heywood put Bullingbrook's words into the mouth of an anxious father who 'meant to have made my son a barrister' (2.105–6); in *2 Henry IV*, Shakespeare gives the mindset of a citizen to the son of John of Gaunt.

Another possible indication that Shakespeare may have had *Captain Thomas Stukeley* in mind when writing *2 Henry IV* is the expletive 'foutre' uttered on two occasions by Pistol (5.3.80, 95). The same word is used by Stukeley on discovering that the expected payment of five thousand ducats by Philip II for an embassy to Rome has come twenty ducats too short: 'Foutre for ducats if he take the tithe!' (18.19). In the light of Pistol's predilection for dialogue taken from plays like *Tamburlaine* and *The Battle of Alcazar*, it seems quite reasonable to think of him as acquainted with *Stukeley* – particularly because the lines 'A foutre for the world and worldlings base! / I speak of Africa and golden joys' (5.3.80–81) are geographically as well as lexically suggestive of the two Alcazar plays. However, the similarities of language, situation and theme that can be observed between *1 Henry IV* and *Captain Thomas Stukeley* are otherwise much less evident in the sequel. This can be interpreted in two ways, depending on whether *1 Henry IV* or *Stukeley* is assumed to have been written first. If the former, then *Stukeley*'s similarities to it, as with *A Midsummer Night's Dream* and *Richard II*, could be straightforwardly attributed to derivativeness on the part of Heywood et al., and there would be no reason to expect that Shakespeare should make substantial use of *Stukeley* in *2 Henry IV*. If *Stukeley* came first, on the other hand, then the fact that *2 Henry IV* has fewer points of likeness to it than *1 Henry IV* could be explained by the fact that Hotspur, the character in whom the thematic concerns of *Stukeley* are most searchingly explored, is no longer present. Though Hotspur could be said to live on in parodic form in Pistol, the humour of that character is to recycle quotations from a variety of heroic dramas: for him to depend too narrowly on Stukeley would be out of keeping.

*

In general, this chapter has not looked beyond the theatre in seeking to identify and explain points of similarity between *Henry IV* and other plays that were being staged in the mid-1590s. The lost play *Harry V* indicates that the Admiral's Men were depicting the historical figure named in its title onstage in 1595–6, setting a precedent for Shakespeare to do so in Prince Hal. *The Battle of Alcazar* was certainly remembered by Shakespeare when writing *2 Henry IV*, where it is parodied, but Shakespeare's treatment of historical causation in the *Henry IV* plays, and the language and attitudes of Hotspur in particular, may also have been shaped by Peele's drama, perhaps recently restaged by the Admiral's and recorded by Henslowe as *Mahomet*. *Captain Thomas Stukeley* demonstrates the ongoing theatrical interest in 1596 in its ambiguous central figure, in the Battle of Alcazar, and in wider questions about the potential for military heroism to disrupt personal relationships and to degenerate into treachery. It may have drawn on an early *1 Henry IV*, or Shakespeare may have found in its comic dialogue and the attitudes of its protagonist useful materials for his own history.

However, the affinities between *Stukeley* and *1 Henry IV*, in particular, may reflect not just the tendency of Elizabethan dramatists to learn from their competitors' successes, but also their common engagement with certain contemporary developments. Firstly, the depiction in *Stukeley* of the protagonist fighting against Shane O'Neill in the Ireland of the 1560s is plainly inflected by the Nine Years' War (1594–1603) taking place in Ireland at the time of the play's production. As well as being a historical figure in his own right, Shane O'Neill can be seen as standing in for Hugh O'Neill, second Earl of Tyrone, the leading figure among England's Irish opponents from 1595. After Shane O'Neill is beheaded by the Scots to whom he has surrendered in Scene 12, the concluding lines, 'And may all Irish that with treason deal, / Come to like end or worse than Shane O'Neill' (12.84–5) are transparent in their contemporary relevance, as Stephen O'Neill points out.[68] Furthermore, the persistent threat that Spain would intervene in the Irish war gives currency to the play's depiction of an earlier figure who tried to involve both Philip II and the Pope in

---

[68] O'Neill, p. 132.

invasions of Ireland. Finally, as Jowitt and O'Neill both note, the location of the Irish scenes in Dundalk is much more relevant to the 1590s situation than to the events of the 1560s. It was at Dundalk that O'Neill was proclaimed a traitor on 24 June 1595, and it was there that he negotiated a short-lived truce in March 1596.[69] As for Shakespeare: *1 Henry IV* does not refer to the Nine Years' War as directly as the later *Henry V*, which also incorporates the Irishman Macmorris. However, Christopher Highley has argued that the play does include 'a displaced representation of Tyrone's resistance to English authority in Ireland' in the form of Owen Glendower, another Celtic enemy of the English who like O'Neill is seen as blending wildness and incivility with a courtly upbringing and uses marriage to forge alliances with disparate malcontented parties. The play uses mockery to defuse the threat posed by Glendower, who is led by prophecies to avoid the Battle of Shrewsbury, but Hal's defeat of Hotspur in the liminal territory of the Welsh Marches constitutes a symbolic victory over con-temporary Celtic enemies.[70] If Highley is right in seeing *1 Henry IV* as shaped in this way by the anxieties of the Nine Years' War, then these anxieties are thematic territory that it shares with *Stukeley*, a play that voices them rather more obviously.[71]

The second feature of *Captain Thomas Stukeley* that seems pertinent in the light of its date is the decision to have Stukeley set out for Cadiz immediately after the Dundalk scenes, although in reality it was Viviero at which he landed after leaving Ireland following his release from prison in 1570. In the play, Stukeley's doings there are the stuff of romantic fantasy: after the Governor imprisons him over his refusal to hand over the horses, he persuades the Governor's wife to release him so that he can remonstrate with King Philip and then, having pledged to return on his honour as a soldier and a gentleman, does so before the Governor has noticed his absence. By autumn 1596, though, it must have been difficult to think of Cadiz without remembering the Earl of Essex's naval venture in June of that year, in which he destroyed the Spanish fleet and looted and burned the city. While it is hard to identify any way in which the play comments

---

[69] Jowitt, p. 88; Nicholas Canny, 'O'Neill, Hugh, second earl of Tyrone (c.1550–1616)', *Oxford Dictionary of National Biography* (Oxford University Press, 2004); online edn, Jan 2008 www .oxforddnb.com/view/article/20775 (accessed 23 August 2015); O'Neill, pp. 126–7.

[70] Christopher Highley, *Shakespeare, Spenser, and the Crisis in Ireland*, Cambridge Studies in Renaissance Literature and Culture, 23 (Cambridge: Cambridge University Press, 1997), pp. 87, 89–97, 105.

[71] Highley briefly compares *Stukeley* with *1 Henry IV* as two plays that 'trade in wish-fulfillments about quelling rebellion in Ireland', p. 97.

upon those events directly (unless the business with the horses relates to Queen Elizabeth's subsequent fury over 'how much of the plunder had been hidden from royal officials'), the play perhaps invites its audiences to make some sort of connection between Essex and the reckless chivalry of Stukeley.[72] Although she does not comment on the Cadiz scenes, Jowitt does link Stukeley with Essex, arguing that the play reflects contemporary anxieties about the lack of a male monarch who might be able to control such 'Audacious, aggressive characters', while Simpson implies that the play's positive depiction of Stukeley is evidence that it was revised by Shakespeare, who is assumed to have been a supporter of Essex.[73] While Simpson's identification of Shakespeare as a contributor to *Stukeley* has not found favour, a number of commentators have linked his second tetralogy of history plays to Essex one way or another. I leave aside the tendency to read the Act 5 Chorus of *Henry V* as a reference to Essex, which has been questioned by Richard Dutton.[74] However, Grady suggests that the four plays' interest in Machiavellian political theories relates to the 'spectacular climax' of Essex's career between 1595 and 1601; Robin Headlam Wells finds in the histories 'a consistently sceptical view of the kind of heroic masculinity that was exemplified by the Earl of Essex'; and Barker notes the importance of neo-chivalric ideas of honour 'in the self-fashioning of the Earl of Essex, a celebrity whose qualities and personal connections to the Percy family could have encouraged spectators to link him to Hotspur'.[75] In autumn 1596, Essex's disastrous Irish campaign was still two and a half years in the future, although I suspect that *Stukeley*'s depiction of a character who fights against an O'Neill before in effect turning against his own monarch could have rendered the play very difficult to perform from about 1600 onward. At the time of the plays' writing, though, their common interest in the militaristic values identified with Essex, as well as the backdrop of war in Ireland, could be a reason why the dramatist or dramatists behind one play could find congenial material in the other.

[72] Paul E. J. Hammer, 'Devereux, Robert, second earl of Essex (1565–1601)', *Oxford Dictionary of National Biography* (Oxford University Press, 2004); online edn, Oct 2008 www.oxforddnb.com/view/article/7565 (accessed 23 August 2015).

[73] Jowitt, p. 94; *The School of Shakespere*, vol. I, pp. xx–xxii, 143.

[74] Richard Dutton, '"Methinks the Truth Should Live from Age to Age": The Dating and Contexts of *Henry V*', *Huntington Library Quarterly*, 68 (2005), 173–203.

[75] Grady, p. 26; Robin Headlam Wells, *Shakespeare on Masculinity* (Cambridge: Cambridge University Press, 2000), p. 24; Barker, p. 302. The Ninth Earl of Northumberland married Essex's sister in 1594.

CHAPTER 4

'Sundrie variable and pleasing humors'
New Comedies, 1597–98

The material surveyed in Chapter 3 appears to indicate that by the time of *Captain Thomas Stukeley*, the creative relationship between Shakespeare and some Admiral's Men dramatists had become a reciprocal one. Not only did Shakespeare's work in his first years with the Lord Chamberlain's Men draw on plays that were being staged by the Admiral's; by 1596, Shakespeare's plays were themselves discernibly influencing the work of at least one dramatist writing for the other company. This adds a further level of detail to Roslyn Knutson's observation that playing companies sought 'to have dramatists duplicate the successes in other companies' repertories', as with the 'set of plays on the Wars of the Roses' staged by several companies in the early 1590s.[1] Companies bought plays on subjects that had featured in other companies' repertories; but moreover, when writing those plays, dramatists also picked up on points of style, theme and characterisation.

The current chapter attempts to explore this dynamic in more detail by focusing on four comedies that are all assumed to have appeared during the years 1597–8. Two of these can be fairly securely dated to that period: George Chapman's *An Humorous Day's Mirth*, printed in 1599, is generally agreed to equate to 'the comodey of vmers' first performed by the Admiral's Men on 11 May 1597, and the play printed in 1616 as *English- men for My Money: or, A Pleasant Comedy, Called, A Woman Will Haue Her Will* is surely the 'comodey called A womon will haue her wille' for which Henslowe recorded payments to the dramatist William Haughton on 18 February and in early May 1598, probably indicating performances a few weeks later.[2] Henry Porter's play *The Two Angry Women of Abington*,

[1] Roslyn Lander Knutson, *The Repertory of Shakespeare's Company 1594–1613* (Fayetteville: University of Arkansas Press, 1991), pp. 7, 48. The plays in question include the Queen's Men *True Tragedy of Richard III*, the Strange's Men *Henry VI*, and the Pembroke's Men *First Part of the Contention Between York and Lancaster* and *True Tragedy of Richard Duke of York*.

[2] For 'the comodey of vmers', see *Henslowe's Diary*, ed. by R. A. Foakes [and R. T. Rickert], 2nd edn (Cambridge: Cambridge University Press, 2002), p. 58. Holger Schott Syme calls the identification 'a

printed in 1599, is not recorded by Henslowe, at least not under that title, but the fact that payments for a second part to the play were made to Porter in December 1598, January 1598–9 and February 1598–9 suggests that Part I appeared not long before then.[3] The precise date of the fourth play has been most controversial: Shakespeare's *The Merry Wives of Windsor* is sometimes dated as early as 23 April 1597 because its references to the Order of the Garter may link it to the Garter Feast held in Westminster on that date, while at the other extreme Giorgio Melchiori flatly asserts that 'the comedy could not have been written before late 1599' because it contains a character apparently introduced in *Henry V*.[4] These problems of dating will be addressed in more detail later in the current chapter.

One reason for choosing these four comedies is their relative chronological proximity to each other: they could all have appeared within a period as short as eighteen months. Another, though, is the considerable overlap between them in terms of idiom and theme. The influence of Chapman's humours comedy may be reflected in the fact that the title page of *The Two Angry Women* advertises 'the humorous mirthe of *Dick Coomes* and *Nicholas Prouerbes*', and that of the 1602 Quarto of *Merry Wives* offers 'sundrie variable and pleasing humors, of Syr *Hugh* the Welch Knight, Iustice *Shallow*, and his wise Cousin M. *Slender*. With the swaggering vaine of Auncient *Pistoll*, and Corporall *Nym*.'[5] Three of the plays have English settings, and two of those – *Englishmen for My Money* and *The Merry Wives of Windsor* – make extensive mockery of foreigners who speak accented and unidiomatic English. Both *Englishmen* and *Merry Wives*, along with *Two Angry Women*, focus on characters who (with acknowledgement of the term's limitations) might be called members of

---

reasonable conjecture rather than a certainty', but the entries for 'Verones sonnes hosse' and 'Labesyas clocke' in two inventories of clothing that Henslowe dates to March 1598 name two characters that appear in the printed play, indicating that it was in the Admiral's repertory for that date. Holger Schott Syme, 'The Meaning of Success: Stories of 1594 and Its Aftermath', *Shakespeare Quarterly*, 61 (2010), 490–525 (p. 507n.); *Henslowe's Diary*, pp. 318, 321. For 'A womon will haue her wille', see *Henslowe's Diary*, pp. 87, 89; *English-men for My Money: or, A Pleasant Comedy, Called, A Woman Will Haue Her Will* (London, 1616; STC: 12931).

[3] Andrew Gurr takes this position in *Shakespeare's Opposites: The Admiral's Company 1594–1625* (Cambridge: Cambridge University Press, 2009), p. 241n, modifying his argument in 'Intertextuality at Windsor', *Shakespeare Quarterly*, 38 (1987), 189–200, where he dated the play much earlier.

[4] William Shakespeare, *The Merry Wives of Windsor*, ed. by Giorgio Melchiori (London: Thomas Nelson and Sons, 2000), p. 21.

[5] Henry Porter, *The Two Angry Women of Abington*, ed. by W. W. Greg (Oxford: Malone Society, 1912); William Shakespeare, *A Most Pleasaunt and Excellent Conceited Comedie, of Syr Iohn Falstaffe, and the Merrie Wiues of Windsor* (London, 1602; STC: 22299). Subsequent references to Porter's play use this edition.

the middling sort: a London merchant and his household, and the non-aristocratic gentry of Windsor and Abingdon, as the town is usually spelled nowadays.[6] Sexual jealousy of husbands for their wives, or vice versa, is a prominent theme of *An Humorous Day's Mirth*, *Merry Wives* and *Two Angry Women*. And finally, the interest in women's right to choose their husbands that is indicated by Haughton's alternative title *A Woman Will Have Her Will* is also a concern of Shakespeare's, Porter's and to a lesser extent Chapman's plays.

These and other points of contact, which seem to indicate a collective participation in theatrical fashion beyond the bounds of any one company, will be discussed in more detail in the paragraphs that follow. However, the plays' similarities of form, setting and theme also make them a useful sample in which to address some of the critical debates mentioned in the introduction: whether the Admiral's had a distinct company style; whether their plays articulated a distinct view of class or gender politics, perhaps reflecting majority opinions in their audience; and whether playwrights' and audiences' familiarity with existing plays in the company's repertory was a factor in the shaping of new plays. In a group of four plays that have important features in common, other points of resemblance and difference should be easier to identify.

The chapter is divided into four sections, each of which adds a new play to the discussion. The Admiral's Men plays are put into their probable chronological order: *An Humorous Day's Mirth*, then *Englishmen for My Money*, then *The Two Angry Women of Abington*. However, it is impossible to be sure where *The Merry Wives of Windsor* ought to fit in the sequence. I place it between *An Humorous Day's Mirth* and *Englishmen for My Money*, but this represents a reasonable guess rather than anything more substantial. Accordingly, the sections below do not purport to offer a linear narrative in which playwright A wrote X and then playwright B wrote Y. Instead, the discussion of successive individual plays is cross-cut with discussion of matters relating to more than one of them, including dramatic form, the use of distinctive verbal habits to differentiate between characters, class relations in the comedies, the treatment of foreigners and themes of female desire and agency. The

---

[6] As Theodore B. Leinwand points out, 'it is not easy to describe the middling sort': 'we can do no more than set as criteria an unspecified amount of property, income, and voice rather than any fixed quantity. Such indefinition results in a status group broad enough for commentators at different times to include among its ranks some nonratepayers and some of the lesser gentry'. Theodore B. Leinwand, 'Shakespeare and the Middling Sort', *Shakespeare Quarterly*, 44 (1993), 184–303 (p. 289).

important question of intertextuality, and the extent to which the dramatists allude to other plays in the Admiral's or Chamberlain's repertory, is left to the end.

An Humorous Day's Mirth

Echoing Muriel Bradbrook, Andrew Gurr describes *An Humorous Day's Mirth* as the play with which the Admiral's Men 'initiated "humours" comedy', and both the novelty and the ultimate success of the formula may be reflected in the fact that, unusually, its box-office takings grew over time rather than peaking at its premiere, as well as in John Chamberlain's oft-quoted letter to Dudley Carleton of 11 June 1597:

> We have here a new play of humours in very great request, and I was drawn along to it by the common applause, but my opinion of it is (as the fellow said of the shearing of hogs) that there was a great cry for so little wool.[7]

Chamberlain's underwhelmed reaction notwithstanding, the fact that the play seems to have appeared in print under a slightly different title from that under which it was first staged perhaps reflects its immediate influence. By 1599 Ben Jonson's *Every Man in His Humour* and possibly *Every Man out of His Humour* had appeared, while the title pages of *1 Henry IV*, *The Two Angry Women of Abington* and Chapman's own *The Blind Beggar of Alexandria* had advertised the 'humours' of characters appearing therein, so perhaps a more distinctive title than 'The Comedy of Humours' was now called for.[8]

In some respects, to describe *An Humorous Day's Mirth* as the first humours comedy is an overstatement. In *The Blind Beggar of Alexandria*, first staged (with considerable success) in 1596, Chapman had made his protagonist adopt a series of personae (a blind prophet, an exiled duke, a moneylender and a braggart count) for material gain.[9] All of these have

---

[7] Andrew Gurr, *Playgoing in Shakespeare's London*, 2nd edn (Cambridge: Cambridge University Press, 1996), p. 152. See also Muriel Bradbrook's comment that the play 'initiated the whole Jonsonian comedy of humours', *The Growth and Structure of Elizabethan Comedy* (London: Chatto and Windus, 1955), p. 144. On the box-office takings, see Syme, p. 510. *The Letters of John Chamberlain*, ed. by Norman Egbert McClure, 2 vols (Philadelphia: American Philosophical Society, 1939) vol.I, p.32.

[8] William Shakespeare, *The History of Henrie the Fovrth; With the Battell at Shrewsburie, betweene the King and Lord Henry Percy, Surnamed Henrie Hotspur of the North. With the Humorous Conceits of Sir Iohn Falstalffe [sic]* (London, 1598; STC: 22280); George Chapman, *The Blinde Begger of Alexandria, Most Pleasantly Discoursing His Variable Humours in Disguised Shapes Full of Conceite and Pleasure* (London, 1598; STC: 4965).

[9] Syme places it third in his table of 'Top-grossing productions in Henslowe's *Diary*', p. 507.

their own verbal and behavioural peculiarities, anticipating the idiom of humours comedy, while the count in particular is repeatedly referred to as 'humorous' (1.255, 1.328–37, 2.101, 4.94, 4.151). Moving away from Chapman's previous work, a recent editor of *An Humorous Day's Mirth*, Charles Edelman, notes how frequently the word 'humour' is used in Shakespeare's early plays, and one feature in particular of Chapman's humours comedy may have a Shakespearean antecedent: in Scenes 2 and 8, the play's central character, the witty and manipulative Lemot, accurately predicts the responses that a series of gallants will give when he speaks to them.[10] This derivation of comedy from the spectacle of people being made to act like machines seems to me to owe something to Prince Hal's tormenting of Francis in *1 Henry IV*, where the Prince correctly anticipates that the drawer will be so caught between his questions and Poins's demands 'that his tale to me may be nothing but "Anon"' (2.4.25–6).[11]

The Francis scene, however, is but one episode in a play that is not primarily comic. Moreover, the real innovation of *An Humorous Day's Mirth* is in its form, or rather its apparent lack of form: in the second scene Colinet and Lemot agree to spend the day with 'so humorous acquaintance as rains nothing but humour all their lifetime' (2.10–11), and the remainder of the play largely consists of Lemot, in particular, deriving amusement from manipulating the other characters into exhibiting attitudes of jealousy, lust, affectation and so forth. Although there is a romantic plot of sorts, which sees the melancholic Dowsecer brought out of his humour through falling in love with Martia, this is subordinate to the play's main business of depicting the absurdities of contemporary social types. To the modern reader the effect, in some ways, is of a play made entirely out of Shakespearean subplots like that of Malvolio in *Twelfth Night* and Beatrice and Benedick in *Much Ado About Nothing* – although both of those plays, of course, came after Chapman's and may reflect his influence. Perhaps the play's nearest Shakespearean predecessor, at least in terms of structure, is *Love's Labour's Lost*, in so far as that play offers a sequence of set-pieces in which characters like Armado and Moth, Holofernes and Nathaniel manifest their oddities of speech and attitude through comic interaction. Much as Chapman's Lemot hopes to make 'excellent sport' out of a gallant's affected 'manner of taking acquaintance' (2.25–6), so we are told by

---

[10] George Chapman, *An Humorous Day's Mirth*, ed. by Charles Edelman (Manchester: Manchester University Press, 2010), p. 9. References to the play use this edition.

[11] William Shakespeare, *The First Part of King Henry IV*, ed. by Herbert Weil and Judith Weil (Cambridge: Cambridge University Press, 1997).

Longaville that during the three years of cloistered study planned by him, the King, Berowne and Dumaine, 'Costard the swain' and Armado 'shall be our sport' (1.1.177): characters in both plays find it amusing to surround themselves with people they deem inherently ridiculous, and the idea of 'sport' as a motive for behaviour occurs repeatedly in *Love's Labour's Lost* at 4.1.92, 5.2.153 and 5.2.511, and in *An Humorous Day's Mirth* at 2.30, 4.250, 5.204, 7.31, 8.182, and 8.262.[12] One thus suspects that, although Shakespeare's title alludes to a familiar phrase, it may not be coincidence that Lemot uses a variant of it when he says 'my labour is not altogether lost' in *An Humorous Day's Mirth*, 6.102. However, while Edelman's edition notes a handful of verbal parallels between the two plays, they are relatively minor.[13] Although it would be entirely wrong to suggest that Chapman's play somehow came out of nowhere, it does not exhibit the more substantial stylistic and thematic similarities to *Love's Labour's Lost* that can be observed between, for example, *1 Henry IV* and *Captain Thomas Stukeley*.

Both in its formal disparateness, whereby instead of a single overall plot there are a set of discrete actions that converge in the shared social space of Verone's Ordinary, and in its urbane comedy of manners, *An Humorous Day's Mirth* differs markedly from its few extant comic predecessors in the Admiral's Men repertory: the romantic comedies *A Knack to Know an Honest Man* and (possibly) *John a Kent and John a Cumber*, and Chapman's own romance pastiche, *The Blind Beggar of Alexandria*. It also seems to contradict the generalisations of some critics about the Admiral's repertory and audiences, such as Robert Boies Sharpe's contention (referred to in the Introduction) that the Rose was frequented by unfashionable citizen types. Not only does this play concern itself very much with the behaviour of the fashionable (their ways of talking, their tennis and tobacco, their frequenting of modish eateries); Chamberlain's letter gives the impression that *le tout-Londres* was flocking to see it. *An Humorous Day's Mirth* is also an exception to Brian Gibbons's argument that late Elizabethan plays staged at the Rose 'largely continue to evoke an air of cheerful patriotism and national self-satisfaction' lacking the satirical edge of drama performed by the Chamberlain's Men and the children's companies.[14] Admittedly, the children's companies did not recommence

---

[12] References are to William Shakespeare, *Love's Labour's Lost*, ed. by William C. Carroll (Cambridge: Cambridge University Press, 2009).

[13] They are: 'pretty and pathetical' in *An Humorous Day's Mirth* 1.36 / *Love's Labour's Lost* 1.2.80; 'preambulate' at 3.54 / 5.1.65; 'desolation' at 4.137 / 1.2.129; 'break your shin' at 13.5 / 3.1.59 ('broken in a shin'); and 'Alisander' at 13.174 / 5.2.554.

[14] Brian Gibbons, *Jacobean City Comedy*, 2nd edn (London: Methuen, 1980), p. 34.

playing until two years or so after Chapman's play appeared, so if (as Gurr has suggested) it was their revival that opened up the alleged split between the repertories there would be nothing untoward in the Admiral's Men staging a play like *An Humorous Day's Mirth* in 1597.[15] Furthermore, the fact that Chapman ultimately chose to write plays such as *Monsieur d' Olive* and *Sir Giles Goosecap* for the Children of Blackfriars suggests that he would find them more congenial partners than the Admiral's. Neverthe-less, the assumption that any differences between the companies and their plays evident after 1599 merely exacerbated existing tendencies (as is suggested by Gibbons' words 'continue to') does not square with what we see in *An Humorous Day's Mirth*, and it is worth noting that Gibbons himself refers to Chapman's play as an 'experiment' that anticipated the satirical dramas of Jonson and others, although he neglects to mention which company staged it.[16]

Despite its theatrical novelty – or, to put it another way, perhaps because its novelty was influential – *An Humorous Day's Mirth* does display certain characteristics that are also to be found in the other plays discussed in this chapter. One, integral to the whole idea of humours comedy, is its interest in the way individuals' peculiarities manifest themselves in their speech. This is most obvious in the 'stale proverb[s]' (8.223) with which the gallants Rowley, Labesha and Foyes answer Lemot, as he has predicted; but it is present throughout the piece, whether in the melancholic invective of Dowsecer, the affected melancholy of Labesha, or the puritanical self-scrutiny of Florilla:

> What have I done? Put on too many clothes?
> The day is hot, and I am hotter clad
> Than might suffice health.
> My conscience tells me that I have offended,
> And I'll put them off.
> That will ask time that might be better spent;
> One sin will draw another quickly so.
> See how the devil tempts! (4.1–7)

A second theme of the play that will recur in *The Merry Wives of Windsor* and *The Two Angry Women of Abington* is that of marital jealousy, which, here, is a trait that Lemot exploits in other characters for his own amuse-ment. The elderly Labervele, whose wife Florilla longs for the child 'which yet, alas / I cannot get' (1.24–5), is made to watch Lemot court her under

[15] Gurr, *Playgoing*, p. 156.   [16] Gibbons, pp. 46–8.

the pretext of proving her constancy. Countess Moren, jealous of her younger husband, allows him to Verone's on Lemot's assurance that 'No ladies use to come to ordinaries, madam' (7.235), only for Lemot to contrive that ladies will be present and promptly alert the Countess to the fact. Finally, Lemot enjoys tormenting the Queen with news of the King's attraction to Martia, along with a misleading story that the King's love-rival has threatened to castrate him.

A possible third feature of *An Humorous Day's Mirth* that is more unambiguously present in the other three plays relates to its setting. Gurr surely overstates his case when he writes that Chapman's play 'launched London-set comedy at the Rose in May 1597': the location of the play is clearly Paris (see, e.g., 5.124, 8.84, 8.293).[17] However, as Edelman writes, it is 'Paris in name only', in that the play satirises 'the manners, habits, and social pretensions of English men and women – the same men and women sitting or standing at the Rose'.[18] In so far as the characters of *An Humorous Day's Mirth* are participating in contemporary urban life, the play can be said to present its audience members with a reflection of themselves and their environment, or at least of a version of the same. It would be excessive to insist that this play was the decisive factor behind the more vividly realised London setting of *Englishmen for My Money*, or the location of Shakespeare's and Porter's dramas in provincial English towns: the argument for Chapman's priority in this regard depends on our ignoring his play's Parisian setting, and excluding plays that are not primarily comic such as *The Three Ladies of London* and *1 Henry IV*. Nevertheless, his play's focus on the manners and types of a recognisable urban world, rather than (say) Alexandria, medieval England or ancient Athens, is a characteristic it shares with the other three discussed in this chapter. While *An Humorous Day's Mirth* goes further than any of them in its departure from plot-driven comedy, this does not seem to have harmed its commercial fortunes: as Syme points out, 'The Comedy of Humours' (which, it should be said, he is wary of identifying with *An Humorous Day's Mirth*) is the fourth highest-grossing play recorded by Henslowe, and 'may have been the most successful play the company ever staged, but since Henslowe's daily receipts break off in early November 1597, a day after its last recorded performance, we will never know'.[19]

[17] Andrew Gurr, *The Shakespeare Company, 1594–1642* (Cambridge: Cambridge University Press, 2004), p. 133.
[18] *An Humorous Day's Mirth*, p. 4.   [19] Syme, pp. 507, 510.

The Merry Wives of Windsor

The Merry Wives of Windsor – whose quarto, as we have seen, refers to humours on its title page – is sometimes treated as an early response to the success of *An Humorous Day's Mirth*, as for example by Martin Wiggins who sees Shakespeare as being driven by Chapman's innovation into producing a comedy 'quite unlike his usual style'.[20] On a different but related tack, both Arthur Kinney and Giorgio Melchiori regard the play as a 'burlesque' (Kinney) or 'satire' (Melchiori) of humours comedy, which they deem as having passed its sell-by date by the time Shakespeare came to write *Merry Wives* – although both seem more concerned with the humours comedies of Ben Jonson than of Chapman.[21] How one chooses between these possibilities, or indeed whether one rejects them both, depends on the date that is assumed for Shakespeare's play.

Recent editors of *The Merry Wives of Windsor* invariably discuss the question of whether it was first performed on 23 April 1597 on the occasion of the feast held at Whitehall in connection with the ceremony due to take place at Windsor the following month to mark the installation of new Knights of the Order of the Garter. This argument was first made in detail by Leslie Hotson in 1931 and expanded by William Green in 1962, and some critics of the play have found it an attractive one, for various reasons.[22] For example, it provides an explanation for the play's location in Windsor, a town that does not figure in the other plays in which Sir John Falstaff appears, as well as for the incorporation of a 'long speech by the Queen of Fairies about Windsor Castle and the Garter Chapel' within the final scene at 5.5.48–65.[23] It also provides a referent for Caius' assertion at 1.4.43, '*Je m'en vais voir à le* court *la grande affaire*', leading Green to state, 'To an Elizabethan it was apparent that Shakespeare in the *Merry Wives* had depicted contemporary Windsor at the time of an Order of the Garter celebration'.[24] The year 1597 saw the first Garter installation since

---

[20] Martin Wiggins, *Shakespeare and the Drama of His Time* (Oxford: Oxford University Press, 2000), p. 72.

[21] Arthur F. Kinney, 'Textual Signs in *The Merry Wives of Windsor*', *Yearbook of English Studies*, 23 (1993), 206–34 (p. 207); *The Merry Wives of Windsor*, ed. Melchiori, p. 5.

[22] Leslie Hotson, *Shakespeare Versus Shallow* (London: Nonesuch Press, 1931), pp. 111–22; William Green, *Shakespeare's Merry Wives of Windsor* (Princeton: Princeton University Press, 1962); William Shakespeare, *The Merry Wives of Windsor*, ed. by T. W. Craik (Oxford: Clarendon Press, 1989), pp. 1–6; William Shakespeare, *The Merry Wives of Windsor*, ed. by David Crane, updated edn (Cambridge: Cambridge University Press, 2010), pp. 1–5. References to the play use Crane's edition.

[23] *The Merry Wives of Windsor*, ed. Crane, p. 1.   [24] Green, p. 12.

1593, and one that would be of particular importance to Shakespeare because it included the election to the Order of his company's patron George Carey. One of the other knights admitted in 1597 was Frederick of Mömpelgard, First Duke of Württemberg, and the sub-plot in which the Host is fooled into thinking he has been robbed of his horses by three visiting Germans has been read as alluding to the fact (while Caius' assurance that 'dere is no duke that the court is know to come', 4.5.69–70, may refer to the Duke's actual inability to attend the ceremony). The 1602 Quarto's reading of 'three sorts of cosen garmombles' for 'three cozen-Germans' at 4.5.61 certainly looks like a garbling of the Duke's name. If these details are taken to imply a performance in April 1597, then that obviously means that *The Merry Wives of Windsor* cannot have been influenced by *An Humorous Day's Mirth*.

However, while it is difficult to deny that *The Merry Wives of Windsor* has a thematic interest in the Order of the Garter or that it alludes to Duke Frederick, not all commentators are agreed that this requires the play to have been performed on 23 April 1597. For one thing, as Barbara Freedman forcefully observes, 'no scholar has provided evidence of any topical satire – indeed of any full-length play – performed at any Garter ceremony at any time. Nor has any scholar offered proof that Hunsdon or anyone else ever commissioned a play for either Elizabeth or the Garter'. Furthermore, the play does not really seem to suit that context: 'Garter ceremonial feasts, installations, and investitures would be inappropriate occasions for full-length bedroom farces with jokes about urinals, codpieces, and turds; or for topical satires on those to be inducted; or for mocking treatment of foreign ambassadors' accents and mishaps.'[25] The part of the play most amenable to a Garter feast is the final scene, where the Queen of Fairies requires her elves to bless Windsor Castle in a speech that refers to the Garter and its motto, *Honi soit qui mal y pense* (5.5.62), and indeed both G. R. Hibbard (tentatively) and Giorgio Melchiori (more confidently) suggest that Shakespeare may have written that section in 1597 and later incorporated it in a drama intended for the public stage.[26] Even if Hibbard and Melchiori are right, however, this would still mean that the vast majority of the play was written after April 1597, which would allow Chapman's drama to have influenced it.

---

[25] Barbara Freedman, 'Shakespearean Chronology, Ideological Complicity, and Floating Texts: Something is Rotten in Windsor', *Shakespeare Quarterly*, 45 (1994), 190–210 (pp. 195–7).

[26] William Shakespeare, *The Merry Wives of Windsor*, ed. by G. R. Hibbard (Harmondsworth: Penguin, 1973), p. 50; *The Merry Wives of Windsor*, ed. Melchiori, pp. 18–30.

Indeed, Hibbard and Melchiori go further than this, and separately argue that *Merry Wives* must date from after 1599 because it includes Corporal Nim, a character from *Henry V*.[27] Given that the play's main character, Sir John Falstaff, first appeared in the *Henry IV* plays, perhaps it is natural to assume that the other shared characters first appeared in the histories too. However, Nim is repeatedly introduced by name in *Merry Wives*, including by himself: 'My name is Corporal Nim. I speak and I avouch. 'Tis true. My name is Nim' (2.1.110–11; see also 1.1.100, 2.1.104). At the very least, this does not assume familiarity on the audience's part. Furthermore, although Melchiori sees Nim's peculiarity of using the word 'humour' in almost every speech (all except 1.3.71) as part of the play's 'satire of the conventions of the "comedy of humours"', this need not imply a late date: as we have seen, the same word is used by and about Count Hermes in *The Blind Beggar* with comparable regularity.[28]

One reason why the date of *Merry Wives* matters to this chapter is because it affects the way we locate it in relation to *An Humorous Day's Mirth*: did it come before, soon after, or years after Chapman's play? But the question of its date is inseparable from that of its auspices, in so far as the argument for an early date rests on the assumption that *Merry Wives* was written for a Garter Feast. This would make the play an occasional drama, originally intended for a socially elite audience, that subsequently joined the repertory of the Lord Chamberlain's Men, possibly after some reworking. Hibbard, however, vigorously contests this view:

> The play says in almost every line that it was written for the public theatre, not for a courtly audience. It was clearly intended, more than any other play in the canon, to reflect the life, to meet the expectations, and to endorse the values of the Elizabethan bourgeoisie, the class from which its author came and to which he belonged.[29]

Plainly, more is at stake in the 'Garter Feast' debate than the question of when *Merry Wives* was written. Hibbard's explanation of the values he sees the drama as upholding by reference to its having been written for the public theatre rather than a court occasion exemplifies how our assumptions about its origins are likely to shape our reading of class politics in

---

[27] Shakespeare, *The Merry Wives of Windsor*, ed. Hibbard, p. 48; ed. Melchiori, p. 20.
[28] See for example 1.324–37, in which it appears five times. *The Plays of George Chapman: The Comedies: A Critical Edition*, gen. ed. Allan Holaday (Urbana: University of Illinois Press, 1970). Subsequent references to *The Blind Beggar* use this edition (by Lloyd E. Berry).
[29] *The Merry Wives of Windsor*, ed. Hibbard, p. 14.

this play, which stages a sexualised conflict between Windsor's lower gentry (the Fords, the Pages) and outsiders (Falstaff, Fenton) who come from a higher social sphere – or think they do. This chapter will return to the matter of class later on; suffice it to say that there is plenty of evidence for a date of 1597–8 for *The Merry Wives*, roughly contemporaneous with the other plays discussed in this chapter, and for seeing Shakespeare as capitalising on the popularity both of humours comedy in general and of his own character Falstaff. The play's references to the Garter do not require it to have been performed on 23 April 1597: it is quite possible that Shakespeare wrote them envisaging a later performance before George Carey, who is known to have arranged private performances by his players such as that of 'Sir *John Old Castell*' (which could be part of *Henry IV*, or conceivably *Merry Wives*, or another play entirely) on 6 March 1600.[30] This, indeed, would entail a view of the play neither as primarily courtly nor as primarily popular, but as always intended to negotiate between those two positions.

*

The attempt over the preceding paragraphs to argue for the feasibility of reading *The Merry Wives of Windsor* as a response to *An Humorous Day's Mirth* may seem odd in light of the fact that, on the surface, the two plays are not much like each other. The rather aimless nature of Chapman's play, consisting of sequences distinguished 'by their lack of relation to a narrative or main plot', as Gibbons puts it, is a world away from Shakespeare's farcical comedy, in which the Italianate intrigue of the Falstaff/wives plot is skilfully interwoven with the romantic comedy of Anne Page and Fenton and the two strands converge at Herne's oak.[31] Taking my cue from the remark of Wiggins quoted earlier, however, I would suggest that Chapman's influence is most clearly discerned in his prompting Shakespeare to adopt an uncharacteristic mode.[32] Numerous critics have suggested that *Merry Wives* somehow stands apart from Shakespeare's other comedies, whether as 'his most purely comic play' (Andrew Gurr), 'Shakespeare's only bedroom farce' (Barbara Freedman), his only citizen comedy (Alexander Leggatt, George K. Hunter), or 'Shakespeare's only

---

[30] The reference appears in a letter dated 8 March 1599 (i.e. 1600) from Rowland Whyte to Sir Robert Sidney. See *Letters and Memorials of State*, ed. Arthur Collins, 2 vols (London, 1746), vol. II, p. 175.

[31] Gibbons, p. 50. On *Merry Wives* and Italian comedy, see Leo Salingar, *Shakespeare and the Traditions of Comedy* (Cambridge: Cambridge University Press, 1974), pp. 228–36.

[32] See note 20.

comedy set in England' (Wendy Wall).[33] It does not really fit the festive model of Shakespearean comedy associated with C. L. Barber, who mentions it only as a play 'where Shakespeare's creative powers were less fully engaged' than in other comedies of the same time.[34] Nor does it quite square with Northrop Frye's view that 'At the core of most Renaissance comedy, including Shakespeare's', is a New Comic action consisting of 'the effort of a young man to get possession of a young woman who is kept from him by various social barriers': as Peter F. Grav puts it, 'its romantic storyline is subordinated; in short, the young lovers play second fiddle to the Falstaff plot'.[35] The play's title indicates where its interest lies, the Quarto title more so: this is 'A Most Pleasaunt and Excellent Conceited Comedie, of Syr *Iohn Falstaffe*, and the merrie Wiues of *Windsor*', with the humours of Sir Hugh, Shallow, Slender, Pistol and Nym. Anne and Fenton do not figure in the title, in keeping with the play's relative lack of interest in their relationship: they are seen together only briefly, at the start of 3.4, before their joint entrance thirty lines before the end of the play. This structural relegation of the love plot, and the domination of the play by a series of intrigues – Ford's deception of his wife and Falstaff, Falstaff's attempted seduction of Mistress Ford and Mistress Page and the wives' response, the enmity of Evans and Caius and their revenge upon the Host – mirrors the priorities of Chapman's play, where the lovers Dowsecer and Martia are not shown doing anything more than looking at each other before the final scene. So does the way in which these intrigues allow the characters concerned to manifest their distinctive humours, such as Ford's jealousy, Falstaff's vanity, Sir Hugh's pedantry and Slender's seeming inability to think independently of his uncle: 'I will marry her, sir, at your request; but if there be no great love in the beginning, yet heaven may decrease it upon better acquaintance' (1.1.196–8). By contrast, the lovers are distinctive in being (so to speak) humourless, in keeping with

---

[33] Gurr, 'Intertextuality at Windsor', p. 196; Freedman, p. 191; Alexander Leggatt, *Citizen Comedy in the Age of Shakespeare* (Toronto: University of Toronto Press, 1973), pp. 146–9; George K. Hunter, 'Bourgeois Comedy: Shakespeare and Dekker' in *Shakespeare and His Contemporaries: Essays in Comparison*, ed. by E. A. J. Honigmann (Manchester: Manchester University Press, 1986), pp. 1–15; Wendy Wall, *Staging Domesticity: Household Work and English Identity in Early Modern Drama* (Cambridge: Cambridge University Press, 2002), p. 90.

[34] C. L. Barber, *Shakespeare's Festive Comedy: A Study of Dramatic Form and its Relation to Social Custom* (Princeton: Princeton University Press, 1959), p. 222.

[35] Northrop Frye, *A Natural Perspective: The Development of Shakespearean Comedy and Romance* (New York: Columbia University Press, 1965), p. 72; Peter F. Grav, *Shakespeare and the Economic Imperative: 'What's Aught but as 'tis Valued?'* (New York: Routledge, 2008), p. 62.

the marginality of their romance to the play's main business of humours comedy.

As is the case in *An Humorous Day's Mirth*, different characters' distinctive use of language is key to the dramatic expression of their respective humours – something that Kinney contrasts with Ben Jonson's comedy, where 'characters show their humours primarily in their behaviour'.[36] The play contains a wide array of personal idiolects: for example, Sir Hugh's is typified by pompous redundancies, softened consonants and transpositions of the parts of speech, as in the lines 'There is three umpires in this matter, as I understand: that is, Master Page (*fidilicet* Master Page); and there is myself (*fidilicet* myself); and the three party is (lastly and finally) mine host of the Garter' (1.1.110–12). Nim's is contrastingly brusque, threatening and humour-obsessed: 'Slice, I say. *Pauca, pauca.* Slice, that's my humour' (1.1.107). The Host is almost aggressively convivial, prone to extravagant modes of address: 'Thou'rt an emperor: Caesar, Kaiser, and Pheasar. I will entertain Bardolph; he shall draw, he shall tap. Said I well, bully Hector?' (1.3.6–7). Furthermore, as Melchiori argues, this linguistic variety is explicitly thematised: 'the comedy of languages' is 'the central motif of the play', reaching its zenith in the Latin lesson scene but commented on throughout. Mistress Quickly anticipates Dr Caius' 'abusing of God's patience and the King's English' (1.4.5); Nim is described by Page as 'a fellow frights English out of his wits' (2.1.124–5); and Sir Hugh, to Falstaff, is 'one that makes fritters of English' (5.5.142).[37] In Caius, especially, *Merry Wives* exhibits a tendency that will be evident in *Englishmen for My Money*: the expression of a character's foreignness through his inability to master idiomatic English.

One personality trait that noticeably figures both in *The Merry Wives of Windsor* and in *An Humorous Day's Mirth* is that of marital jealousy, exhibited in Chapman's play by Labervele, Countess Moren and the Queen, and in Shakespeare's by Master Ford. Ford's language is nothing like so distinctively stylised as that of Sir Hugh, Nim or the Host; rather, he adopts a distinctive attitude towards language, in particular towards the abhorred term 'cuckold'. After hearing Falstaff promise him (in the guise of Brook) that Ford will be revealed as 'knave and cuckold' (2.2.223), he goes on to utter a soliloquy in which he harps obsessively upon it: 'Terms! Names! Amaimon, sounds well; Lucifer, well; Barbason, well; yet they are devils' additions, the names of fiends: but Cuckold! Wittol! – Cuckold? The devil himself hath not such a name' (2.2.232–5). And when Mistress

---

[36] Kinney, p. 207.   [37] *The Merry Wives of Windsor*, ed. Melchiori, pp. 6–8.

Ford discourages him from looking too closely into the buck-basket that contains Falstaff with the words, 'You were best meddle with buck-washing!', he cannot help but think of the symbolism of the horned stag: 'Buck? I would I could wash myself of the buck! Buck, buck, buck! Ay, buck! I warrant you, buck – and of the season too, it shall appear' (3.3.120–4). The effect is similar to that in *An Humorous Day's Mirth* when Florilla justifies her willingness to have her purity tried by Lemot with the spurious biblical allusion, 'it is written, "We must pass to perfection through all temptation". Habakkuk the fourth', and Labervele responds, 'Habakkuk! Cuck me no cucks! In-a-doors, I say! Thieves, puritans, murderers!' (4.242–6). In both plays, characters already given to jealousy are cynically exploited by others: Chapman's Lemot, for instance, anticipates that his courtship of Florilla before Labervele 'shall so heat his jealous humour till he be start mad' (2.94–5), while Pistol and Nim tell Ford and Page of Falstaff's adulterous intentions towards their wives in order to avenge his discharging them from his service. The difference is that while Lemot repeatedly intervenes, for his own amuse-ment, in the marriage of Labervele and Florilla, once Pistol has set Ford off Ford requires no further propulsion, but dons the Brook disguise and pays Falstaff to seduce his wife under his own steam – a divergence that reflects the extent to which the action of *An Humorous Day's Mirth* continually relies upon Lemot's prompting, whereas the various characters of *The Merry Wives of Windsor* are more capable of generating their own plots and counter-plots.

A further point of difference between *Merry Wives* and *An Humorous Day's Mirth* is the social world in which the two plays locate themselves. Not only is Chapman's play metropolitan in its setting, whether that metropolis be Paris or London; it also focuses on characters from the upper end of the social scale. Although there is very little to separate the King and Queen (who have no obvious political role) from the other characters, all apart from Verone and his servants seem to be idle gentlefolk devoting their time to amusement. By contrast, as we have seen, *The Merry Wives of Windsor* has repeatedly been regarded by critics as an early citizen comedy, exploring the tension between well-heeled members of the mid-dling sort and impecunious gentlemen that is often to be found in, for example, the work of Middleton. The fact that it is not set in the city, that Ford and Page are themselves gentry, and that (unlike the merchants and tradesmen of citizen comedy) it is not clear how they gain an income, is beside the point; the class dynamic is made clear by Page when he explains why Fenton must not marry his daughter:

The gentleman is of no having. He kept company with the wild Prince and
Poins. He is of too high a region; he knows too much. No, he shall not knit
a knot in his fortunes with the finger of my substance. If he take her, let
him take her simply. The wealth I have waits on my consent, and my
consent goes not that way. (3.2.55–60)

Fenton is simultaneously Page's social superior and his economic inferior,
and the conflict between them anticipates (in more benign form) the
'deadly enmity' between the draper Quomodo and the gallants in
Middleton's *Michaelmas Term*, or the tension between the apprentice
Quicksilver (younger son of gentlefolk) and his goldsmith master, Touchstone, in Jonson, Chapman and Marston's *Eastward Ho*.[38]

The existence of this tension invites the question of whether the play's
sympathies lie ultimately with the Ford and Page families, or with Fenton
and Falstaff, a matter about which there is considerable critical disagreement. On the one hand, it has been noted that the setting for the drama is,
by Shakespearean standards, decidedly non-aristocratic: 'the inn and the
merchant's house displace the more customary quarters of royalty and
nobility', as Kinney says.[39] Peter Holbrook identifies *Merry Wives* as one of
the occasions on which 'Shakespeare's comedies can seem positively anti-
aristocratic': in its 'self-consciously bourgeois setting' we see Falstaff, 'an
out-and-out snob who calls Ford a "mechanical salt-butter rogue,"
"knave," and "peasant"', get his 'comeuppance'.[40] Douglas Bruster and
Richard Helgerson similarly interpret the disciplining of Falstaff in class-
based terms, while feminist critics such as Natasha Korda underline (and
critique) the role of the wives in achieving it.[41] Phil Withington, indeed,
regards the wives as the true embodiment of the bourgeois civic culture
whose development he takes to be the political backdrop of the play.[42]

[38] Thomas Middleton, *Michaelmas Term*, ed. by Theodore B. Leinwand, in *The Collected Works*, ed.
by Gary Taylor and John Lavagnino (Oxford: Clarendon Press, 2007), 1.2.111.

[39] Kinney, p. 213.

[40] Peter Holbrook, 'Shakespeare, Class, and the Comedies', in *A Companion to Shakespeare's Works*,
vol. III: *The Comedies*, ed. by Richard Dutton and Jean E. Howard (Malden, MA: Blackwell, 2003),
pp. 67–89, p. 81.

[41] Douglas Bruster, *Drama and the Market in the Age of Shakespeare* (Cambridge: Cambridge
University Press, 1992), p. 52; Richard Helgerson, *Adulterous Alliances: Home, State, and History
in Early Modern European Drama and Painting* (Chicago: University of Chicago Press, 2000),
pp. 60–2; Natasha Korda, '"Judicious Oeillades": Supervising Marital Property in *The Merry Wives
of Windsor*', in *Marxist Shakespeares*, ed. by Jean E. Howard and Scott Cutler Shershow (London:
Routledge, 2001), pp. 82–103 (pp. 90–92).

[42] Phil Withington, 'Putting the City into Shakespeare's City Comedy', in *Shakespeare and Early
Modern Political Thought*, ed. by David Armitage, Conal Condren and Andrew Fitzmaurice
(Cambridge: Cambridge University Press, 2009), pp. 197–216.

However, as Wendy Wall points out, the humiliation of Falstaff coincides with the defeat of the Pages by Anne's elopement with Fenton, who lectures them over the 'thousand irreligious cursèd hours / Which forcèd marriage would have brought upon her' (5.5.199–200).[43] The play has been read as a critique of bourgeois materialism in respect of marriage, as by Peter Grav.[44] And the extent of Falstaff's defeat has been minimised by some critics: as David Crane writes, '*The Merry Wives of Windsor* is not a play about Falstaff's discomfiture, much less his conversion; rather it is about his invincibility'.[45] While Peter Erickson acknowledges 'victory of a bourgeois solidarity over the aristocratic court' as one possible interpretation of the play's class dynamic, he argues that the emphasis on the Garter ceremonial in the play's final scene generates 'a celebration of national identity that is aristocratic rather than egalitarian in orientation'.[46] And yet, as Freedman points out, the pro-monarchist force of the speech on Windsor Castle and the Garter that appears in that scene is somewhat diminished through being delivered by Mistress Quickly in her get-up as the Queen of Fairies.[47]

The tempting way out of this impasse is to see it as intentional, and to regard *The Merry Wives of Windsor* as striving to avoid an outcome that ostentatiously privileges either the class of gentlemen to which Fenton is assumed to belong or the class of lower gentry/upper bourgeoisie represented by the Fords and the Pages. Admittedly, it may be naïve to suppose that a play can somehow be abstracted from the class tensions attendant on its production. But the problem with *Merry Wives* is that readings of its class dynamic tend to be based on assumptions about its original auspices: for example, Erickson reads it as an occasional play, while Freedman does not. While I would incline towards Freedman's position, the danger of circularity has to be acknowledged. Structurally, though, the play seems to set up the Falstaff and Ford plots in counterpoint to one another. As Leo Salingar puts it, 'the two main plots are antithetical in moral substance and parallel in progression. One action deals with attempted adultery, the other with match-making; in one, lust is the cover for money, in the other, love triumphs over mercenary concerns'.[48] Although the Falstaff plot receives

---

[43] Wendy Wall, 'The Merry Wives of Windsor: Unhusbanding Desires in Windsor', in *A Companion to Shakespeare's Works*, vol. III, pp. 376–92.

[44] Grav, pp. 54–82.   [45] *The Merry Wives of Windsor*, ed. Crane, p. 11.

[46] Peter Erickson, 'The Order of the Garter, the Cult of Elizabeth, and Class-Gender Tension in *The Merry Wives of Windsor*', in *Shakespeare Reproduced: The Text in History and Ideology*, ed. by Jean E. Howard and Marion F. O'Connor (New York: Macmillan, 1987), pp. 116–40, p. 126.

[47] Freedman, p. 197.   [48] Salingar, p. 234.

greater emphasis, the working of the double plot can be interpreted as an attempt to avoid giving the play too explicit a class allegiance – perhaps because the play was always designed to be suitable for transfer between the public theatre and court, or perhaps because the public theatre audience for which Shakespeare was writing was itself socially diverse. This would support Andrew Gurr's contention that prior to the revival of the children's companies in 1599 (at St Paul's) and 1600 (at the Blackfriars), the Admiral's Men and the Chamberlain's Men were essentially performing to similar groups of playgoers: 'Given the limited forms of public entertainment then available, regular attendance by the same people at the suburban playhouses where the two companies performed was inevitable.' Although dramatists writing for the children's companies would come to represent their smaller, more expensive playhouses as socially exclusive spaces, the identification of different venues with different demographics was not yet in evidence. The assumption that both companies performed to mixed audiences would also square with the evidence of *An Humorous Day's Mirth*, which certainly does not seem to have been targeted at the 'citizen' audiences with which Gurr says the Admiral's successor companies at the Fortune would later be associated.[49]

Another feature of *Merry Wives* that helps prevent it from expressing too specific a class allegiance is one that has already been alluded to: the way it creates a comic community based on language. While Falstaff may be able to rescue his position somewhat at the end of the play by telling the Pages that their 'arrow hath glanced' (5.5.205–6) in the matter of Anne's marriage, the two characters who are unequivocally discomfited in the final scene are Anne's unsuccessful suitors, Slender – and Caius: 'By gar, I am cozened. I ha' married *un garcon*, a boy; *un paysan*, by gar, a boy. It is not Anne Page. By gar, I am cozened' (5.5.179–81). Richard Helgerson and Wendy Wall both regard Caius as ultimately excluded through linguistic difference from full participation in the restored community of the play's ending, in which (as Helgerson puts it) the union of Fenton and Anne Page 'confirms the union of classes and conditions in a harmonious national state', and while I do not wholly share their assumption that the Welshman Sir Hugh is similarly excluded, I would concur that one way in which the play defuses its class tensions is through laughing at a foreigner.[50] A similar dynamic can be observed in *Englishmen for My Money*, as will be argued in the next section.

---

[49] Gurr, *Shakespeare's Opposites*, pp. 33, 171.   [50] Helgerson, p. 64; Wall, *Staging Domesticity*, p. 92.

Englishmen for My Money

Like *An Humorous Day's Mirth*, William Haughton's *Englishmen for My Money* has often been regarded as a ground-breaking comedy. This is partly because of its setting: Jean E. Howard describes it as 'the first English stage comedy set specifically in London', and even if the Paris of Chapman's comedy is read as London in disguise it has to be said that Haughton takes much greater pains to localise his drama.[51] We are told that the merchant's house which is the scene for much of the action is in Crutched Friars, a neighbourhood in the east of the City of London; the play's substantial third scene (330 lines in Lloyd Edward Kermode's edition) takes place in the commercial centre of the Exchange; and the nocturnal scenes in Act 3, which rely for their comedy on foreigners being unable to find their way around the city in the dark, are littered with street-names and landmarks: Leadenhall, London Stone, 'the maypole on Ivy-bridge going to Westminster' (3.3.50–51).[52] As Leggatt puts it, Haughton seems 'to use his local colour with the self-consciousness of an innovator'.[53]

Another reason for the foundational status of *Englishmen for My Money*, however, relates to the class dynamics that the play depicts. Pisaro is a naturalised Portuguese merchant and moneylender living in London with his three daughters Laurentia, Marina and Mathea, the fruit of his marriage to an Englishwoman who has since died. The plot centres on his attempts to marry them to three foreign merchants in order to stop them marrying three English gentlemen, Heigham, Harvey and Walgrave, who hope thereby to redeem the lands they have mortgaged to Pisaro. In his use of the 'Plautine conflict between age and youth' as a means of figuring a class conflict between a merchant rich in money and gallants rich in status and land (until they mortgage it), Haughton anticipates a recurrent trope of the citizen comedies of Middleton and others: as Jonathan Haynes observes, the 'social tensions' that it depicts provide the 'groundwork of the city comedy to follow'.[54]

The combination of an English setting with a love-plot that seems to figure a broader class antagonism makes *Englishmen for My Money*

---

[51] Jean E. Howard, *Theater of a City: The Places of London Comedy, 1598–1642* (Philadelphia: University of Pennsylvania Press, 2007), p. 38.
[52] References to *Englishmen for My Money* use the edition in *Three Renaissance Usury Plays*, ed. by Lloyd Edward Kermode (Manchester: Manchester University Press, 2009).
[53] Leggatt, p. 7.
[54] Ibid., p. 10; Jonathan Haynes, *The Social Relations of Jonson's Theater* (Cambridge: Cambridge University Press, 1992), p. 31.

somewhat reminiscent of *The Merry Wives of Windsor*, where one gentleman's courtship of a burgher's daughter, and another gentleman's attempt to seduce a burgher's wife, are played out against a backdrop that is localised with references to the Garter inn (2.1.146), Frogmore (2.3.69), the Little Park and Great Park (3.1.4), Datchet Mead (3.3.115), and the Castle (5.5.49) – albeit more extensively in the Folio than in the Quarto text, as Leah S. Marcus points out.[55] It is difficult to be absolutely sure which play should be given priority, unless one reads the Garter allusions of *Merry Wives* as indicating a first performance on 23 April 1597. Certainly, *Englishmen* refers extensively to Shakespeare's works, in particular *The Merchant of Venice* and *Romeo and Juliet*, as will be shown later. However, one scene that has been used to argue for Haughton's indebtedness to *Merry Wives* may in fact be nothing of the kind. Andrew Gurr and Wendy Wall both assume that the episode in *Englishmen* where the three daughters offer to pull the Dutch suitor up to their chamber in a basket only to leave him suspended half-way is derived from the business with Falstaff and the buck-basket.[56] It is much closer, though, to a medieval tale about 'Virgil the necromancer' that Pamela Allen Brown suggests as one of Shakespeare's sources for *Merry Wives*:

> Besotted with a rich man's daughter who is closely watched, Virgil woos her ardently, despite his gray hairs. The maid agrees to smuggle him into her chamber. Never intending to make good, she tells him to get into a basket tied to a rope so he can be hauled up through her window for a night of love. She leaves him hanging halfway up. Dawn's light turns the great man into a laughingstock.[57]

As Andrew Fleck has recently argued, Haughton could have encountered the tale in *The Lyfe of Virgilius* printed in Antwerp in 1518 and reprinted in London in 1562.[58] This does not necessarily mean that Haughton used the medieval legend and that Shakespeare copied him, but it does pose a stumbling block for any argument about priority that uses the basket as evidence. It might also be worth noting that Haughton's stage device of having three women haul a man aloft seems to have made sufficient impact

---

[55] Leah S. Marcus, 'Levelling Shakespeare: Local Customs and Local Texts', *Shakespeare Quarterly*, 42 (1991), 168–78 (pp. 173–7).

[56] Wall, *Staging Domesticity*, pp. 121–2; Gurr, *Shakespeare's Opposites*, p. 38.

[57] Pamela Allen Brown, *Better a Shrew than a Sheep: Women, Drama, and the Culture of Jest in Early Modern England* (Ithaca: Cornell University Press, 2003), p. 49. Brown cites John Spargo, *Virgil the Necromancer: Studies in Virgilian Legends* (Cambridge: Harvard University Press, 1934), pp. 136–97.

[58] Andrew Fleck, 'The Origins of *Englishmen for My Money*'s "Lover in the Basket" Episode in Doesborch's *Lyfe of Virgilius*', *Notes and Queries*, 57 (2010), 357–9.

on Shakespeare for him to have used it years later in *Antony and Cleopatra*. In the absence of firm evidence one way or the other, then, this chapter regards *Merry Wives* and *Englishmen* as two chronologically proximate plays dealing in similar themes and tropes.

One of the most noticeable of these is the speaking of English by people from other nations, which in *The Merry Wives of Windsor* means Dr Caius in particular, though to some extent Sir Hugh. In *Englishmen*, however, Haughton creates three distinct idiolects: those of the Frenchman Delion, the Italian Alvaro, and the Dutch Vandal. The techniques used to mark Delion out as French are very similar to those used for Caius, including the use of 'me' instead of 'I', as in 'me vill cut his ears' (*Merry Wives*, 2.3.57–8) and 'me sal go home to your house' (*Englishmen*, 1.3.21); the addition of '-a' to the end of words, as in 'Verefore vill you not meet-a me?' (*Merry Wives*, 3.1.64–5) and 'you should love-a me' (*Englishmen*, 2.3.167); and the replacement of 'th' with 'd' or 't' and of 'w' with 'v', as in 'de herring is no dead so as I vill kill him' (*Merry Wives*, 2.3.9) and 'vat be dat?' (*Englishmen*, 2.3.87). Haughton does not, however, employ Caius' distinctive oath 'By gar'.

Just as different characters' linguistic peculiarities are explicitly commented on in *Merry Wives*, so are they made a recurrent theme of *Englishmen*. As A. J. Hoenselaars notes, 'Their proficiency in English is the standard by which the wooers are judged', and accordingly, 'Broken English serves to confirm that the merchants are inadequate suitors'.[59] The three sisters comment at length (with imitations) on the foreigners' bad English and ridiculous manners (2.3.1–42), expressing an attitude encapsulated by Laurentia when she tells Vandal, 'If needs you marry with an English lass, / Woo her in English, or she'll call you ass' (2.3.159–60). Conversely, the play's attitude towards languages other than English seems decidedly xenophobic, from Marina's proud claim to be monoglot (2.1.32) through to the servant Frisco's recollection, 'my great grandfather's grandmother's sister's cousin told me that pigs and Frenchmen speak one language, "awee awee"' (1.1.172–4). However, as Elizabeth Schafer argues, the play's depiction of Anglophone characters (Frisco, the three sisters) imitating foreigners' imitations of English, not to mention the tutor Anthony's success in getting hired to teach Pisaro's daughters through disguising himself as a foreigner and 'simply offering an

---

[59] A. J. Hoenselaars, *Images of Englishmen and Foreigners in the Drama of Shakespeare and His Contemporaries: A Study of Stage Characters and National Identity in English Renaissance Drama* (Rutherford, NJ: Fairleigh Dickinson University Press; London: Associated University Presses, 1992), p. 56.

impression of non-Englishness, speaking a bombastic English which Frisco cannot understand', can be read as a more self-conscious reflection by Haughton on 'the workings of his own language comedy'.[60] And as Emma Smith suggests, all this bluster about language seems to be a way of articulating a more basic anxiety about the mingling of nations: 'the unspeakable possibility of international marriage and its mongrel offspring is transferred to the resultant linguistic progeny', as in Frisco's plea to the English gentlemen, 'do not suffer a litter of languages to spring up amongst us' (1.2.104–5).[61] It is more substantial than anything we see in *Merry Wives*, where Anne Page's statement that she 'had rather be set quick i' th'earth, / And bowled to death with turnips' (3.4.79–80) than marry Dr Caius does not make specific reference to his nationality.

One reason for this heightened anxiety about intermarriage in *Englishmen for My Money*, and for the play's obtrusive interest in questions of national identity, may be its London setting: various commentators have read it as a response to 'popular anxieties about the economic and social consequences of alien merchants and artisans in the city', in Howard's words.[62] On the one hand, Pisaro seems to exemplify the capacity of aliens to be integrated within London society: he has married an Englishwoman, he has three daughters who regard themselves as English, and his speech is indistinguishable from that of the English characters in the play in so far as it does not display the markers of foreignness that colour the dialogue of the French, Italian and Dutch merchants. On the other, the play ambiguously intimates that he may be Jewish: he practices usury, Walgrave says he has a nose 'able to shadow Paul's, it is so great' (1.2.16), and he lives in Crutched Friars, 'the quarter of town where Jews mostly resided in the late-sixteenth century'.[63] His desire to marry his daughters to alien merchants, rather than simply finding three Englishmen who are less objectionable than Heigham, Harvey and Walgrave, implies an ongoing self-identification as non-English, and also raises the prospect that 'all the money Pisaro makes from his foreign trade and his usurious loans' will 'ultimately flow out of English hands into alien ones', as Howard remarks.[64]

[60] Elizabeth Schafer, 'William Haughton's *Englishmen for My Money*: A Critical Note', *Review of English Studies*, n.s., 41 (1990), 536–8 (pp. 536–7).

[61] Emma Smith, '"So Much English by the Mother": Gender, Foreigners, and the Mother Tongue in William Haughton's *Englishmen for My Money*', *Medieval and Renaissance Drama in England*, 13 (2001), 165–81 (p. 173).

[62] Howard, p. 43. See also Hoenselaars; Smith; and Lloyd Edward Kermode, 'After Shylock: The "Judaiser" in England', *Renaissance and Reformation/Renaissance et Réforme*, 20 (1996), 5–26.

[63] Kermode, 'After Shylock', p. 7.   [64] Howard, p. 43.

Haughton's play thus hints at contemporary concerns over the role of aliens and naturalised aliens in London's trade, the nature of their business practices, and their ambiguous national loyalties.

Another reason for the emphasis on international tensions in *Englishmen for My Money*, however, may relate to its class politics: like *The Merry Wives of Windsor*, this is (as Haynes points out) a 1590s play that seems to anticipate the antagonism between citizens and gentlemen that would drive the citizen comedy of the next decade. Pisaro sets out the basic situation in his opening soliloquy:

> by the sweet loved trade of usury,
> Letting for interest, and on mortgages,
> Do I wax rich, though many gentlemen
> By my extortion comes to misery:
> Amongst the rest, three English gentlemen
> Have pawned to me their livings and their lands,
> Each several hoping – though their hopes are vain –
> By marriage of my daughters to possess
> Their patrimonies and their lands again. (1.1.17–25)

This certainly establishes him as something of a villain, and the New Comedy idiom of the play encourages an audience to hope that Pisaro's daughters and their English wooers will succeed in defying him. Nevertheless, the English suitors come across at times as equally cynical, Walgrave promising 'We'll work our lands out of Pisaro's daughters, / And cancel all our bonds in their great bellies' (4.1.114–15). As with Fenton in *Merry Wives*, who confesses to Anne that 'thy father's wealth / Was the first motive that I wooed thee' (3.4.13–14), it is impossible to be sure whether the Englishmen's principal motivation is emotional or financial, and it is noticeable that Walgrave looks forward not to erotic fulfilment but to the pregnancy that will set the seal on their successful redemption of their property. At the end of the play, accompanied by Mathea, he confidently asks Pisaro for his blessing, 'For I have blessed you with a goodly son. /'Tis breeding here, i'faith, a jolly boy' (5.1.284–5). His wife is dehumanised to a deictic 'here', the territory Walgrave has raided in order to establish homosocial and economic bonds with Pisaro. While Pisaro's status as blocking character within the play may discourage too much sympathy for him, Haughton does elsewhere suggest that the Englishmen's attitudes grow out of a sense of entitlement that is not very appealing: 'Gentlemen, you know, must want no coin', Heigham tells Pisaro when asking for another loan (1.3.63), while later in the same scene he and Harvey tease a sunburnt post-carrier in a manner whose class-based aspect is made clear when a merchant tells the unfortunate messenger 'Get home, ye patch! Cannot you suffer gentlemen jest with you?' (1.3.194). In this socially fraught context, the desire to prevent foreigners from running off with English (or at least half-English) women is one thing that can transcend class boundaries, as with the scholar Anthony's explanation, 'To help my countrymen I cast about, / For strangers' loves blaze fresh, but soon burn out' (4.2.58–9), or when Frisco begs the gentlemen not to let a litter of languages spring up. Haynes is sensitive to this aspect of *Englishmen for My Money* when he writes of the play 'submerging (without obscuring) class differences in the interests of a bully nationalism'; from another angle, though, the play can be seen as invoking nationalism in order to submerge class differences, perhaps (as with *The Merry Wives of Windsor*) within the theatre audience as well as wider society.[65]

A final feature of the play that mitigates some of the class tensions it stages, and which is a theme of the other plays discussed in this chapter, is the stress on female choice indicated both by the main title, *Englishmen for My Money*, and more explicitly in the alternative title, *A Woman Will Have Her Will*. While it may be unclear whether the gentlemen are more desirous of the sisters or of the financial liquidity they offer, there is no uncertainty about the feelings of the sisters themselves. In the opening scene, Anthony's arguments in the Englishmen's favour prove needless: 'long ere this I stooped to that fair lure', as Marina explains (1.1.99–100). Laurentia follows suit and the youngest sister, Mathea, asserts her refusal to be bowed by 'Father, friends, nor kin' (1.1.119):

> I'faith I'll have thee Ned, or I'll have none.
> Do what they can, chafe, chide, or storm their fill,
> Mathea is resolved to have her will. (1.1.122–4)

The sisters' status as actively desiring subjects, even as they demonstrate awareness of the financial side of the gentlemen's courtship of them (see 1.3.119–45), is emphasised throughout the play, as is their willingness to act on their desires. Their verbal wit leaves the courting merchants 'beaten in plain field' (2.3.173), while Vandal is left more literally dangling following their trick with the basket; in the final act, Laurentia manages to escape from her father's house in Anthony's attire, while Marina successfully plays along with Harvey's feigned terminal illness. Although Anne Page's role in securing her match with Fenton in *The Merry Wives of Windsor* is not so

---

[65] Haynes, p. 31. On the relationship between the play's class politics and the composition of the Rose audience, see Tom Rutter, '*Englishmen for My Money*: Work and Social Conflict?', in *Working Subjects in Early Modern English Drama*, ed. by Michelle M. Dowd and Natasha Korda (Farnham: Ashgate, 2011), pp. 87–99.

spectacular, Lena Cowen Orlin points out that she apparently 'takes the initiative in setting the scene for their private spousals' in the inaudible conversation that follows her instruction, 'hark you hither!' at 3.4.21; Orlin also understands Anne's letter to Fenton – 'Of such contents as you will wonder at', as he tells the Host at 4.6.13 – as containing the instructions for the plan to deceive her parents and elope with him.[66] And while the printed text of *An Humorous Day's Mirth* elides the means by which Martia and Dowsecer end up with each other, her admiration for him is evident from the first time she sees him and hears him speak: 'Oh, were all men such, / Men were no men but gods, this earth a heaven' (7.90–91).

In making it unambiguously clear that the sisters are attracted to their gentlemen suitors, Haughton to some extent distracts attention from the uncertainty that surrounds the gentlemen's own motives. Tellingly, the fullest male expression of love in the play is feigned: it comes from Harvey, when he is pretending to have been mortally afflicted by the loss of Marina (4.1.191–208). In placing such emphasis on the feelings of the sisters instead, Haughton sets up the play's ending as a triumph of young love over parental opposition, rather than simply a triumph of three spendthrift gentlemen over their creditor. As with the double ending of *The Merry Wives*, which gives qualified victory both the burghers of Windsor and to the courtly Fenton, it feels as if the play is trying to avoid taking sides too explicitly, and it is notable that rather than being punished and departing like Shylock, Pisaro is incorporated within the comic community of the play's ending. He is forced to acknowledge that he has been beaten at his own game by the gentlemen, and outwitted by his daughters:

> Is it even so? Why, then, I see that still,
> Do what we can, women will have their will.
> Gentlemen, you have outreached me now,
> Which ne'er, before you, any yet could do. (5.1.295–8)

He invites the gentlemen to a wedding feast, ushering them in 'for all the storms are passed, / And heaps of joy will follow on as fast' (5.1.307–8). His willingness to concede defeat, and his grudging admiration for the gentlemen's ability to 'outreach' him, places the emphasis on reconciliation rather than conflict at the end of the play.

---

[66] Lena Cowen Orlin, 'Shakespearean Comedy and Material Life', in *A Companion to Shakespeare's Works*, vol. III, pp. 159–81 (pp. 166–7).

The Two Angry Women of Abington

Although it is impossible to be sure whether *Englishmen for My Money* or *The Merry Wives of Windsor* should be given chronological priority, the degree of similarity between them does suggest that one playwright knew the work of the other. These are two comedies set in England where young couples end up together in spite of parental opposition and other suitors, while the class antagonisms implied by the romantic plots are to some extent defused through the mockery of foreigners – whose mangling of English takes much the same form in the two plays. One feature of *Merry Wives* that is perhaps unexpectedly absent from *Englishmen*, however, is its incorporation of humours comedy. Haughton's familiarity with *The Blind Beggar of Alexandria* may be reflected in his use of a similarly daring pun on 'account', and of the Platonic binary of shadow and substance; but the influence of Chapman's techniques of characterisation either there or in *An Humorous Day's Mirth* is not really in evidence in *Englishmen for My Money*.[67] The final play to be considered in this chapter, however, does advertise itself in print as a humours comedy: *The Pleasant Historie of the Two Angrie Women of Abington. With the Humorous Mirthe of Dick Coomes and Nicholas Prouerbes, Two Seruingmen*. Along with its self-proclaimed inclusion of 'humorous mirth', Henry Porter's comedy seems to combine a number of motifs that appear in Haughton's and Shakespeare's plays: a young couple united against the wishes of their parents, a social environment of comfortably-off but not aristocratic families in a town by the Thames, and (as we shall see) an outdoor scene of nocturnal error and confusion, when the angry mothers, with servants in tow, set off in pursuit of their disobedient children.

In spite of these apparent similarities, though, on closer inspection *The Two Angry Women of Abington* proves to be a rather different sort of play, for all its titular similarity to Shakespeare's. For one thing, it is not really a humours comedy at all, at least not in the sense of including a diverse array of eccentric types. Unless one includes the anger of the wives as a humour in its own right, the only humorous characters are the two servants, Coomes (an irascible drunk) and Proverbs (who speaks entirely

---

[67] In *The Blind Beggar*, Elimene refuses to refer to her husband as a Count 'Because it comes so neare a thing that I knowe' (5.19); in *Englishmen*, Antony says he did not teach the sisters 'To keep a merchant's book, or cast account: / Yet to a word much like that word "account"' (1.1.148–9). In *The Blind Beggar*, the main character plans to 'cause the nobles to pursue my shadowe; / As for my substance they shall neuer finde' (3.33–4); in *Englishmen*, Pisaro suggests that the foreigners woo his daughters disguised as the Englishmen and 'under shadows be of substance sped' (2.3.240).

in proverbs, rather like Chapman's gulls but at greater length). What was innovative in Chapman's play, carrying with it a new approach to form and characterisation, is here accommodated to pre-existing dramatic norms: namely, the stereotype of the comic servingman, corporeally selfindulgent in Coomes's case, old and sententious in Proverbs'. The feeling that Porter is taking from humours comedy only so much as he can fit within familiar conventions seems to inform Wiggins's observation that Nicholas Proverbs is incorporated in the play 'not for artistic reasons but to give the clown something to do': Chapman's play represents for Porter a new way of writing clown roles rather than something with more thoroughgoing implications for his dramaturgy.[68] It is also noticeable that where Chapman's humorous characters are fashionable, or would-be fashionable, gentlefolk, Porter's are those of the lowest status in his play.

Another aspect of *The Two Angry Women* that resembles the other plays under discussion less in reality than it does on the surface is the way it opposes a young couple, including a visibly desiring woman, to the wishes of obstructive parents. In some ways, the play fits the New Comedy formula: Frank Goursey woos and wins Mall Barnes at her window (in a scene reminiscent of *Romeo and Juliet*), only for the lovers to be disturbed by their feuding mothers and separately chased through the fields at night as they seek to escape to Oxford. The terms in which Mall pleads with her mother clearly recall the subtitle and dialogue of Haughton's play:

> Now I beseech yee for the loue of Christ,
> To giue me leaue once to do what I list.
> I am as you were when you were a maide,
> Gesse by your selfe, how long you would haue staide,
> Might you haue had your will. (ll. 1652–6)

Alone, outdoors, anxiously trying to evade her mother, Mall expresses her frustration at not being 'release from all my maidens sorrow' (l. 2554), and pledges to the absent Frank, 'Ile runne through hedge and ditch, through brakes & briers, / To come to thee, sole Lord of my desires' (ll. 2567–8). This, it seems, is a young women outspoken in her desires and willing to take risks in order to achieve them, like Anne Page or Pisaro's daughters; and a further point of similarity with *Merry Wives* is in the way the romance of the youngsters is counterpointed with the matrimonial difficulties of the older generation. Barnes and Goursey fall out with their

---

[68] Wiggins, p. 70.

wives when Mistress Barnes accuses Mistress Goursey of having adulterous designs on Master Barnes, and the wives are only reconciled when the husbands (who have remained on good terms throughout) pretend to come to blows over them.

The play's upholding of youthful freedom to choose over parental oppression is not the whole story, however. The idea for Frank and Mall to marry comes not out of their spontaneous desire for each other, but from Master Barnes's idea that "twould be a meanes / To make their mothers friends' (ll. 609–10), a plan with which Master Goursey concurs as soon as he reads Barnes's letter (l. 1122). Frank Goursey is not initially amenable to the plan, insisting that he is 'too young to marry' (l. 1131), fearing that 'mistresse wedlocke' will 'snip / My pleasure ayming minde' (ll. 1144–6), and describing marriage as 'an earthly day of doome' (l. 1186). Earlier conversations (ll. 292–365, 455–82) in which it is intimated that Frank keeps whores offer further insights into his reluctance to be tied down. For her part, Mall's discussion of matrimony with her father seems to imply that she is more concerned to 'not dye a maide' (l. 656) than particular over who she marries: 'If I shall haue a husband, get him quickly', she tells Master Barnes (l. 675). After her father's departure, she seems particularly excited about the 'house authoritie' she will acquire (l. 689) when she can 'Wife it as fine as any woman could' (l. 685) and 'Carry a maistering eye vpon my maide' (l. 687). Admittedly, in the wooing scene Frank does show himself able to withstand Mall's rudeness and respond with innuendo in a way that suggests their mutual compatibility. Nevertheless, in this play the romantic comedy structure supports a patriarchal world in which fathers choose their children's partners, young men are reluctant to give up their whoring for matrimony, and young woman are motivated by the twin prospects of devirgination and movement up the domestic pecking-order.

These rather unidealistic sexual politics make *The Two Angry Women of Abington* a potentially fruitful play to bring to bear on the question raised by Andrew Gurr over whether plays staged by the Chamberlain's and Admiral's companies consistently articulated different views of the legitimacy of young love in the face of parental opposition. In *Playgoing in Shakespeare's London*, Gurr argues that in contrast to Shakespeare plays like *Romeo and Juliet* and *A Midsummer Night's Dream*, which 'uphold the power of love over parental authority', from 1600 the 'Henslowe playwrights' – that is, dramatists writing for the Admiral's Men and for Worcester's Men, who would move to the Rose in 1602 – opposed this position 'and the challenge to citizen views about marriage which it embodied'.[69] In *The Shakespeare Company*, indeed, he seems to give the phenomenon an earlier date when he asserts that the support for the young lovers in *Englishmen for My Money* was 'a rare feature in the Admiral's repertory'.[70] Although more recently Gurr has modified this position somewhat, *The Two Angry Women* seems to offer support for it in so far as it depicts a young couple who are willing to be guided by their fathers in matrimonial choice, presents their union as a happy ending, and makes the obstacle to it not inter-generational tension per se but the more specific maternal intransigence of unreasonable wives.[71]

Another way of interpreting the gender politics of *The Two Angry Women of Abington*, however, is suggested by the work of Mary Bly and Charles Cathcart, both of whom point to the profusion of references to *Romeo and Juliet* in the play. For example, in the scene where Frank courts Mall at her window she talks of him speaking 'without the booke' (l. 1517), and he asks her to 'come seale the bargaine with a kisse' (l. 1583) only for her mother to disturb them and utter a speech containing the words 'Ile rather haue her married to her graue' (l. 1628). These lines seem to allude to *Romeo and Juliet*, 1.5.109 ('You kiss by th'book'), 5.3.114–15 ('seal with a righteous kiss / A dateless bargain to engrossing Death'), and 3.5.140 ('I would the fool were married to her grave'), while Porter's precedent for the spectacle of a man courting a woman aloft has already been noted.[72] Another echo of Shakespeare's play appears in a lyrical speech uttered by Mall's brother Philip, who notes that 'The skye that was so faire three houres ago, / Is in three houres become an Etheope' (2024–5), recalling Romeo's lines 'It seems she hangs upon the cheek of night / As a rich jewel in an Ethiop's ear' (1.5.44–5).[73]

Bly and Cathcart are in agreement that the effect of Porter's courting scene is essentially parodic, not least because of the way in which Romeo and Juliet's 'metaphors of romantic love' in their own balcony scene 'are here replaced by puns of sexual wit' and images of masts, steeples and the like. For Bly, this is testimony to the influence of 'Juliet's erotic fluency' on 'the shaping of comic heroines in the four to five years after the play's first performances': Porter develops Juliet's expressions of desire

[69] Gurr, *Playgoing*, p. 154.   [70] Gurr, *The Shakespeare Company*, p. 136.

[71] Gurr, *Shakespeare's Opposites*, p. 180.

[72] William Shakespeare, *Romeo and Juliet*, ed. by G. Blakemore Evans (Cambridge: Cambridge University Press, 1984). Subsequent references are to this edition.

[73] See Mary Bly, 'Bawdy Puns and Lustful Virgins: The Legacy of Juliet's Desire in Comedies of the Early 1600s', *Shakespeare Survey*, 49 (1996), 97–100 (pp. 102–3); Charles Cathcart, '*Romeo* at the Rose in 1598', *Early Theatre*, 13 (2010), 149–62 (pp. 152–3).

in her soliloquies into bawdy repartee.[74] Cathcart, however, finds that the strain of parody in the window scene does not extend to, for example, Philip's speech on night: thus, 'any systematic strategy in Porter's use of the tragedy' is hard to find, and the comedy's intertextuality should be seen as 'playful' in the manner of the early comedies staged by the revived children's companies. I would suggest, though, that the modified version of *Romeo and Juliet* that underlies the play's structure – as Cathcart puts it, 'two families with a background of friendly relations rather than enmity, but between whose mistresses a sudden quarrel breaks out' – does suggest a coherent underlying project.[75] For warring families Porter substitutes comically angry women; for defiant offspring, two young people willing to accede to their fathers' wishes; for romantic idealism, pragmatic submission to the need for sex, material satisfaction and good neighbourliness. One explanation for this is a playwright anticipating the tastes of an audience unsympathetic to the romantic illusions of ungoverned youth – although this hardly squares with what we see in *An Humorous Day's Mirth* or *Englishmen for My Money*. Another, though, is a playwright consciously subverting the tragic dignity of a highly popular drama through a shift of genre and an appropriately materialistic set of values.

As Cathcart notes, *The Two Angry Women of Abington* is not the only Admiral's Men comedy of its time to allude to *Romeo and Juliet*. *Englishmen for My Money* begins with Pisaro's line, 'How smug this grey-eyed morning seems to be' (1.1.1), an echo of Friar Laurence's 'solitary aubade' beginning 'The grey-eyed morn smiles on the frowning night' (2.3.1); the words, 'Night's candles burn obscure' (2.3.345), uttered as Pisaro looks forward to the disguised foreigners' trick on his daughters, recalls 'Night's candles are burnt out' (3.5.9); and the crafty-sick Harvey's line to Pisaro, 'would you wed your daughter to a grave?' recycles the words of Lady Capulet referred to earlier.[76] In the first scene of Act 4, the sisters repeatedly appear above to be wooed from below, anticipating *The Two Angry Women* in offering a visual image reminiscent of *Romeo and Juliet*; earlier on, Harvey's words, 'but soft, forbear. / The cloud breaks up, and our three suns appear' (1.2.110–11) seem modelled on Romeo's words 'But soft, what light through yonder window breaks? / It is the east, and Juliet is the sun' in the same scene (2.2.2–3). Nor is this the only Shakespeare play to which *Englishmen* alludes. As a moneylender who loses his daughters to improvident gentlemen, Pisaro finds himself in a predicament analogous to that of Shylock in *The Merchant of Venice*, and it is noticeable that one of his daughters escapes his house, like

---

[74] Bly, pp. 104, 97.   [75] Cathcart, pp. 151–3, 155–6.   [76] Cathcart, p. 151.

Jessica, in male disguise. (As Kermode points out, however, it is unclear whether Pisaro is meant to be Jewish, or whether Haughton gives him quasi-Jewish attributes such as the distinctive nose because he exercises the trade of usury with which Jews were associated.)[77] Pisaro's house, like Shylock's, is described as hell (1.2.5–7), and Harvey's observation that he has 'grown kind' (1.3.222) when, distracted by business concerns, he invites the English suitors to dinner, recalls Antonio's comment after the fateful bond has been agreed.[78]

Haughton's characterisation of Pisaro, however, is much less indebted to Shakespeare's Shylock than it is to a character from another Admiral's Men play: Barabas, from *The Jew of Malta*. As Kermode says, 'The opening of the play with Pisaro, *solus*', where the main character lyrically imagines the ships bringing wealth to him from across the seas and boasts of his 'Judas-like' (1.1.27–8) deceptions, is very like that of Marlowe's play, and Pisaro shares both Barabas's 'oral eloquence and sense of superiority' and his habit of 'breaking-off into a contradictory aside'.[79] The third scene of the play, set in the Exchange, is particularly rich in allusion to Marlowe. In stating his willingness to lend the gentlemen 'half the substance that I have', Pisaro calls to mind the demand for Malta's Jews to pay one half of their estate to Malta's rulers, and particularly Barabas's observation, 'Half of my substance is a city's wealth' (1.2.86).[80] And while Haynes is right to say that the scene 'mimics the rhythm of a business session', with its succession of messengers each bringing slightly different news about the progress of Pisaro's ships, it does so partly by mimicking Marlowe's opening scene, where two merchants in succession relay similar information to Barabas.[81] Pisaro's distraction at the supposed loss of two English ships is conveyed using a sequence of lines that end with half-rhyming dactyls, recalling Barabas's calmer use of that foot in the same scene:

> PISARO ... What a bots made the dolts near Italy!
> Could they not keep the coast of Barbary,
> Or having passed it, gone for Tripoli,
> Being on the other side of Sicily,
> As near, as where they were, unto the straits? (1.3.122–6)

---

[77] Kermode, 'After Shylock', p. 8.
[78] See William Shakespeare, *The Merchant of Venice*, ed. by M. M. Mahood (Cambridge: Cambridge University Press, 2003), 2.3.2 ('Our house is hell'), and 1.3.171 ('The Hebrew will turn Christian, he grows kind').
[79] *Three Renaissance Usury Plays*, pp. 44, 42, 267n.
[80] Christopher Marlowe, *The Jew of Malta*, ed. by N. W. Bawcutt (Manchester: Manchester University Press, 1978). Subsequent references are to this edition.
[81] Haynes, p. 28.

Compare:

> BARABAS. . . . As one of them indifferently rated,
> And of a carat of this quantity,
> May serve in peril of calamity
> To ransom great kings from captivity. (1.1.29–32)

More generally, Pisaro's distress at his 'late excessive loss' (1.3.137) recalls Barabas's feigned distress at the expropriation of his estate. Elsewhere in the play, other characters three times ring the changes on Ferneze's enquiry of the Bashaw, 'What wind drives you thus into Malta road' (3.5.2).[82]

The allusions to Shakespeare and to Marlowe in *Englishmen for My Money* and *The Two Angry Women of Abington* have somewhat contradictory implications. On the one hand, Haughton's use of Marlowe could be interpreted as an example of repertorial self-awareness: the dramatist gives his work the look and feel of an Admiral's Men play by incorporating references to the work of that company's most famous dramatist, and simultaneously bolsters a sense of company identity by giving Marlowe's play canonical status. Chapman can be seen as doing something similar in *The Blind Beggar of Alexandria*, which is full of Marlovian allusions such as 'what is dalliance sayes my seruant then' (1.160) and 'The haplesse Infant of a haplesse father' (10.43), while in *Englishmen* Haughton goes beyond *The Jew of Malta* to reference other Admiral's Men staples like *The Spanish Tragedy* ('It may be I may live to fit you yet', 1.1.203) and *Doctor Faustus* ('as the ancient English Roman orator saith, 'So-lame-men, misers, housewives', and so forth').[83] However, the fact that Haughton and Porter both allude to Shakespeare seems to indicate the opposite: far from creating a sense of repertorial identity, it means that at least two Admiral's Men plays contained lines and scenes that resembled (albeit, at times, parodically) the work of the other company's principal dramatist, and as a dramatic technique it seems to rely on the assumption that playgoers at the Rose were familiar with

---

[82] 'What wind, a-God's name, drives you forth so late?' (2.3.363); 'He's reckoning what wind hath drove him hither' (3.2.146); 'what wind drives you to our house so late?' (3.4.14–15)

[83] On *The Blind Beggar of Alexandria*, see Tom Rutter, 'The Communities of George Chapman's *All Fools*', *Community-Making in Early Stuart Theatres: Stage and Audience*, ed. by Roger D. Sell, Anthony W. Johnson and Helen Wilcox (Abingdon: Routledge, 2017), pp. 218–38. The references are to 'What is beauty, sayeth my sufferings, then?', in Christopher Marlowe, *Tamburlaine the Great*, ed. by J. S. Cunningham (Manchester: Manchester University Press, 1981), Part I, 5.1.160; 'The hopeless daughter of a hapless Jew' in *The Jew of Malta*, 1.2.316; 'Why then I'll fit you' in Thomas Kyd, *The Spanish Tragedy*, ed. by J. R. Mulryne, 2nd edn (London: A & C Black; New York: Norton, 1989), 4.1.70; and *Solamen miseris socios habuisse doloris* in Christopher Marlowe, *Doctor Faustus: A- and B- Texts (1604, 1616)*, ed. by David Bevington and Eric Rasmussen (Manchester: Manchester University Press, 1993), A-Text, 2.1.42.

Shakespeare's plays. These two ways of reading dramatic allusion in Admiral's Men plays are not altogether incompatible: the dramatists may have tried to imprint a company identity on their own works while simultaneously alluding to those of another company. However, sustaining both readings requires a willingness to interpret different allusions in different ways – a critical practice that may seem inconsistent and selective. Nevertheless, the presence of Shakespearean allusions in the two plays does have one clear implication: that Admiral's men dramatists not only knew Shakespeare's work, they expected their audience to as well. Playgoers who went to the Rose must also have attended the Theatre; and it follows logically from this that playgoers who went to the Theatre must also have attended the Rose. Shakespeare's audiences were undoubtedly familiar with the plays of the Admiral's Men, and the evidence for the two companies drawing on the same body of playgoers is stronger than that for them appealing to different groups.

The view of Shakespeare and the Admiral's Men as drawing upon a common stock of theatrical reference-points gains a little support from one final feature that is shared by all four plays discussed in this chapter. Cathcart suggests that the nocturnal scenes in *Englishmen for My Money* and *The Two Angry Women of Abington* again show the influence of *Romeo and Juliet*, which similarly has 'significant scenes set at night'; but a more obvious resemblance is to *A Midsummer Night's Dream*, so much of which takes place by night in the wood outside Athens. Disorientation, confusion and mistaken identity beset the characters in all three plays: Puck leads the lovers a merry dance, Frisco misdirects the Dutchman and adopts his identity while the English gentlemen dupe their foreign competitors and make them lose their way, and in *Two Angry Women* the presence outdoors of Sir Rafe Smith and his man on a hunting expedition makes an already chaotic situation even more so. In *Englishmen*, as Frisco pretends to identify a sequence of locations that are actually some distance apart (London Stone, then Westminster, then Shoreditch), a remark from Delion hints at the ancestry of the scene in which he finds himself: 'O Dio! Dere be some nautie tinge, some spirit do lead us' (3.3.56–7). London in the dark takes on the character of the countryside by night, where Puck might 'Mislead night-wanderers, laughing at their harm' (2.1.39). However, the role of the mischievous sprite has been taken on by the all too human Frisco, who enjoys the confusion he sows among the foreign suitors:

> I shall lead you such a jaunt that you shall scarce give me thanks for. – Come, sirs, follow me. [*Aside*] Now for a dirty puddle, the pissing conduit, or a great post, that might turn these two from asses to oxen by knocking their horns to their foreheads. (3.3.34–8)

The ascription of a Puckish role to a human character recurs in *Two Angry Women*, where Master Goursey's servant Hodge watches his mistress and her other servant departing in pursuit of her son and suggests to his master, 'faith if I were there, I would haue some knauery with them, good maister will ye carry the torche your selfe, & giue me leaue to play at blind man buffe with my Mistresse' (ll. 1900–3). Later on he boasts of pretending to be Coomes and leading her 'such a dance in the darke' (l. 2204), while Coomes himself mentions the will o' the wisp when he glimpses Frank's boy in the dark and mutters, 'And ye be a sprite Ile fraie the bug beare' (l. 2018). Sir Rafe shows that social superiority is no guarantee against superstition when he observes, 'I thinke some spirit leads me thus amisse: / As I haue often heard, that some haue bin thus in the nights' (ll. 2439–40).

But of course, as both plays make clear, the sources of the confusion and mistaken identity that beset the characters are human, not supernatural: they evoke the chaotic nocturnal world of *A Midsummer Night's Dream* only to dispel it. Shakespeare, in fact, does something very similar in *The Merry Wives of Windsor*, whose final scene features the Queen of Fairies, Hobgoblin and 'Fairies black, grey, green, and white' (5.5.30). In despatching the elves to 'Strew good luck . . . on every sacred room' of Windsor Castle, the Fairy Queen recalls Oberon's injunction, 'Every fairy take his gait, / And each several chamber bless / Through this palace with sweet peace' (5.1.394–6); but the audience knows that these fairies are children dressed according to Mistress Page's plan 'Like urchins, oafs, and fairies, green and white, / With rounds of waxen tapers on their heads' (4.4.47–8), while the part of the Fairy Queen is taken by Mistress Quickly and that of Hobgoblin by Pistol. To use Kinney's term, Shakespeare's earlier play is here 'burlesqued' in one of the drama's many self-referential moments; and the fact that supernatural characters are recycled in thoroughly non-supernatural forms is testimony to the fact that *The Merry Wives of Windsor* inhabits a different comic universe from *A Midsummer Night's Dream*, as a comedy of 'material life', in Orlin's phrase.[84] A similar quality is identified by Wiggins when he likens *Merry Wives* to *An Humorous Day's Mirth* in its stress on 'the importance of human agency': 'the events remain tightly under human control, created not by chance, still less by any supernatural force, but by the machinations, not always benevolent, of particular characters'.[85] In Chapman's play, Labervele's attempt to convince his wife that the engraved jewels that have appeared in her private

---

[84] Kinney, p. 209; Orlin, pp. 159–61.   [85] Wiggins, p. 72.

garden were placed there by heaven or by the fairies meets with disbelief: 'Fairies were but in times of ignorance, / Not since the true pure light hath been revealed; / And that they come from heaven I scarce believe' (4.18–20). Florilla's words are echoed by Philip in *Two Angry Women* as the night's confusions near their end:

> Father, O Fathe[r] I haue heard them say,
> The dayes of ignorance are past and done,
> But I am sure the nights of ignorance
> Are not yet past, for this is one of them. (2495–8)

The ignorance, though, is the result of human anger, human stupidity and coincidence, rather than supernatural intervention. The moment of intertextuality underscores the extent to which all four plays invoke the fairies only to reject them: they serve as markers of the enchanted world from which *An Humorous Day's Mirth*, *The Merry Wives of Windsor*, *Englishmen for My Money* and *The Two Angry Women of Abington* all distance themselves, with their recognisable locations, stress on human agency and (particularly in Shakespeare, Haughton and Porter) materialistic view of courtship and marriage.

CHAPTER 5

'Nor pure religion by their lips profaned'
Oldcastle, Robin Hood and *As You Like It*

The previous chapter of this book attempted to address questions both of cross-repertorial influence and of intra-repertorial identity. It put the case for reading Shakespeare's *The Merry Wives of Windsor* – along with plays by Chapman, Haughton and Porter likely to have been staged at the Rose around the same time – as part of a trend towards 'humours' comedy, often in English settings, often featuring non-aristocratic characters and dealing with themes of choice before marriage and jealousy within it. At the same time, the similarities among all four plays were used as a means of throwing into relief any divergences between Shakespeare's company and the Admiral's Men in terms of audience and general ethos: of establishing whether the plays staged at the Rose express ideologies that seem to imply an attempt to appeal to particular groups of theatregoers, and the extent to which those plays seem to create a distinctive identity for themselves as Admiral's Men plays.

The answers to these questions proved less than straightforward. On the one hand, for example, the allusions to *The Jew of Malta* in Haughton's *Englishmen for My Money* may be read as an attempt to fashion an identity for the newer piece as an Admiral's Men play. Furthermore, Porter's *The Two Angry Women of Abington* seems to display a sympathy for arranged marriage that Andrew Gurr has identified as increasingly prevalent in Admiral's Men plays from the turn of the century onward. On the other hand, though, there is the recurrent allusion to Shakespeare both by Haughton and by Porter, and the apparent approval of women's free marital choice in *Englishmen* and, less explicitly, in Chapman's *An Humorous Day's Mirth*. The class allegiances of the Admiral's plays are similarly inconsistent: although *The Two Angry Women* and *Englishmen for My Money* are both set in non-aristocratic environments, in the latter play it is the gentlemen who come out on top, while *An Humorous Day's Mirth* is resolutely focused on the fashionable world. In so far as any conclusions can be drawn from this evidence, it would appear that Admiral's Men dramatists expected audiences to recognise allusions to Admiral's Men plays, but also to Shakespeare; and that those audiences were sufficiently heterogeneous as to preclude any consistent identification of the plays with the outlook of a particular social group.

The current chapter begins by raising another question relating to the corporate identity of the Admiral's Men, namely that of religious affiliation. It does so by considering perhaps the best known instance of the company appearing to lay its confessional cards on the table: the two-part play *Sir John Oldcastle*, the first part of which was probably first staged late in 1599 and was printed in 1600 as *The First Part of the True and Honorable Historie, of the Life of Sir John Old-castle, the Good Lord Cobham* (Part 2 is not extant).[1] Not only does it provide a sympathetic portrayal of the title character, a Lollard martyr; it explicitly distances itself from Shakespeare's *Henry IV*, where the name Sir John Oldcastle was initially applied to the less-than-saintly character who would become Falstaff. Accordingly, *Sir John Oldcastle* has been read as marking a fault-line between the religious allegiances of the Admiral's and Chamberlain's companies, a view of the play that this chapter examines in detail. The second part of the chapter examines another two-part play about another potentially divisive figure: Robin Hood, depicted in Anthony Munday's *Robert, Earl of Huntingdon* plays (the second of which was written with Henry Chettle). Not only does the dramatists' focus on this folk hero and on the controversial Prince John (later King) enmesh them inescapably in the materials of religious debate; I will argue that their treatment of those materials, as of other themes and tropes, influences the practice of Shakespeare in *As You Like it*.

Sir John Oldcastle

The earliest reference to *Sir John Oldcastle* in Philip Henslowe's records is a note in the hand of the Admiral's Man Thomas Downton dated 16 October 1599 and recording receipt of 10 pounds to pay Anthony Munday, Michael Drayton, Robert Wilson and Richard Hathaway 'for the first pte of the lyfe of Sr Jhon Ouldcasstell & in earnest of the Second pte'.[2] Evidently, the play was conceived early on as a two-part drama, rather than the second part being a response to the success of the first; and Part I accordingly leaves the

---

[1] *The First Part of the True and Honorable Historie, of the Life of Sir John Old-castle, the Good Lord Cobham* (London, 1600; STC: 18795).
[2] Philip Henslowe, *Henslowe's Diary*, ed. by R. A. Foakes [and R. T. Rickert], 2nd edn (Cambridge: Cambridge University Press, 2002), p. 125.

plot dangling, with Lord and Lady Cobham en route to Wales in flight from the ecclesiastical authorities. The fact that the authors were being paid for Part II before Part I had demonstrated its marketability, and that the dramatists opted for a treatment of the materials that would necessitate a second part if the story were not to be left incomplete, does suggest that the company and playwrights had some confidence in the play's popularity. The unusual bestowal of a gift of ten shillings upon the playwrights 'at the playnge of Sr John oldcastell the ferste tyme', recorded in Samuel Rowley's hand as received from Henslowe at some point in early November, may also reflect anticipated (or immediate) success, or it may stem from other causes to be discussed later in this chapter.[3]

If *Oldcastle* was indeed expected to do well, one reason for this may have been its relationship with another successful two-part play based on English history: the Chamberlain's *Henry IV*. As is well known, Shakespeare's Falstaff had originally been called Sir John Oldcastle, only for the name to be changed due to 'offence beinge worthily taken by personages descended from his title, as peradventure by manie others allso whoe ought to haue him in honourable memorie', as the antiquary Richard James (1591–1638) would later write.[4] The 'personages descended' presumably included Sir Henry Brooke, eighth Lord Cobham (1564–1619) and (depending on the date of Shakespeare's play; see Chapter 3) his father Sir William Brooke, seventh Lord Cobham (1527–97). Although descended from Oldcastle's wife rather than Oldcastle himself, the Cobhams shared his title, and seem to have been aggrieved at the mockery of the earlier Lord Cobham in Shakespeare's play. If *1 Henry IV* was written before Sir William became Lord Chamberlain on 8 August 1596 following the death of his predecessor Henry Carey (or, recklessly, during the period of Brooke's tenure), then as the official in charge of court entertainment Sir William would have been in a position of particular power in relation to Shakespeare's company, whose patronage passed to Carey's son George. At any rate, the character Oldcastle was evidently renamed, and it has been suggested that the publication of *1 Henry IV* in 1598, a relatively short time after the play's presumed appearance on stage, with Oldcastle appearing as 'Falstaff', was intended as a public gesture of retraction that gave the new character name the materiality of print, while *2 Henry IV* (printed 1600)

---

[3] *Henslowe's Diary*, p. 126.
[4] Quoted in Gary Taylor, 'The Fortunes of Oldcastle', *Shakespeare Survey*, 38 (1985), 85–100, p. 86. Taylor cites James's autograph epistle 'To my Noble friend S^r. henry Bourchier' in his manuscript edition of Hoccleve's *The Legend and Defence of [th]e Noble Knight and Martyr Sir Jhon Oldcastel*.

includes an explicit disavowal: 'Oldcastle died martyr, and this is not the man'.[5]

Although the Admiral's Men *Oldcastle* appeared more than two years after the death of Sir William Brooke, by which time George Carey himself had become Lord Chamberlain, it begins with a clear reference to the old controversy. The Prologue ostentatiously dispels any ambiguity caused by the new play's 'doubtful title':

> It is no pampered glutton we present,
> Nor agèd counsellor to youthful sins;
> But one whose virtues shone above the rest,
> A valiant martyr and a virtuous peer,
> In whose true faith and loyalty expressed
> To his true sovereign and his country's weal,
> We strive to pay that tribute of our love
> Your favours merit. Let fair truth be graced,
> Since forged invention former time defaced. (Pro.1, 6–14)[6]

The Prologue asserts the 'faire truth' of the current play as against the 'forged invention' of former time, apparently referring to the play by Shakespeare that presented Oldcastle as a 'pampered glutton' and 'agèd counsellor to youthful sin'. It claims that the true history of Oldcastle is of a man both loyal to king and country, and a 'valiant martyr'; and in doing so, it implicitly casts the Lord Chamberlain's Men as traducers of a proto-Protestant hero. Before discussing what the play may tell us about the Admiral's Men, it may be worth considering the validity of their accusation against the other company, and whether the ascription to the character later known as Falstaff of the name of a man treated by John Foxe as a 'valeaunte Christen knighte' and martyr implies anything about the religious subtext of *Henry IV*.[7]

Perhaps the most formidable arguments to this effect are offered by Gary Taylor in a 1985 article that defends the decision to use the name 'Sir John Oldcastle', not 'Falstaff', in the edition of *1 Henry IV* printed in the Oxford *Complete Works*. Restoring the original name, Taylor writes,

---

[5] See Taylor, p. 89; David Scott Kastan, *Shakespeare After Theory* (New York: Routledge, 1999), p. 94; James M. Gibson, 'Shakespeare and the Cobham Controversy: The Oldcastle/Falstaff and Brooke/Broome Revisions', *Medieval and Renaissance Drama in England*, 25 (2012), 94–132 (p. 111). William Shakespeare, *The Second Part of King Henry IV*, ed. by Giorgio Melchiori (Cambridge: Cambridge University Press, 1989), Epilogue, pp. 24–5.

[6] *Sir John Oldcastle, Part I*, in *The Oldcastle Controversy: 'Sir John Oldcastle, Part I' and 'The Famous Victories of Henry V'*, ed. by Peter Corbin and Douglas Sedge (Manchester: Manchester University Press; New York: St. Martin's Press, 1991). References to the text of *Oldcastle* use this edition.

[7] John Foxe, *Actes and Monuments* (London, 1563; STC: 11222), p. 277.

'restores the meaning and the shape which that identification gave to the character and the play'. The historical Oldcastle's dissolute youth, service as a soldier and friendship with the young Prince Henry all tally with the character as treated by Shakespeare, while lines like 'I'll be a traitor then, when thou art king' (1.2.119), the repeated references to gallows in the play, and the description of Sir John as 'that roasted Manningtree ox with the pudding in his belly' (2.4.374–5) seem to glance at Oldcastle's eventual conviction as a traitor and heretic and his execution by being hanged in chains and burnt. The decision to portray 'a Protestant martyr as a jolly hypocrite' is not an innocent one but part of the play's design: when considered alongside the character's original name, 'Sir John's moralizing, swearing, threats of repentance, and mimicry of Puritan idiom' look like satire against the more militant elements of Protestantism.[8]

The tentative conclusions that Taylor draws from his evidence relate more to Shakespeare's private religious views, which he thinks may have involved a degree of sympathy towards Catholicism than to any coherent position on the part of the Chamberlain's Men, and this reluctance to ascribe the treatment of Oldcastle in *Henry IV* to any corporate religious outlook typifies commentary on the play. When critics have discussed it as a Lord Chamberlain's Men play, they have instead tended to invoke the company's patrons the Careys, whether citing disgruntlement over the fact that William Brooke, not George Carey, succeeded Henry Carey as Lord Chamberlain in 1596 or the Careys' membership of the Essex faction at court, who opposed the Cobhams.[9] Others have expressed doubt as to whether it was meant to offend the Cobhams at all: as Janet Clare, Richard Dutton and Peter Corbin and Douglas Sedge all note, Oldcastle had already been depicted as the disreputable 'Jockey' in *The Famous Victories of Henry V*, apparently without negative consequence.[10] Still others dispute the assumption that Shakespeare's treatment of Oldcastle implies anything other than conformity to Church of England orthodoxy: Kristen Poole, for

---

[8] Taylor, pp. 93–5, 98. William Shakespeare, *The First Part of King Henry IV*, ed. by Herbert Weil and Judith Weil (Cambridge: Cambridge University Press, 1997).

[9] Robert Boies Sharpe, *The Real War of the Theaters: Shakespeare's Fellows in Rivalry with the Admiral's Men, 1594–1603: Repertories, Devices and Types* (New York: Modern Language Association of America, 1935), p. 90; Paul Whitfield White, 'Shakespeare and the Cobhams', in *Shakespeare and Theatrical Patronage in Early Modern England*, ed. by Paul Whitfield White and Suzanne R. Westfall (Cambridge University Press, 2002), pp. 64–89, p. 74.

[10] Janet Clare, *'Art Made Tongue-Tied by Authority': Elizabethan and Jacobean Dramatic Censorship* (Manchester: Manchester University Press, 1990), p. 77; Richard Dutton, *Mastering the Revels: The Regulation and Censorship of English Renaissance Drama* (Basingstoke: Macmillan, 1991), p. 102; The Oldcastle Controversy, p. 12.

example, compares it to the anti-Puritan satire to which dramatists contributed in the wake of the Martin Marprelate pamphlets.[11]

Critics commenting on the Admiral's Men, however, have been readier to identify a consistent religious position within their repertory, one that reflects the presumed makeup of their audience. In *Tudor Drama and Politics*, David Bevington ascribes the company a 'dominant audience of respectable Puritan citizens inclined to old-fashioned, unsophisticated morality and anti-Catholic ridicule'.[12] Along similar lines, Andrew Gurr speculates that *Sir John Oldcastle* may have been the stimulus to the Admiral's mounting 'a series of plays about Protestant heroes' that he thinks would have been in keeping with 'citizen values'.[13] Richard Helgerson, identifying an interest in 'Protestant or proto-Protestant martyrs' such as Oldcastle in the repertories of the Admiral's Men and the Earl of Worcester's Men, argues that the 'situation of the citizen and the Protestant – both figures who identify strongly with the nation and its ruler but both of whom are intent on keeping some part of themselves and their community free from the encroachment of national power – is central to the Henslowe version of English history'.[14] Finally, Paul Whitfield White sums up his reading of the Oldcastle/Falstaff affair with a comparison between the companies. The Lord Chamberlain's Men 'did not adopt any political or religious allegiance', he writes, because 'Shakespeare was too much of a pragmatist and his company managed to balance a range of demands made by their various patrons at court and in the commercial playhouses'. However, the Admiral's Men 'with the launching of their own rival *Oldcastle* [play] at the Rose in November of 1599 reaffirmed an identity with London's puritan-leaning audiences'.[15] The centrality of Sir John Oldcastle to the question of the two companies' putative allegiances could hardly be made more explicit.

There are other possible explanations, though, for the decision of the Admiral's Men to stage an Oldcastle play beyond sympathy for this historical figure (and the religious attitudes he symbolised) on the part of playwrights, players or expected audiences. One is sheer opportunism: by

---

[11] Kristen Poole, 'Saints Alive! Falstaff, Martin Marprelate, and the Staging of Puritanism', *Shakespeare Quarterly*, 46 (1995), 47–75 (p. 54). See also Kastan, p. 100.

[12] David M. Bevington, *Tudor Drama and Politics: A Critical Approach to Topical Meaning* (Cambridge, MA: Harvard University Press, 1968), p. 256.

[13] Andrew Gurr, *Playgoing in Shakespeare's London*, 2nd edn (Cambridge: Cambridge University Press, 1996), p. 154.

[14] Richard Helgerson, *Forms of Nationhood: The Elizabethan Writing of England* (Chicago: University of Chicago Press, 1992), p. 240.

[15] White, 'Shakespeare and the Cobhams', p. 86.

late 1599, both parts of *Henry IV* and *Henry V* had all appeared, and the company may have felt that a multipart history purporting to tell the real story of the man behind Falstaff was likely to be a success. As will be outlined below, the first part of *Oldcastle* invokes and imitates its Shakespearean predecessors in ways that would support this reading. Another relates to company patronage. The ten-shilling gift to the playwrights at the time of the play's premiere was an unusual gesture for Henslowe, which prompts the question of whether it reflected something special about the play itself. Perhaps that something was merely a matter of commercial success: Corbin and Sedge note the 'increased box office takings of the week of 3 November', around the time when the play first appeared. However, the figure of £8 16s is not outstanding, and would be surpassed over the next few months in the weeks of 30 December (£10 8s), 6 January (£9 9s), 30 March (£11 14s) and 18 May (£12 14s).[16] An alternative explanation links the gift to the growing alliance between Lord Admiral Charles Howard and the eighth Lord Cobham after Howard fell out with Cobham's enemy the Earl of Essex in the wake of the Cadiz expedition of 1596. Cobham would marry Howard's daughter, the dowager countess of Kildare Frances Fitzgerald, on 21 May 1601, although the relationship between the two men cooled when Cobham took part in negotiations over James's succession to the English throne via channels of which Howard did not approve.[17] If the Lord Admiral was allying himself to Cobham in the late 1590s, then it may be that he encouraged his players to stage a riposte to the plays that Cobham felt had insulted the honour of his title, and that the money Henslowe gave to the dramatists was a reward for service to the company's patron.[18]

As well as there being alternative reasons for the Admiral's staging of an Oldcastle play beyond an identification of the company with puritan attitudes, it is debatable whether the other plays in their repertory would support such a reading. Gurr rightly points to the fact that in the early seventeenth century the Admiral's Men (now the Prince's Men, under the patronage of Prince Henry) would stage '"Foxean" plays flaunting an overtly Protestant view of English history' such as Samuel Rowley's *When You See Me You Know Me* and Thomas Dekker's *The Whore of Babylon*.[19]

---

[16] *The Oldcastle Controversy*, p. 9; *Henslowe's Diary*, pp. 120–1.
[17] Robert W. Kenny, *Elizabeth's Admiral: The Political Career of Charles Howard Earl of Nottingham 1536–1624* (Baltimore: Johns Hopkins Press, 1970), p. 203, 252.
[18] The possibility is considered by Clare, p. 79; White, 'Shakespeare and the Cobhams', p. 87. See also Irving Ribner, *The English History Play in the Age of Shakespeare* (Princeton: Princeton University Press, 1957), pp. 199, 202.

However, as this book has shown, some of their plays of the 1590s had included caricatures of puritanism such as Servio in *A Knack to Know an Honest Man* and Florilla in *An Humorous Day's Mirth*. Either the company changed direction at the turn of the century, or its Protestantism was sufficiently mainstream as to permit anti-puritan satire; or perhaps it simply lacked a consistent religious allegiance. The relatively small proportion of its post-1600 repertory to have survived in print means that we lack the information necessary for a confident choice between these possibilities. Furthermore, while the first part of *Sir John Oldcastle* undeniably presents itself as a positive treatment of a figure whom Protestants identified as a martyr, its religious position is far from being straightforward, as will be argued over the paragraphs that follow.

In some respects, this complexity reflects the inherently problematic nature of Oldcastle as a historical figure: as a number of critics have demonstrated, his reputation in the sixteenth century was an extremely controversial one. Early Tudor chroniclers recycled the official narrative according to which he had been treasonably involved in the intended Lollard rising of 1414 against the 'noble Kinge' Henry V and justly punished as a consequence.[20] With the advent of the Reformation, Oldcastle acquired renewed currency as an exemplary heretic and traitor: Thomas More referred to him in an account of 'the great parell and ieopardy that the realme was lyke to haue fallen in' through heresy in Henry V's time that showed why 'the repressynge and greuous punyshement' of heretics was necessary.[21] William Tyndale and other Protestant writers, however, were more inclined to share Oldcastle's views on transubstantiation, the use of images and the temporal and spiritual power of the Catholic Church, and consequently sought to clear him from the accusation of treachery. John Bale, for example, rejected the story that the Lollards 'had made a great assemblye in saynct Gyles felde at London / purposynge the destruccyon of the lande and the subuersyon of the

[19] Andrew Gurr, *Shakespeare's Opposites: The Admiral's Company 1594–1625* (Cambridge: Cambridge University Press, 2009), p. 45.

[20] C. L. Kingsford, *The First English Life of King Henry the Fifth* (Oxford: Clarendon Press, 1911), p. 23, cited in Alice-Lyle Scoufos, *Shakespeare's Typological Satire: A Study of the Falstaff-Oldcastle Problem* (Athens, Ohio: Ohio University Press, 1979), p. 59. My account of Oldcastle's reputation is indebted to Scoufos, pp. 44–69. See also *The Oldcastle Controversy*, pp. 1–8; Poole. See also Annabel Patterson, 'Sir John Oldcastle as Symbol of Reformation Historiography', in *Religion, Literature, and Politics in Post-Reformation England, 1540–1688*, ed. by Donna B. Hamilton and Richard Strier(Cambridge: Cambridge University Press, 1996), pp. 6–26; Poole.

[21] *A Dyaloge of Syr Thomas More Knyghte ... Wheryn be Treatyd Dyuers Maters, as of the Veneracyon & Worshyp of Ymagys & Relyques, Prayng to Sayntis, & Goynge on Pylgrymage* (London, 1530; STC: 18085), fol. cxliiii.

common welthe' as a lie spread by the bishops: when the King 'with a great nombre of menne entred the same felde . . . he founde no soche companye'.[22] Bale's account was incorporated wholesale in John Foxe's *Actes and Monuments* in 1563; when Foxe's Catholic opponent Nicholas Harpsfield insisted both on the reality of the insurrection and on Oldcastle's leadership of it, this prompted Foxe's 'Defence of the Lord Cobham' in the 1570 *Acts and Monuments* in turn.[23] As Alice-Lyle Scoufos shows, 'disparate accounts of the history of Sir John Oldcastle' continued to circulate, including republications of Tudor chroniclers such as Fabyan, Stow's *Annales*, which depicted Oldcastle as 'a most peruerse enimie to the state of the church', and Holinshed's *Chronicles*, where he is exonerated of responsibility for the rising and called 'a valiant capteine and a hardie gentleman'.[24] As David Womersley points out, though, historians seeking to rehabilitate Oldcastle were faced with the problem of how to avoid criticism of Henry V, the hero of Agincourt, for allowing his death to happen (not to mention the more general persecution of Lollards during his reign); like his predecessor John Bale, Foxe could only exculpate Henry by depicting him as the 'tool of the clergy', a 'puppet worked by the priests'.[25] Furthermore, as dramatists working in the late 1590s Munday, Drayton, Wilson and Hathaway had to deal with the additional baggage of Oldcastle's relationship to the character now known as Sir John Falstaff.

The *Oldcastle* dramatists use a number of strategies to navigate these treacherous historical waters. While they do include the planned Lollard rising, they emphatically distance Oldcastle from it while showing how he could have acquired the reputation of being involved: the rebels propose him as their general (5.38) and the report that he is the 'chief man on whom they do depend' is subsequently brought to the King (6.104). Once they have been apprehended, however, and Oldcastle directly asks them whether he had anything to do with them, their leader Sir Roger Acton is obliged to confess, 'To clear my conscience ere I die', that 'we have no other ground / But only rumour to accuse this lord' (12.112–14). Moreover, Oldcastle is separately depicted as the active enemy of treason: he refuses to be drawn into the plot of the Earl of Cambridge, Henry Scrope and Sir Thomas Grey against Henry, and goes on to reveal it to the King. In

---

[22] John Bale, *A Brefe Chronycle Concernynge the Examinacyon and Death of the Blessed Martyr of Christ Syr Iohan Oldecastell the Lorde Cobham* ([Antwerp], 1544; STC: 1276), fol. 47v.

[23] The passage cited from Bale appears in Foxe, p. 275. See Scoufos, p. 62.

[24] Scoufos, p. 69; John Stow, *The Annales of England* (London, 1592; STC: 23334), p. 550; Raphael Holinshed, *The Third Volume of Chronicles* (London, 1587; STC: 13569), p. 544.

[25] David Womersley, *Divinity and State* (Oxford: Oxford University Press, 2010), pp. 97–8.

his earlier exchanges with Henry, Oldcastle adopts a position that seems to anticipate that of the Church of England in combining loyalty to the monarch with non-recognition of papal power:

> My gracious Lord, unto your Majesty,
> Next unto my God, I owe my life,
> And what is mine either by nature's gift
> Or fortune's bounty, all is at your service;
> But for obedience to the Pope of Rome,
> I owe him none. (6.7–12)

For his part, Henry is absolved of responsibility for Oldcastle's apprehension and imprisonment by the simple expedient of making him unaware of it: the Bishop of Rochester has Oldcastle arrested using a warrant signed by the King before he learned of Oldcastle's non-involvement in the planned rising, and does so at a time when Henry, en route to France, has other things on his mind. Henry's final line in the play refers to Oldcastle as the 'True perfect mirror of nobility' (15.57).

In addition to clearing Oldcastle of treason and Henry of knowledge of his arrest, the playwrights use two techniques to distance him from the Shakespearean character who once bore his name. One is the invention of a third Sir John, the parson of Wrotham, 'A priest in show, but in plain terms a thief' (2.157). This purse-taker, drinker and gambler, with 'Doll, my concubine' (2.167) in tow, is clearly modelled on Falstaff, but as Benjamin Griffin suggests, the resemblance between the two may be more than a matter of exploitative imitation. 'Sir John the parson is a kind of pressure valve: the audience attention that might have gone to meditating on the differences, and similarities, between Shakespeare's Oldcastle and the Admiral's Men's now goes to work on something else.'[26] By including a Falstaffian character, the dramatists discourage the audience from identifying their Oldcastle with his Shakespearean predecessor. At the same time, however, the play does make explicit references to Shakespeare's Falstaff (as opposed to Oldcastle). When Wrotham robs the disguised King Henry, the latter muses, 'Where the devil are my old thieves that were wont to keep this walk? Falstaff, the villain, is so fat he cannot get on's horse; but methinks Poins and Peto should be stirring hereabouts' (10.52–5). Hearing that his victim is 'one of the King's servants' (10.64), Wrotham enquires whether it might be possible to arrange for him to be pardoned, should that prove necessary:

[26] Benjamin Griffin, 'Marring and Mending: Treacherous Likeness in Two Renaissance Controversies', *Huntington Library Quarterly*, 60 (1997), 363–80 (p. 374).

SIR JOHN Methinks the King should be good to thieves because he has
    been a thief himself; though I think now he be turned true man.
KING HENRY 'Faith, I have heard, indeed, he has had an ill name that
    way in his youth; but how can'st tell he has been a thief?
SIR JOHN How? Because he once robbed me before I fell to the trade
    myself; when that foul villainous guts, that led him to all that roguery,
    was in's company there, that Falstaff. (10.77–83)

Aside from the comedy that arises out of Sir John speaking, without
knowing it, to the very man who robbed him, this exchange has several
effects. Firstly, by reminding us that the King was once a thief, by
depicting Wrotham as one of his victims, and by insinuating that the
experience of being robbed was one of the things that corrupted him, the
exchange makes Wrotham somewhat more sympathetic as a character,
with traces of the loveable rogue à la Falstaff. Secondly, as Corbin and
Sedge point out, the dramatists 'would have been at pains to emphasise
that Falstaff and Oldcastle are different characters in order to vindicate
Oldcastle's reputation', and this vignette works to that end by treating
Falstaff as a distinct personage.[27] Thirdly, though, there is a sense in which
moments like this create a dynamic whereby the fictions of Shakespeare
and of the Admiral's Men dramatists mutually reinforce each other. The
Admiral's play gains legitimacy by presenting itself as belonging to the
same fictional world as *Henry IV*, one in which Prince Hal associates with
Falstaff, Poins and the rest before his reformation as Henry V. The events
of *Henry IV* are depicted as the back-story to *Sir John Oldcastle*. But the
gain is not all on the side of the Admiral's Men. In asserting the existence
of Falstaff as a character within the world of their play, and emphasising his
non-identity with Oldcastle, Munday, Drayton, Wilson and Hathaway aid
the cause of the Lord Chamberlain's Men by widening the circulation of
the character's new name beyond the Chamberlain's repertory and
allowing him to function as a pseudo-historical figure rather than an
offensive travesty of a Lollard martyr. This may not have been their
intention; indeed, Gurr suggests that the revival of *Oldcastle* by the Earl
of Worcester's Men, another company managed by Henslowe, when they
began playing at the Rose in August 1602 was meant as a snub to their
neighbours at the Globe, which would support a reading of the play as a
hostile gesture in relations between the companies.[28] However, if, as was
earlier noted, the early printing of *1 Henry IV* may indicate a need on the

---

[27] *The Oldcastle Controversy*, p. 92n.

part of the Lord Chamberlain's Men to publicise the fact that their celebrated character was Sir John Falstaff, not Sir John Oldcastle, then it has to be said that the Admiral's Men play also served this purpose.

The references to Poins and Falstaff are not the only ways in which *Sir John Oldcastle*, for all its disparagement of 'forged invention', can be read as a supplement to the Henriad rather than simply a 'riposte', to use Womersley's term.[29] As was noted earlier, as well as exonerating Oldcastle from involvement in the Lollard rising, the later play shows him revealing the so-called Southampton plot by means of 'articles' (12.119) which he has cunningly led Scrope, Cambridge and Grey to sign. Clearly, Oldcastle does not feature in *Henry V* (although the play does give a role to an ex-Lollard, Sir Thomas Erpingham). However, Shakespeare's explanation of the discovery of the plot, 'The king hath note of all that they intend / By interception which they dream not of' (2.2.7), is one that *Oldcastle* does not so much contradict as expand upon: the 'interception which they dream not of' proves to have been Oldcastle himself. Conversely, the Admiral's Men play seems to rely on *Henry V* later on when Oldcastle himself is arrested for high treason and demands of the Bishop of Rochester, 'Let me be brought before his majesty':

> ROCHESTER We are not bound to do kind offices
> For any traitor, schismatic, nor heretic.
> The King's hand is our warrant for our work
> Who is departed on his way for France,
> And at Southampton doth repose this night. (13.64–8)

While the King's confrontation with the conspirators is depicted later on in the play, at this point any playgoers familiar with *Henry V* would be likely to read the action as contemporaneous with Act Two, Scene Two of Shakespeare's drama. Furthermore, their recollection of *Henry V* could be ironised by the awareness that while publicly and deliberately unmasking 'This dangerous treason' that 'God so graciously hath brought to light' (2.2.180–81), Shakespeare's monarch was blithely unaware of Oldcastle's own wrongful arrest for the same crime.[30] Once again, rather than straightforwardly contradicting the Shakespearean play, the Oldcastle dramatists create a complex relationship of allusion, interdependence and retrospective irony.

---

[28] Gurr, *Shakespeare's Opposites*, p. 32. On the revival of *Oldcastle*, see *Henslowe's Diary*, p. 213.

[29] Womersley, p. 360.

[30] William Shakespeare, *King Henry V*, ed. by Andrew Gurr, updated edn (Cambridge: Cambridge University Press, 2005).

If the *Oldcastle* dramatists' introductory show of distancing their drama from Shakespeare's is allowed to be, if not misleading, at least disingenuous, then this raises the question of the play's broader religious and political position. Undeniably, its depiction of Oldcastle's persecution by the Catholic clergy is much more robust than anything we see in Shakespeare: the Bishop of Rochester gloatingly expresses his hope of ending Oldcastle's 'disdainèd life' (12.73) and, when his plans prove unsuccessful, is perfectly willing to make fraudulent use of the royal warrant. The Summoner who is given the task of ordering Oldcastle to appear before the bishop is a 'drabmonger' (4.73). As for Sir John of Wrotham: not only does he enthusiastically encourage Rochester's persecution of Oldcastle (2.32–6,141–5), he himself is depicted as a thief, whoremaster and hypocrite. In the words of Larry S. Champion: 'If Rochester reflects the Machiavellian tactics of the Church leaders, the parson and the summoner reflect the utter corruption of its ministers and agents'.[31] While there is nothing in this hostile depiction of Catholic clergy that is noticeably out of keeping with Church of England orthodoxy, there is one moment where the play does seem to sail close to the wind, and that, ironically, is the very moment when it seems to insist most loudly on its conformity: when the King responds to Sir Roger Acton's plea that it was his conscience that led him to 'join with peasants' (12.7) in rebellion.

> KING Thy conscience? Then thy conscience is corrupt,
>   For in thy conscience thou art bound to us,
>   And in thy conscience thou shouldst love thy country;
>   Else what's the difference 'twixt a Christian
>   And the uncivil manners of the Turk?
> BEVERLEY We meant no hurt unto your Majesty,
>   But reformation of religion.
> KING Reform religion? Was it that ye sought?
>   I pray who gave you that authority?
>   Belike then, we do hold the sceptre up
>   And sit within the throne but for a cipher.
>   Time was, good subjects would make known their grief,
>   And pray amendment, not enforce the same,
>   Unless their king were tyrant, which I hope
>   You cannot justly say that Harry is. (12.10–24)

---

[31] Larry S. Champion, '"Havoc in the Commonwealth": Perspective, Political Ideology, and Dramatic Strategy in *Sir John Oldcastle* and the English Chronicle Plays', *Medieval and Renaissance Drama in England*, 5 (1991), 165–79 (p. 167).

The insistence that subjects do not have the right to 'reform religion' seems like an assertion of the idea of Royal Supremacy – if, indeed, an anachronistic one given that it is being uttered by Henry V, not Henry VIII. But after it comes the more subversive notion, concealed in a subjunctive clause, that subjects might have the right to 'enforce' change if 'their king were tyrant'. Henry, of course, is no tyrant. But even to grant this possibility flies in the face of the Homily against Disobedience and Wilful Rebellion, which insists that 'kynges and princes, aswell the euill as the good, do raigne by Gods ordinaunce, and that subiectes are bounden to obey them'. Rather than rebelling against bad rulers, subjects should recognise their own sinfulness and leave their prince to God: 'a rebell is worse then the worst Prince, and rebellion worse then the worste gouernment of the worst prince that hitherto hath ben'.[32] In suggesting that tyrants might forfeit their right to be obeyed, and to determine their state's religion, the *Oldcastle* dramatists gesture towards a position that was arguably treasonous.

Aside from being placed in the mouth of a king, one reason why this statement seems to have slipped under the radar is its being delivered in response to a religious rising that the play strives hard to undermine. Although the rebels identify themselves as 'Professed friends to Wycliffe, foes to Rome' (5.9), we are encouraged to question their motives and principles. Acton obtains large sums of money from Murley, the brewer of Dunstable, by appealing to his 'hope of honour' (5.98) and desire to be made a knight; Murley demonstrates his willingness to contemplate treason in suggesting that if the rebels kill the king they can 'make another' (8.32); and in Marlovian phrase, Henry himself attributes the rising to the rebels' 'aspiring minds' (12.1), while treating with scorn their appeal to conscience. Griffin rightly compares the way the dramatists set up Oldcastle in contrast to the Falstaffian Sir John of Wrotham with the way they divide in two 'the figure of the Lollard ... in order that its unacceptable side may be conquered. They endeavour to establish that Henry V was mainly persecuting *bad* Lollards'.[33] And yet one is tempted to ask: apart from Sir John and Lady Cobham, where are the good Lollards in the play? We hear of critics of the Church who 'give themselves the name of Protestants, / And meet in fields and solitary groves' (2.20–21), but it is unclear what, if anything, these shadowy figures have to do with Acton, Murley and company. The anachronistic nomenclature seems significant: these, the play seems to imply, are the true ancestors of *Oldcastle*'s Elizabethan

---

[32] *The Second Tome of Homilees* (London, 1571; STC: 13669), pp. 547, 553.   [33] Griffin, p. 375.

audience, while the 'Lollard extremists', to use David Bevington's term, are repudiated in a gesture that associates the play with moderate, rather than radical reform.[34]

There are other features of *Sir John Oldcastle* beyond its treatment of the Lollard rising that complicate its religious position. One is its depiction of Oldcastle himself, who is first introduced to us in a scene that sits uncomfortably with any view of the play as simple hagiography. A group of starving beggars approaches his gate, expressing relief that 'we are now come to the good Lord Cobham's, to the best man to the poor that is in all Kent' (3.21–2). And yet when Oldcastle enters, his servant Harpoole seemingly berates him for his expenditure, not on relieving the poor, but on fine clothes: 'Your backs, your backs, the devil, and pride / Has cut the throat of all good housekeeping' (3.28–9). (This may owe something to the historical Oldcastle's confession, 'in my frayle youthe I offended the (lorde) most greuouslye in pryde / wrathe / and glottonye / in couetousnesse and in lechere'.)[35] In turn, Cobham criticises the servant's willingness to give to the poor:

> OLDCASTLE Yea, except thou have a crew of seely knaves
> And sturdy rogues still feeding at my gate,
> There is no hospitality with thee.
> HARPOOLE They may sit at the gate well enough, but the devil of
> anything you give them, except they will eat stones. (3.32–6)[36]

Although Harpoole does attempt to eject the beggars – 'Out, you rogues, you knaves! Work for your livings!'(3.50) – the histrionic excess of his manner seems intended as a statement of disagreement with Oldcastle, as becomes apparent when he laments the hard-heartedness of the rich:

> Alas, poor men. O Lord, they may beg their hearts out;
> There's no more charity amongst men
> Than amongst so many mastiff dogs.
> – What make you here, you needy knaves?
> Away, away, you villains! (3.51–5)

He goes on to complain, not of Oldcastle's sartorial pride, but of his miserliness: 'You are grown so beggarly you have scarce a bite of bread to give at your door. You talk of your religion so long that you have banished charity from amongst you' (3.60–62). It is surprising to see a play

---

[34] Bevington, p. 257.   [35] Bale, fol. 26v; cp. Foxe, p. 266.
[36] Corbin and Sedge replace the first edition's commas after 'Yea' and 'gate' with a semicolon and a full stop, but this seems to lose the point of Oldcastle's remark.

ostensibly intended to present Oldcastle as 'one whose virtues shone above the rest' making him the target of a complaint we have already encountered in the Strange's Men play *A Knack to Know a Knave* (see Chapter 1): that radical Protestantism, with its stress upon faith rather than works as the key to salvation, risks undermining charity and good neighbourliness.

As the source of this complaint in *Sir John Oldcastle*, Harpoole merits further attention. While his loyalty to Oldcastle is beyond question, their difference of opinion over almsgiving seems to reflect the fact that their religious positions do not coincide. When Oldcastle is placed under arrest by the Bishop of Rochester, Harpoole objects to being described by the Bishop as a 'grizzled heretic':

> 'Sblood, my Lord Bishop, ye do me wrong. I am neither heretic nor puritan, but of the old church. I'll swear, drink ale, kiss a wench, go to mass, eat fish all Lent, and fast Fridays with cakes and wine, fruit and spicery, shrive me of my old sins afore Easter, and begin new afore Whitsuntide. (13.129–33)

Although Womersley seems to take this as a statement of loyalty to Catholicism, it is hardly a straightforward one: a defence of that faith on the grounds that it permits one to sin, repent and sin again also serves as a criticism of it. It is also unclear whether any such irony is intended by Harpoole, as Champion thinks, or works at his expense.[37] However, Womersley is surely right to find a degree of nostalgia in the play's evocation of a faith 'tolerant of human frailty, appreciative of fleshly pleasure in all its forms'.[38] To some extent, this nostalgia even informs the depiction of the 'wolf ... in sheep's coat' Wrotham (2.155): a corrupt priest who is 'a singer, a drinker, a bencher, a wencher', who can 'say a mass and kiss a lass' (4.182–3) is more sympathetic, because more frank in his admission of fleshly frailty, than an ideologue like the Bishop of Rochester.

Harpoole's criticisms of Oldcastle's lack of charity, and the play's identification of him with a Catholic English past that is remembered with some affection, make it difficult to regard *Sir John Oldcastle* as doctrinally puritan in any consistent or programmatic way – in White's words, 'as close as one could get to Protestant propaganda in the theatre'.[39] Womersley resolves the inconsistency by arguing that the character was intended to appeal to those in the audience who 'shared

---

[37] Champion, p. 168.   [38] Womersley, p. 373.
[39] White, 'Shakespeare and the Cobhams', p. 86.

his unreconstructed religious attitudes', and to show them that their medieval Catholic forebears had themselves been oppressed by a Roman Church with little sympathy for national cultures: when Rochester orders the burning of Oldcastle's English Bible and devotional texts, Harpoole fights to save his *Bevis of Hampton* and *Robin Hood* (13.152–6).[40] However, by stressing the religious differences between Harpoole and his master, while treating both sympathetically, the playwrights emphasise the difficulty of dividing Christians into good Protestants and bad Catholics, both in the play's medieval setting, where loyal and disloyal Catholics coexist with loyal and disloyal Lollards, and, by implication, in the 1590s, where theatregoers are expected to sympathise with a range of religious positions.

Indeed, a final argument against reading *Sir John Oldcastle* as propaganda is to be found in the hints it drops that it is not able to address all the topics it would like to. One example is in the opening scene, where the First Judge responds to public disorder with the decree that

> There be no meetings; when the vulgar sort
> Sit on their ale-bench with cups and cans,
> Matters of state be not their common talk,
> Nor pure religion by their lips profaned. (1.120–23)

Bevington reads this speech as a statement of support for the suppressing of conventicles in the 1580s and 1590s, an expression of the dramatists' own conformism in a play that is generally 'wary of the people'.[41] However, as Womersley notes, it also testifies to 'the depth of interest amongst the "vulgar sort" in how "matters of state" might connect with questions of "pure religion"'.[42] More specifically, I would argue, it can be read as an allusion to the fact that the theatre itself was not allowed to address these topics directly: it was precisely 'matters of Divinity and State' that were ordered by the Privy Council to be censored in 1589.[43] Another episode in the play that takes on a new significance when considered in relation to this ban is Harpoole's treatment of the Sumner who tries to serve a process upon Oldcastle. The play's editors note that in forcing him to eat the process, seal and all, Harpoole re-enacts a scene from the old play *George a Greene*, as well as recalling the moment in *Henry V* where Fluellen makes Pistol eat the leek. In the context of *Oldcastle*, however, the action is not merely comic:

---

[40] Womersley, p. 373.   [41] Bevington, p. 257–8.   [42] Womersley, p. 4.
[43] *English Professional Theatre, 1530-1660*, ed. by Glynne Wickham, Herbert Berry and William Ingram (Cambridge: Cambridge University Press, 2000), pp. 94–5.

HARPOOLE Is this process parchment?
SUMNER Yes, marry.
HARPOOLE And this seal wax?
SUMNER It is so.
HARPOOLE If this be parchment, and this wax, eat you this parchment
    and this wax, or I will make parchment of your skin and
    beat your brains into wax. Sirrah Sumner, dispatch!
    Devour, sirrah, devour! (4.38–44)

By insisting on the edible materiality of the Bishop's summons, Harpoole
gestures towards a topic that the play does not discuss, but which was of
central importance in Oldcastle's second examination by the Bishops: the
nature of the Eucharist. In Bale, the parties dispute at length the question
of what happens to the bread once it has been consecrated, in an argument
that culminates in Oldcastle uttering his considered opinion:

> Therfor I saye now ageyne / lyke as I sayd afore. As our lorde Jesus Christ is
> verye god and verye manne / so in the most blessed sacrament of the aultre/
> is Christes verye bodye and breade.
>   Than sayd they all with one voyce. It is an heresye.
>   One of the bysshoppes stode vp by & by / and sayd. What yt is an
> heresye manyfest / to saye that yt is breade after the sacramentall wordes be
> ones spoken / but Christes bodye onlye.[44]

Oldcastle's belief in consubstantiation, that the bread is materially bread
even once it has been turned into the body of Christ, is paralleled by
Harpoole's insistence that the parchment and wax continue to be 'dry
meat' (4.69) and 'the purest of the honey' (4.58) even when they contain
an episcopal summons. His observation, 'you shall eat more than your own
word, for I'll make you eat all the words in the process' (4.71–2) puns not
only on the saying, 'to eat one's words', but on the idea of eating the Word
as made flesh in Christ; and his unknowing allusion to the doctrine for
which his master will be vilified gains in irony for being uttered by one of
the 'old church'.

The covertness with which *Oldcastle* alludes to the actual doctrines in
which its protagonist believed suggests that this is a play whose true
allegiances may be hard to identify. Simply in choosing Oldcastle as its
subject, it implies sympathy for a Foxean narrative of English history.
However, it departs from Foxe in its insistence that the planned Lollard
rising was real, thus depicting Lollardy as a potential threat to political
stability. While Oldcastle himself is kept scrupulously apart from the rising

---

[44] Bale, fol. 28v; cp. Foxe, p. 267.

and treated as a paragon of loyalism, the play touches on the highly controversial question of whether a bad ruler might be deposed, an idea comprehensively dismissed in the *Homily upon Disobedience*. In a further twist, the play seems to regard England's Catholic past with some nostalgia, while making Oldcastle the butt of insinuations about puritan miserliness. Irving Ribner has suggested that one reason for the play's ambivalence towards puritanism may be its joint authorship; there is also the intriguing suggestion of Donna B. Hamilton that Anthony Munday, one of its dramatists, had Catholic sympathies and 'only outwardly conformed to Protestantism', although the nature of her argument, which takes Munday's anti-Catholic writings and recusant-hunting as a front, makes it a difficult one to prove.[45] At any rate, the play's tensions and evasions make it impossible to read it with confidence as a statement of the religious position of the Admiral's Men, as opposed to a product of patronage, commercial imperatives, or a combination of the two.

As You Like It and the *Huntingdon* Plays

As a two-part play where the comic ending of Part I was (presumably) followed by a tragic Part II, *Sir John Oldcastle* was not a novelty in the repertory of the Admiral's Men. *Tamburlaine* is the obvious point of comparison; the lost *Hercules* (first staged on 7 and 23 May 1595) may have been another.[46] More significant for the current chapter, however, is the two-part play about Robin Hood written by Anthony Munday in early 1598 (the second part in collaboration with Henry Chettle). Not only would Munday go on to collaborate on *Oldcastle* in autumn 1599; in choosing Robin as his subject he selected a figure who, like Oldcastle, had a complex and controversial significance in relation to England's religious past and present. This makes the Robin Hood plays, *The Downfall of Robert, Earl of Huntingdon* and *The Death of Robert, Earl of Huntingdon*, useful territory on which to explore further the question of the religious identity (if any) of the Admiral's Men; and as I shall go on to explain, another reason why they are of interest to this book is their apparent influence on Shakespeare's *As You Like It*, identified more than a century ago by Ashley Thorndike. While Thorndike focused primarily on the plays' depiction of the freedom enjoyed by exiles who take refuge in

---

[45] Ribner, p. 204. Donna B. Hamilton, *Anthony Munday and the Catholics, 1560-1633* (Aldershot: Ashgate, 2005), p. xvi.

[46] *Henslowe's Diary*, pp. 28–9.

the forest, Munday and Chettle also anticipate Shakespeare in their treatment of the religious themes with which the motif of exile is associated.

It is difficult to think of a folk hero so profoundly afflicted with such contradictory social, religious and political meanings as Robin Hood. Early poems and ballads depict him as an outlaw of yeoman origin, the enemy of the Sheriff of Nottingham (of course) and of bishops, ultimately murdered by a treacherous prioress. The anti-monasticism of these descriptions, however, goes hand in hand with a veneration of the Virgin Mary: Robin may be suspicious of monks, but he is a loyal Catholic, and this combination of subversiveness and piety seems to have characterised his identity in pre-Reformation England.[47] On the one hand he was associated with ribaldry and licence, as Peter Stallybrass demonstrates, and came to be incorporated in the 'carnivalesque festivities of the May-games'.[48] On the other, as Alexandra F. Johnston and Paul Whitfield White have shown, such games seem to have had an important role in parochial events that redirected Robin's subversive energies towards Church-sanctioned charity: 'the figure of Robin Hood in his various manifestations emerges from the records as the chief fundraiser for the parishes of the Thames Valley and the west of England'.[49]

The post-Reformation fortunes of Robin Hood need to be understood in the light of Robin's complex prior relationship to religious institutions. It hardly seems surprising to find the Lord Chancellor's secretary Sir Richard Morrison urging the King *circa* 1535 to suppress the 'plays of Robin Hood, Maid Marion, Friar Tuck wherein beside the lewdness and ribaldry that there is opened to the people, disobedience also to your officers is taught' in favour of anti-Catholic propaganda.[50] It is slightly more surprising to find the Bishop of Winchester, Stephen Gardiner, accused in the rather different climate of 1545 of forbidding 'the players of London ... to play any moe playes of Christe / but of robin hode and

---

[47] J. C. Holt, *Robin Hood*, rev. edn (London: Thames & Hudson, 1989), pp. 15–39.

[48] Peter Stallybrass, '"Drunk with the Cup of Liberty": Robin Hood, the Carnivalesque, and the Rhetoric of Violence in Early Modern England', in *Robin Hood: An Anthology of Scholarship and Criticism*, ed. by Stephen Knight (Cambridge: D. S. Brewer, 1999), pp. 113–45 (p. 299).

[49] Alexandra F. Johnston, 'The Robin Hood of the Records', in *Playing Robin Hood: The Legend as Performance in Five Centuries*, ed. by Lois Potter (Newark: University of Delaware Press; London: Associated University Presses, 1998), pp. 27–44 (p. 39). See also Paul Whitfield White, 'Holy Robin Hood! Carnival, Parish Guilds, and the Outlaw Tradition', in *Tudor Drama Before Shakespeare, 1485-1590: New Directions for Research, Criticism, and Pedagogy*, ed. by Lloyd Edward Kermode, Jason Scott-Warren and Martine van Elk (Houndmills: Palgrave Macmillan, 2004), pp. 67–89.

[50] *English Professional Theatre*, p. 20.

litle Johan': in this case, Robin Hood plays seem not merely to have been tolerated, but to have been actively encouraged by the forces of Counter-Reformation as an alternative to Protestant drama.[51] Robin Hood's earlier role as a fundraiser evidently survived, as White shows, into the reign of Elizabeth; however, the culture of May-games with which he was associated encountered the same resistance both from puritans and from the established church as morris-dancing did (see Chapter 2).[52] They are discursively linked to the pre-Reformation past, or an insufficiently reformed present, in the Marprelate tract *Hay any Work for Cooper* (1589), when a priest called Glibbery is accused of ending his sermon prematurely so as to join 'either the Summer Lord with his May Game, or Robin Hood with his Morris dance', who have been heard passing by outside.[53]

Munday's decision to write (or agree to write) a play about Robin Hood thus recalls his incorporation of morris dancing in *John a Kent and John a Cumber*. In both cases, he made use of cultural materials that could be traced back to pre-Reformation England and that had become controversial in part because of their association with the pre-Reformation English Church. The problematic nature of these materials may be one reason for the complex framing device Munday uses in *The Downfall*, whereby the Robin Hood play we are watching is understood to be a rehearsal of a drama written by the Tudor poet John Skelton for performance at the court of Henry VIII. Rather than having Elizabethan actors dress up as Robin Hood and his men, Munday has them impersonate Henrician courtiers preparing to perform those roles in the altogether different cultural context of pre-Reformation England.[54] By metadramatically placing his Robin Hood play eighty years in the past, Munday thus dodges the question of what it might mean to perform a Robin Hood play in the present.

This is not the only way in which Munday can be seen as diminishing the subversive potential of his dramatic materials. He follows the

---

[51] William Turner, *The Rescuynge of the Romishe Fox* ([Bonn], 1545; STC: 24355), sig. G2r; cited in Johnston, p. 27.

[52] White, 'Holy Robin Hood!', p. 76. On opposition to Robin Hood and May games, see John Forrest, *The History of Morris Dancing 1458-1750* (Cambridge: James Clark, 1990), pp. 117, 138, 140, 150.

[53] Joseph L. Black, ed., *The Martin Marprelate Tracts: A Modernized and Annotated Edition* (Cambridge: Cambridge University Press, 2008), p. 108; see also Johnston, p. 28.

[54] As Womersley points out (p. 367), the allusion to 'good king *Ferdinand*' at line 11 places the fiction before the death of Ferdinand II on 23 January 1516. References are to Anthony Munday, *The Downfall of Robert, Earl of Huntingdon*, ed. by John C. Meagher (Oxford: Malone Society, 1965).

chroniclers John Leland and Richard Grafton in making Robin an outlawed earl rather than (as Jeffrey L. Singman puts it) 'the lawless yeoman leader of a band of highway robbers', making him less of a 'challenge to social authority' than the figure from the popular tradition.[55] He also distances the play explicitly from the Robin Hood games by having Sir John Eltham step out of character to express his anxiety that the King will not like a play with 'no ieasts of *Robin Hoode*, / No merry Morices of Frier *Tuck*' (ll. 2210–11). Skelton explains that 'merry ieasts, they haue bene showne before' (l. 2221):

> Our play expresses noble *Roberts* wrong,
> His milde forgetting trecherous iniurie:
> The Abbots malice, rak't in cinders long,
> Breakes out at last with *Robins* Tragedie. (ll. 2226–9)

Munday's play is thus presented as a drama not about Robin Hood, but 'noble Robert', associated with the elevated form of tragedy rather than disreputable 'merry jests', and privileging the Christian virtues of mildness and forgiveness. Maid Marian, too, is purged of some of her associations, being neither the 'smurkynge wench' of the popular tradition nor a man dressed as a woman, as in some morris dances, but Matilda, the daughter of Robert Fitzwater, a figure from the reign of King John whose story had recently been told in verse by Michael Drayton.[56] The insistence that she is 'No *Marian*, but *Fitzwaters* chast *Matilda*' (l. 2758) elevates her both socially and morally.

A third way in which Munday makes his Robin Hood materials amenable to an Elizabethan audience is his exploitation of a feature of the tales identified by Lois Potter: 'the ease with which they could be co-opted to support a post-Reformation view of the church with its corrupt priests and lecherous friars'.[57] In *The Downfall* the outlawing of Robin results from the machinations of the Prior of York (Robin's uncle) and the Bishop of Ely; the Prior's hubristic assurance that all the King's power 'Cannot preuaile against my holy order' (l. 1726) condemns him in the terms of an Elizabethan polity that assumed royal supremacy. The description of Ely as 'a wolfe in a sheepes skinne' (l. 2106) employs the imagery of Reformation polemic, while Robin's opposition to the power of a clerical estate ungoverned by the monarch is conveyed through the revelation that

---

[55] Holt 162; Jeffrey L. Singman, 'Munday's Unruly Earl', in *Playing Robin Hood*, pp. 63–76 (p. 69).
[56] See Stallybrass, p. 306; Forrest, p. 168; Michael Drayton, *Matilda. The Faire and Chaste Daughter of the Lord Robert Fitzwater* (London, 1594; STC: 7205).
[57] Lois Potter, 'Introduction' to Part I, in *Playing Robin Hood*, pp. 21–5, p. 22.

he 'vrg'd the king to sesse the clergie, / When to the holy land he tooke his iorney' (ll. 1393–4).[58] In Part II it is the Prior, along with Sir Doncaster of Hothersfield, who is responsible for Robin's poisoning and death, and he insists that his clerical status need not prevent him from succeeding to the earldom of Huntingdon: 'Ile haue a dispensation, and turne temporall' (l. 304).[59] Munday's incorporation of the Matilda material adds a further religious dimension to the two plays, in that by placing Robin within the reigns of King Richard and King John (rather than Edward I, as in earlier versions of the legend) he makes John's struggles with the Church of Rome part of the implied backdrop to the main plot. Even before John has become King, Part I gestures towards these conflicts: 'this proude Priest I can not brooke' (ll. 543-4), he complains of King Richard's regent, the Bishop of Ely, while the fact that Robin himself is not only outlawed but 'excommunicate' (l. 1191) anticipates the future papal interdiction of John and of the realm.

Despite these allusions to the religious politics of John's reign, though, the two plays ultimately resist a Foxean narrative that would see it as a time of 'calamitie' brought about by 'the subtile conueyaunce of his Clergy'. Although *The Downfall* depicts a power-struggle between Prince John and the Bishop of Ely, the waters are muddied by the fact that Ely is not simply a representative of papal power but the designated regent of King Richard, who is fighting in the Crusades. *The Death* does anticipate the Foxean narrative (taken by Foxe from John Bale, as with the Oldcastle story) of John's death at Swineshead or Swinested Abbey, 'where as most writers testifie [tha]t he was most trayterously poisoned, by a Monke of that Abbey, of the sect of Sisteanes, or sainct Bernardes brethren called Simon of Swinsted'.[60] Although the play does not depict John's demise, it is clearly alluded to when John swears over the dying Robin never to attempt Matilda's chastity, and announces that if he should do so,

> He craues to see but short and sower daies,
> His death be like to *Robins* he desires,
> His periur'd body proue a poysoned prey,
> For cowled Monkes, and barefoote begging Friers. (ll. 782–5)

---

[58] For the image of the wolf in sheep's clothing, derived from Matthew 7:15, see the September eclogue in Spenser's *Shepheardes Calender*, and John Bale's *Three Lawes*, where a bishop's mitre is made to signify 'The mouth of a wolfe': John Bale, *A Comedy Concernynge Thre Lawes, of Nature Moses, & Christ, Corrupted by the Sodomytes* (Wesel, 1538; STC: 1287), sig. D4r.

[59] References are to Anthony Munday, *The Death of Robert, Earl of Huntingdon*, ed. by John C. Meagher (Oxford: Malone Society, 1967).

[60] Foxe, p. 69.

The proleptic irony of these lines, however, makes a very different point from Foxe, who treats John's death as a graphic example of Catholic interference in domestic politics by means of treacherous monks: 'I would ye did marke well the wholesome procedinges of these holye votaries, howe vertuously they obey their kynges, whome god hath appoynted'. By contrast, Munday and Chettle, notwithstanding the anti-Catholic language of John's speech, make his anticipated death the consequence of his inability to contain his lustful desires – not a feature of his reign in which Foxe shows the remotest interest.

Two relatively recent critics who consider the religious position of the *Huntingdon* plays, Donna Hamilton and David Womersley, both see it as ambivalent and contradictory, albeit with differences of emphasis. Hamilton acknowledges Robin's status as victim of 'the greed of a Catholic prior' and the corruption of the monks and nuns to whose protection Matilda entrusts herself after his death early in the second play. However, she also stresses the stories' 'strong associations with Catholic traditions', the emphasis on John's pursuit of Matilda rather than his conflicts with the Pope, and the similarities between the wrongful accusations and expropriations that Robin suffers and the treatment of Elizabethan Catholics.[61] Womersley, too, accepts that the plays' ostensible anti-Catholicism is tempered by 'positive depictions of indisputably Catholic places, objects, and activities' such as the dying Robin's request to be buried with 'My beades and Primer' (l. 808) and the broadly sympathetic treatment of Matilda's decision to become a nun. However, he treats these elements as 'touches of ecumenical longing' that temper the 'strident Protestantism' revealed by the plays' allusions to touchstones of Reformation historiography such as the donation of Constantine and Henry II's quarrel with Beckett.[62]

In their different ways, both Hamilton and Womersley regard the plays as having a final religious allegiance, be that Catholicism (albeit protectively concealed) or Protestantism (albeit tinged with nostalgia). Another way of reading *The Downfall* and *The Death*, however, might be to recognise them as inherently, even deliberately fluid in this respect, rather than seeking to identify a definitive position. The way Robin combines opposition to the ungoverned temporal power of the Catholic Church, and death of the hands of its corrupt ministers, with a request to be buried with beades and primer 'At *Wakefield*, vnderneath the Abbey wall' (l. 805), not to mention chaste adoration of a virgin called Marian, is but one example of

---

[61] Hamilton, pp. 129–30, 137.   [62] Womersley, pp. 364–5, 368.

the plays' tendency to endow the same figure with apparently contradictory attitudes and characteristics. Another is their depiction of Friar Tuck. At times, the Friar is an attractively subversive figure: in *The Downfall* he helps Robin rescue Scarlet and Scathlock from hanging (allotted the vivid stage direction, 'the Frier, making as if he helpt the Sheriffe, knockes downe his men, crying, keepe the kings peace' (ll. 989–91)), and he subsequently determines to join Robin and his men in Sherwood. However, he also anticipates Sir John of Wrotham in his conformity to the stereotype of the worldly prelate, such as when he leers after Maid Marian 'Now by the reliques of the holy Masse, / A prettie girle, a very bonny lasse' (ll. 830–1). The plays are no less ambivalent towards nuns than they are towards the friar. In *The Downfall*, in an evocative account of his life on the run with Scathlock, Scarlet remembers how 'The Nunnes of Farnsfield, pretty Nunnes they bee, / Gaue napkins, shirts, and bands to him and mee' (ll. 1288–9). Here, the nuns' charity is assimilated to a picaresque outlaw narrative in a way that mildly sexualises them without really impugning their chastity. But when the Prior of York tries to tempt Friar Tuck into betraying Robin, he offers his co-conspirator a rather different image of the religious life: 'Come good sir *Doncaster*, and if we thriue, / Weele frolicke with the Nunnes of Leeds beliue' (ll. 1465–6). This promise, though light on detail, presumably extends to more than just cadging shirts, and suggests the kind of activities that are hinted at in the Queen's Men play *The Troublesome Raigne of John King of England* (printed 1591), where a nun is found hiding in an abbot's chest.

The Death of Robert, Earl of Huntingdon is, if anything, even more radically contradictory in its treatment of the religious life than is the first play. Matilda's decision to escape the pursuit of John by fleeing 'to *Dunmow* Abbey, / Where I will end my life a votary' (ll. 1958–9) is treated without irony, and is welcomed by her father (ll. 2066–7). The refusal of the Abbess to let the King within its walls, pleading the right to sanctuary of 'honorable maids distrest, / Religious virgins, holy Nunnes profest' (ll. 2134–5) presents the nunnery as a place of refuge from a tyrannical monarchy. However, the Abbess's stance is immediately undercut by the revelation that 'there is a Monke of *Bury*, / That once a weake comes thither to make merry' (ll. 2140–4), and indeed we later see the Monk and the Abbess attempting to persuade Matilda to give in to John, who has promised the Abbey a hundred marks a year in return. As with Abigall in Marlowe's *The Jew of Malta*, a woman's decision to take the veil is presented with sympathy as the product of personal integrity, while the institution she joins is shown to be profoundly corrupt: 'Where shall a

maid haue certaine sanctuary, / When Ladie Lust rules all the Nunnery?'
(ll. 2554–5). In this play, though, the tableau of the final scene seems to
reassert the dignity of the spiritual ideals for which Matilda has died,
whatever the shortcomings of religious houses in practising those ideals:
'A march for buriall, with drum and fife. Enter Oxford, Matilda borne with
Nuns, one carrying a white pendant. These words writ in golde; Amoris,
Castitatis, & Honoris honos. The Queene following the Biere, carrying a
Garland of flowers: set it in the midst of the Stage' (ll. 2908–11). This
powerful image, along with the concluding epitaph to 'Matilda martyrde,
for her chastitie' (l. 3049), at least complicates the anti-monastic attitudes in
evidence elsewhere in the play.

Contradictions such as these render The Downfall and The Death of
Robert, Earl of Huntingdon unexpectedly open plays, susceptible to readings from diverse confessional perspectives. One feature of The Downfall
that reveals some suggestive facets when viewed from an angle that does
not assume 'strident Protestantism' is its treatment of the exile to which
Robin and his supporters submit. Robin's decision, following his
outlawing and the expropriation of his goods, 'To keepe in Sherewodde,
till the kings returne, / And being outlawed, leade an outlawes life'
(Downfall, ll. 1013–14), has been read as an allegory for the experience of
radical puritans, whose 'attempt to carry through a further reformation of
the Church was temporarily abandoned' following the prosecutions of
leading ministers in the Court of High Commission and the Star Chamber
from 1589 onwards.[63] David Bevington, for example, writes of the outlaws
creating a 'Puritan world in exile' in the face of 'an elaborate fable of an
oppressive administration and church, which drive all well-intentioned
men into outlawry'.[64] The motif of exile, however, was not an inherently
Protestant one in the sixteenth century: as Jane Kingsley-Smith points out,
'The Reformation and counter-Reformation inspired waves of religious
exile, with conspicuous numbers of high-ranking Catholics and Protestants
either leaving for or returning from the Continent upon the succession of
each Tudor monarch'.[65] In The Downfall, while the foresters jointly
undertake never to 'spare a Priest, a vsurer, or a clarke' (l. 1355) from their
predations, their collective vow of chastity and the central importance
among them of a maiden who renames herself Marian could equally be
read as implying a Catholic religious community. Furthermore, the

---

[63] Patrick Collinson, The Elizabethan Puritan Movement (London: Jonathan Cape, 1967), p. 432.
[64] Bevington, pp. 295–6.
[65] Jane Kingsley-Smith, Shakespeare's Drama of Exile (Basingstoke: Palgrave Macmillan, 2003), p. 175.

description by Warman (the Sheriff of Nottingham) of Scarlet and Scath-lock as 'scapethrifts, vnthrifts' (l. 934) and of Robin as one of those 'That reuell, wast and spende, and take no care' (l. 976) arguably identifies Warman himself, rather than the outlaws, with the social and economic attitudes associated with puritanism, although Womersley (for one) would contest this view.[66]

The potential for exile, as a theme, to be read in specifically Catholic terms is evident from the way it has been approached by critics of another text from the late 1590s that depicts outlawed aristocrats in a woodland setting. That is, of course, Shakespeare's *As You Like It*, where the deposed Duke Senior and his followers take refuge in the forest of Arden, '*dressed as foresters*' (2.1.0s.d.), and are said to live 'like the old Robin Hood of England' (1.1.93–4).[67] Peter Milward notes that in the source, Thomas Lodge's *Rosalynde*, the forest of Arden is identified 'with the Ardennes in the Low Countries (where many Catholics had gone into exile from the beginning of Elizabeth's reign)'; accordingly, in *As You Like It* 'the situation of the former Duke, deposed and in exile, clearly corresponds in Elizabethan terms to that of the Catholic exiles in the Low Countries'.[68] Carol Enos goes further, identifying parallels between the play and 'the story of the exile Thomas Hoghton I, who left the country "for con-science's sake" and placed his property in the hands of a brother', while Richard Wilson, as well as noting the Ardennes connection, links *As You Like It* to the 'unofficial seminary in the Forest of Arden' started by Shakespeare's relative Edward Throckmorton, who 'left Stratford for Rome in 1580'.[69] Admittedly, these readings depend to some extent on the associations of Arden / Ardennes as a location, and so do not apply to the Robin Hood plays. But they also point to the inherent ambivalence of exile as a theme when it is interpreted as a comment on the situation of a persecuted religious minority in Elizabethan England. As used by Munday,

---

[66] Womersley links the outlaws' wastefulness with the parable of the prodigal son, used 'as a statement of the Protestant doctrine of justification by faith alone, and of the insufficiency of good works in the business of salvation', p. 363.

[67] References are to William Shakespeare, *As You Like It*, ed. by Michael Hattaway, updated edn (Cambridge: Cambridge University Press, 2009).

[68] Peter Milward, *The Catholicism of Shakespeare's Plays, Renaissance Monographs*, 23 (Tokyo: Renaissance Institute, 1997), p. 25.

[69] Carol Enos, 'Catholic Exiles in Flanders and As You Like It; or, What if You Don't Like It at All?', in *Theatre and Religion: Lancastrian Shakespeare*, ed. by Richard Dutton, Alison Findlay and Richard Wilson (Manchester: Manchester University Press, 2003), pp. 130–42, p. 130; Richard Wilson, *Secret Shakespeare: Studies in Theatre, Religion and Resistance* (Manchester: Manchester University Press, 2004), p. 16.

it can certainly be read as alluding to the puritan experience; but that is far from being the only possible interpretation.

The prominence of forest exile in *As You Like It* and the Huntingdon plays may well be the result of direct influence, as critics including Meredith Skura and Michael Hattaway have suggested.[70] *The Downfall* and *The Death* were licensed for performance in late March 1598 and revised 'for the corte' in November, which would have both allowed ample opportunity for Shakespeare to have encountered them before the presumed date of his play and provided evidence of the suitability of Robin Hood materials for court performance.[71] Furthermore, Shakespeare's knowledge of the two plays is apparent from the echoes of them that Womersley finds in *Othello* and *Macbeth*.[72] Finally, as A. H. Thorndike pointed out in 1902, there are several elements of *As You Like It* that do not appear in *Rosalynde* but do appear in *The Downfall* or *The Death*, suggesting that Shakespeare's treatment of his source material was influenced by Munday and Chettle. Shakespeare devotes much more space to the depiction of the woodland life enjoyed by the Duke than does Lodge, and the Duke's opening speech, which asks, 'Hath not old custom made this life more sweet / Than that of painted pomp? Are not these woods / More free from peril than the envious court?' (2.1.2–4) has its counterpart in a speech in *The Downfall* that begins, 'Marian, thou seest though courtly pleasures want, / Yet country sport, in Sherewodde is not scant' (ll. 1366–7), and describes the birdsong, flora and 'Christall brooke' (l. 1377) that surpass their court equivalents. In both plays, the cheerful outlook of the foresters is depicted as a conscious response to misfortune and grief: 'happy is your grace', comments Amiens, 'That can translate the stubbornness of Fortune / Into so quiet and so sweet a style' (2.1.18–20), while Robin has to charge his followers to 'neuer more let woefull sound / Be heard among yee; but what euer fall, / Laugh griefe to scorne; and so make sorrowes small' (ll. 1318–20). The hunting of deer is made a feature of life in Shakespeare's Arden in a way that it is not in Lodge, and the fourth scene of *The Death* begins with '*Frier* Tuck *carrying a Stags head, dauncing*' (ll. 333–4) in a way that foreshadows the curious 'What shall he have that killed the deer?' song in *As You Like It* (4.2.8). And in Robin's forgiveness of his murderers in *The Death* Thorndike finds the source of the 'spirit of repentance and forgiveness' that informs Duke Senior's hospitality

---

[70] Meredith Skura, 'Anthony Munday's "Gentrification" of Robin Hood', *English Literary Renaissance*, 33 (2003), 155–80 (p. 155); *As You Like It*, p. 51.

[71] *Henslowe's Diary*, pp. 88, 102. On dating, see *As You Like It*, pp. 49–54.

[72] Womersley, pp. 379, 302. The relevant lines are 'The dewe doth them a little rust' (*Downfall*, 2571) and 'The multitudes of seas died red with blood' (*Death*, 1391).

to Orlando, the latter's forgiveness of Oliver, and the conversion of Frederick; by contrast, in Lodge Torismond (the usurping duke) is 'sl[a]ine in battaile' at the story's climax, denying him the unexpected redemption that is made available to his equivalent in Shakespeare.[73]

Beyond these features of language, plot, setting and mood, however, I would argue that an important point of similarity between *As You Like It* and the Huntingdon plays is the playwrights' selection of motifs that are unmistakeably religiously coded yet at the same time ultimately ambivalent. One is the theme of exile, Shakespeare's treatment of which at first sight seems to provide ample basis for a Catholic reading such as is offered by Milward and others. Characters in *As You Like It* sometimes express a nostalgia that readily lends itself to this sort of interpretation, most obviously in the 'better days' exchange between Orlando and Duke Senior on their first meeting:

> DUKE SENIOR True is it that we have seen better days,
> And have with holy bell been knolled to church,
> And sat at goodmen's feasts, and wiped our eyes
> Of drops that sacred pity hath engendered. (2.7.120–23)

The idea of 'better days' of churchgoing and communal living that now lie in the past can be more easily fitted into a Catholic than a Protestant understanding of English history, while the fact that the old order is restored not by violence, but by the conversion of the reigning monarch encourages a reading of the difference between the past and present as being a specifically religious one. And as Arthur F. Marotti comments, the 'old religious man' on 'the skirts of this wild wood' (5.4.143–4) who is the means of Duke Frederick's conversion is himself arguably 'a figure from England's Catholic past: he recalls the older Marian clergy in hiding in the Warwickshire of Shakespeare's youth'.[74]

Details like these, however, can equally be read from the opposite perspective: Chris Butler, for example, takes the play's non-violent ending as a rejection of 'the necessity for papally-sponsored military intervention' to restore Catholicism, in keeping with what he sees as Shakespeare's Anglican rewriting of Lodge.[75] More radically, as the Huntingdon plays show, it is perfectly possible to read Elizabethan depictions of woodland

[73] Ashley Thorndike, 'The Relation of *As You Like It* to Robin Hood Plays', *Journal of Germanic Philology*, 4 (1902), 59–69 (p. 68); Thomas Lodge, *Rosalynde. Euphues Golden Legacie: Found after His Death in His Cell at Silexedra* (London, 1590; STC: 16664), sig. S1v.

[74] Arthur F. Marotti, 'Shakespeare and Catholicism', in *Theatre and Religion*, pp. 218–41 (p. 228).

[75] Chris Butler, 'Religion, Cognition and Author-Function: Dyer, Southwell, Lodge and *As You Like It*', unpublished PhD thesis, Sheffield Hallam University, 2013, p. 185.

exile in puritan terms; we might also remember the Protestants in *Oldcastle* who meet in 'solitary groves', or the Huguenots in Marlowe's *The Massacre at Paris* 'Which in the woods do hold their synagogue' (11.21).[76] One aspect of *As You Like It* that might encourage an identification of Duke Senior and his followers with a Protestant rather than a Catholic community is the emphasis on the Bible, and on preaching, that is evident at the end of his opening speech: 'this our life exempt from public haunt / Finds tongues in trees, books in the running brooks, / Sermons in stones, and good in everything' (2.1.15–17). Another is the fact that his name is and was a synonym for the controversial term 'elder', which presbyterians followed William Tyndale in preferring to 'bishop' when translating the New Testament. The doctrinally loaded nature of this debate would be illustrated in the King James Version of the Bible, where (as Gordon Campbell explains) 'The decision to retain "bishop" (instead of "elder" or "senior") reflects a decision to favour episcopacy rather than presbyterianism as a model of church government'.[77] For Elizabethan puritans, by contrast, the term was a shibboleth that implied the role of locally appointed officers in exercising 'powers of correction which were properly congregational' but had been usurped by 'bishops and archdeacons and their officials'.[78] As Martin complained in *Hay any Work for Cooper*, the hierarchy of the Church of England 'think that the offices of pastors, doctors, elders and deacons, or the most of them, may be as well now wanting in the church, as the offices of apostles, prophets and evangelists'. However, St Paul's first letter to the Corinthians shows 'that the platform of government by pastors, doctors, elders and deacons' is the invention of Christ – unlike 'the government of the church by lord archbishops and bishops'.[79]

The Marprelate pamphlets themselves seem to be glanced at in *As You Like It* with the inclusion of the character Sir Oliver Martext, the 'vicar of the next village' (3.4.31–2) whom Touchstone asks to marry him and Audrey, but who, Jaques objects, will merely 'join you together as they join wainscot' (65–6). The precise nature of the allusion, though, is difficult to gauge. Juliet Dusinberre suggests that it harks back to the anti-Martinist satire into which the bishops had enlisted playwrights and actors a decade earlier, a reading that would place the play's sympathies

[76] Christopher Marlowe, '*Dido Queen of Carthage' and 'The Massacre at Paris*', ed. by H. J. Oliver (London: Methuen, 1968).
[77] Gordon Campbell, *Bible: The Story of the King James Version* (Oxford: Oxford University Press, 2010), p. 82.
[78] Collinson, p. 346.   [79] *The Martin Marprelate Tracts*, pp. 112–14.

with the ecclesiastical hierarchy.[80] Milward, however, reads the Marprelate allusion differently, suggesting that Martext is 'a Puritan parson such as were commonly intruded into Elizabethan churches by the Protestant bishops to take the place of the Marian clergy'.[81] Finally, Hattaway ventures that 'Sir Oliver Martext is presumably what Spenser termed "a popish priest", unfamiliar with God's word'.[82] This alignment of the play with a puritan perspective would make sense in light of Martin's use of the 'mar' epithet against the archbishops and bishops in *Hay any Work for Cooper*: 'you Mar-state, Mar-law, Mar-prince, Mar-magistrate, Mar-commonwealth, Mar-church, and Mar-religion'.[83] The salient point, though, is the openness of Sir Oliver to wildly divergent readings: what looks like an unmistakeable allusion to a *cause célèbre* of religious politics proves impossible, under closer inspection, to pin down. The same may be true of Duke Senior's allusion to the 'holy bell' in his 'better days' speech: Hattaway notes that 'In pre-Reformation England bells were regularly consecrated, a practice decried by the Protestant John Foxe and others, who abjured in particular the ringing of the "holy bell" to help the soul of one recently dead out of purgatory', an observation that would appear to confirm the appearance of Catholic nostalgia in this speech. Hattaway, however, continues: 'it is conceivable that the phrase aligns itself with Reformation opinion on this matter'.[84] The same evidence can be made to yield up contradictory implications depending on preconception. It may be, of course, that such ambiguities would not have existed for early audiences of *As You Like It*: for example, if, as Dusinberre argues, the character Touchstone was played by Will Kemp, and the Martext material was designed to give him the chance to reprise 'one of his favourite comic turns: anti-Martinist satire, through the medium of a renowned jig', this would have been apparent in the theatre in a way that it is not on the page.[85] However, a strategy of conscious ambivalence on Shakespeare's part would have suited a commercial context in which it made sense to maintain as broad an appeal as possible given what Arthur Marotti describes as the 'religiously heterogeneous audience' of early modern drama.[86] It would also have been in keeping with the play's title, which seems to refer the task of interpretation to the preference of the speaker.

[80] Juliet Dusinberre, 'Topical Forest: Kemp and Mar-text in Arden', in *In Arden: Editing Shakespeare: Essays in Honour of Richard Proudfoot*, ed. Ann Thompson and Gordon McMullen (London: Arden Shakespeare, 2003), pp. 239–51.
[81] Milward, p. 31.   [82] *As You Like It*, p. 32.   [83] *The Martin Marprelate Tracts*, p. 118.
[84] *As You Like It*, 2.7.121n.   [85] Dusinberre, p. 247.   [86] Marotti, p. 228.

The view of Shakespeare's drama that this reading implies – as ambivalent and undetermined, in its religious position or in other respects – is a familiar one. In her recent book on Shakespeare and religion Alison Shell writes of the 'disengagements, tactfulnesses and voids by which Shakespeare defers to the sagacity of a paying audience', in similar language to Marotti's reference (in the chapter quoted above) to the 'indirection and ambiguity' with which Shakespeare handled 'both general and specifically topical religious subject matter'.[87] Leaving religion to one side, the openness and ambiguity of his plays is a characteristic that critics have regularly lauded: A. P. Rossiter and Norman Rabkin are two outstanding twentieth-century examples.[88] However, this chapter's reading of *Sir John Oldcastle* and the Huntingdon plays has suggested that such openness was not unique to Shakespeare or his company: even in plays that seem to be markedly protestant in their sympathies, Admiral's Men dramatists expressed attitudes and deployed motifs open to interpretation from other religious perspectives, from Catholic nostalgia to radical puritanism. This casts doubt on the assumption that their audience, at least in the 1590s, was dominated by a contingent of stolidly protestant citizens, while the reliance of *Sir John Oldcastle* on playgoers' familiarity with the *Henry IV* plays is one more piece of evidence suggesting significant overlap between their audience and that of the Lord Chamberlain's Men.

---

[87] Alison Shell, *Shakespeare and Religion* (London: Arden Shakespeare, 2010), p. 165; Marotti, p. 219.

[88] A. P. Rossiter, *Angel with Horns and Other Shakespearean Lectures*, ed. by Graham Storey (London: Longmans, 1961); Norman Rabkin, *Shakespeare and the Common Understanding* (New York: Free Press, 1967).

Conclusion

The openness of *As You Like It, Sir John Oldcastle* and the two *Earl of Huntingdon* plays to readings from diverse religious perspectives testifies to the problems involved in answering one of the questions posed by this book: whether the Admiral's Men's plays of the 1590s exhibit an identifiable company style or allegiance distinct from what is visible in Shakespeare. On the surface, the dramas' explicitly Protestant sympathies, evident from the choice of Oldcastle as a hero and from the negative depiction of Catholic prelates in the Robin Hood plays, as well as their focus on the victims of royal (or ecclesiastical) power rather than its exercisers, supports the position of Helgerson and others who would align the company with the views of Protestants of the middling sort, possibly tending towards puritanism. This would also chime with the interest in non-aristocratic characters evident in plays like *Englishmen for My Money* and *The Two Angry Women of Abington*, as well as plays not discussed in detail in this book such as *The Shoemakers' Holiday*.

On further consideration, though, this argument proves harder to sustain. For one thing, despite the critiques of papal power offered in *Oldcastle* and the Huntington plays, they incorporate an array of contradictory attitudes, including nostalgia for Catholic devotional practices, acclaim for monastic chastity and suspicion of the doctrine of salvation *sola fide*. For another, there are numerous features of the company's 1590s repertory that do not fit this model, such as the mockery of puritans in *A Knack to Know an Honest Man* and *An Humorous Day's Mirth*; the victorious position of the gentlemen characters at the end of *Englishmen for My Money*; the focus of *Captain Thomas Stukeley* on a Catholic traitor who plans to invade Ireland; and the continued presence in the repertory of the plays of Christopher Marlowe, hardly a figure one associates with citizen heroes or Protestant orthodoxy.

The presence of Marlowe does, admittedly, represent one factor that arguably gave the Admiral's repertory a distinctive quality. Not only did the company continue to stage his plays, as well as paying £4 for additions to *Doctor Faustus* in 1602 and nearly twice as much for costumes for *The Massacre at Paris* in 1601; its dramatists can frequently be seen alluding to or otherwise engaging with his work, whether in the Mediterranean setting and usurer's daughter plot of *A Knack to Know an Honest Man*, the rhetorical flights of Stukeley, the magic of *John a Kent* (if it was *The Wise Man of West Chester*), or the parodic Barabas of *Englishmen for My Money*.[1] These plays provide some substantiation for Andrew Gurr's forceful claim, 'It can hardly be wrong to identify Marlowe with the Admiral's long career as much as we do Shakespeare with their opposites.'[2]

The same plays, however, also provide evidence for contrary arguments, in that they demonstrate the influence upon Admiral's Men dramatists of Shakespeare himself. *Stukeley*'s echoes of *A Midsummer Night's Dream* and *Richard II*, the allusions to *Romeo and Juliet* in *Englishmen* and *The Two Angry Women*, not to mention the explicit engagement with the *Henry IV* plays in *Oldcastle*: all of these show the company's repertory to have been shaped by the innovations of the principal dramatist of the Lord Chamberlain's Men as well as by Marlowe's example. Not only that: in assuming their audience's familiarity with Falstaff, the *Oldcastle* dramatists indicate that 1590s playgoers did not confine themselves to the offerings of one company, but moved between their playhouses. This further suggests that we should read the echoes of (for example) *Romeo and Juliet* in *The Two Angry Women* not simply as imitations, but as allusions designed to be recognised as such.

The direction of influence between Shakespeare and the Admiral's Men was not all one way, however. Most obviously, the Marlowe plays in the Admiral's repertory, as well as providing artistic models, continued to be performed, and to offer Shakespeare examples of what a profitable play might look like. It is against the background of *The Jew of Malta* and *Doctor Faustus* that *The Merchant of Venice* and *A Midsummer Night's Dream* were written and staged. However, as this book has demonstrated, new plays in the company's repertory also affected Shakespeare's choice of subject matter, idiom and dramatic structure: plays like the Venetian comedy of faithful friends, *A Knack to Know an Honest Man*, and the Robin Hood plays, with their depiction of woodland exile. In some cases it

---

[1] *Henslowe's Diary*, ed. by R. A. Foakes [and R. T. Rickert], 2nd edn (Cambridge: Cambridge University Press, 2002), pp. 183–5, 206.
[2] Andrew Gurr, *Shakespeare's Opposites: The Admiral's Company 1594–1625* (Cambridge: Cambridge University Press, 2009), p. 199.

is impossible to be absolutely sure which play came first: *Captain Thomas Stukeley* or *1 Henry IV*, *An Humorous Day's Mirth* or *The Merry Wives of Windsor*. However, if *1 Henry IV* did precede *Stukeley*, then it has implications for the dating of Shakespeare's play, while there is no doubt that both were preceded by the lost Admiral's Men play *Harry V*, and *The Merry Wives of Windsor* by Chapman's proto-humours comedy, *The Blind Beggar of Alexandria*. Similarly, while it cannot be conclusively proved that *The Wise Man of West Chester* is the same play as *John a Kent and John a Cumber*, at the very least its title shows that magician plays in the *John a Kent* vein, as well *The Grecian Comedy* and the Chaucerian *Palamon and Arcite*, were being staged by the Admiral's Men, demonstrating the saleability of a play like *A Midsummer Night's Dream*.

I therefore hope this book has done something to deepen understanding of the dramatic culture of the mid- to late-1590, and of Shakespeare's place within it. In this period, the impact of Marlowe continued to be felt, although dramatists chose to transform the tragic materials of *Doctor Faustus* and *The Jew of Malta* into comedy and to diminish the religious threat posed by magic in the former play. Shakespeare followed the practice of other playwrights when he did likewise in *A Midsummer Night's Dream* and *The Merchant of Venice*. His subjection of the Tamburlaine-style hero to scrutiny in the form of Hotspur in *1 Henry IV* paralleled that in *Captain Thomas Stukeley* around the same time, not to mention the much earlier Admiral's play *The Battle of Alcazar*. Shakespeare's early work for the Lord Chamberlain's Men proves to have been very much of its dramatic moment, and informed by work of Admiral's Men dramatists.

The development of a new style of comedy – contemporary, materialistic, 'humours'-based – with *An Humorous Day's Mirth*, *Englishmen for My Money* and *The Two Angry Women of Abington* was another trend in which Shakespeare participated with *The Merry Wives of Windsor*. At the same time, though, Shakespeare's own influence was making itself felt by Admiral's Men dramatists: an awareness of *Love's Labour's Lost*, *The Merchant of Venice* and *Romeo and Juliet* is evident in those offerings. *Sir John Oldcastle* responds explicitly to the work of Shakespeare, offering a revised depiction of the Lollard martyr, although its relationship to *Henry IV* proves to be one of interdependence as well as riposte. Furthermore, the example of *As You Like It* shows Shakespeare at the end of the 1590s to have remained sensitive to what the Admiral's were doing: his reshaping of his source was informed by Munday and Chettle's Robin Hood plays, while his ambivalent treatment of the religious overtones inherent in the theme of exile parallels theirs.

Oldcastle also forces us to confront another of the questions posed earlier in this book: that of the influence on the company of its patron, Charles Howard. The unusual cash gift from Henslowe to the playwrights on the occasion of its premiere can be more plausibly linked to the content of the play than to its box office receipts, which seem to have been good rather than exceptional. Howard's alliance with the current Lord Cobham, whom his daughter would later marry, provides a possible explanation, although that does not answer the question of exactly who commissioned the play. The success of *Henry IV* would in itself have given the Admiral's Men a good reason to stage a drama purporting to tell the real story of Oldcastle, irrespective of any interference by Privy Councillors (or any attempt by Henslowe to curry favour with them). There is also the related problem of whether Howard intended his company to stage plays that articulated a particular religious or political position, as McMillin and MacLean hypothesised for the Queen's Men. As has already been noted, there are aspects of *Oldcastle* and the Huntingdon plays that seem fit the agenda McMillin and MacLean identify for the earlier company: 'to spread Protestant and royalist propaganda ... and to close a breach within radical Protestantism', as *Oldcastle* does in insisting on the protagonist's political loyalism. That play's claim, in its prologue, to be presenting 'fair truth' rather than 'forged invention' also echoes the emphasis on 'truth' that McMillin and MacLean find in the English history plays of the Queen's Men; indeed, one of its dramatists, Robert Wilson, had written and acted for the other company.[3] However, the Catholic sympathies that are also evident in parts of these plays make it hard to argue for a consistently implemented religious agenda, whether in carrying out a hypothetical policy of the company's patron or in appealing to the prejudices of its audience. Unlike the Queen's Men, the Admiral's were very much a London company, with a long-term base at the Rose and then the Fortune. The need to attract playgoers on a daily basis from London's diverse population, rather than arriving, performing and then moving on to the next town, may have encouraged a more ambivalent treatment of England's religious divisions.

Whether the company attempted to maintain a diversity of appeal, in religious, social or other terms, beyond the year 1600 is a question this book does not attempt to answer. In my first book, *Work and Play on the Shakespearean Stage*, I followed Andrew Gurr's precedent in supposing that the turn-of-the-century revival of the children's companies, whose dramatists

---

[3] Scott McMillin and Sally-Beth MacLean, *The Queen's Men and Their Plays* (Cambridge: Cambridge University Press, 1998), pp. 166, 33.

rhetorically aligned them with the upper social strata, encouraged the Admiral's to appeal more specifically to London's citizenry by way of response.[4] Certainly, as we saw in the Introduction, by the second decade of the sixteen century some references to the Fortune in print were associating it with old plays, spectacle and non-elite audiences. However, the small number of plays that have survived from the repertory of the Admiral's successor companies, the Prince's and then the Palsgrave's Men, makes it difficult to chart any such development with precision. On the one hand, plays such as Samuel Rowley's *When You See Me You Know Me* (1604) and Thomas Dekker's *The Whore of Babylon* (1606) offer loyalist Protestant accounts of England's history. On the other, Thomas Middleton's *No Wit, No Help Like a Woman's* (1611), and his and Dekker's *The Roaring Girl* (1611), seem much less stolid fare, embracing themes such as transvestism, incest and homosexuality. The former is generically playful, parodying the miraculous revelations of Shakespeare's late plays; the latter is shifting in its social allegiances, satirising cuckolded citizens and lecherous gallants alike. In the absence of further evidence, it is impossible to know whether these or plays like Rowley's were more typical of the company's Jacobean repertory.

As far as its 1590s repertory is concerned, though, the company's offerings were extremely diverse. They staged comedies of love and friendship such as *A Knack to Know an Honest Man*, of fashionable urban life such as the ground-breaking *An Humorous Day's Mirth*, and of family tensions between provincial bourgeois neighbours such as *The Two Angry Women of Abington*. With *Englishmen for My Money* they apparently invented London city comedy. In *Captain Thomas Stukeley* they depicted the life and death of a notorious adventurer, reflecting indirectly on contemporary affairs. In *Oldcastle* and the Robin Hood plays they took on the vexed question of modern England's relationship to its religious past, combining a rejection of papal power with a nostalgia for aspects of medieval Catholicism. A longer book than the present one could have addressed the urban festivity of *The Shoemakers' Holiday* or the strange blend of marital test and comical satire that is *Patient Grissil*. All of this is to say that, while a repertory-based approach may encourage the identification of a company style, perhaps the best response to the varied, innovative and ideologically unfixed drama of the Admiral's Men between 1594 and 1600, open to the influence of Shakespeare while shaping his own dramatic development, is to refrain from doing so.

---

[4] Tom Rutter, *Work and Play on the Shakespearean Stage* (Cambridge: Cambridge University Press, 2008), p. 110.

Bibliography

WORKS PUBLISHED BEFORE 1700

Where available, entries include Short-Title Catalogue number (STC) as given in A. W. Pollard and G. R. Redgrave, *A Short-Title Catalogue of Books Printed in England, Scotland, & Ireland, and of English Books Printed Abroad 1475-1640*, 2nd edn, rev. W. A. Jackson, F. S. Ferguson and Katharine F. Pantzer, 2 vols. (London: Bibliographical Society, 1986).

Anon, *The Famous Historye of the Life and Death of Captaine Thomas Stukeley* (London, 1605; STC: 23405)

Anon, *The Famous History of Fryer Bacon* (London, 1629; STC: 1184)

Anon, *A Most Pleasant Comedie of Mucedorus* (London, 1610; STC: 18232)

Anon, *A New and Mery Enterlude, Called the Triall of Treasure* (London, 1567; STC: 24271)

Anon, *The Second Tome of Homilees* (London, 1571; STC: 13669)

B., M., *The Triall of True Friendship or Perfit Mirror, Wherby to Discerne a Trustie Friend from a Flattering Parasite* (London, 1596; STC: 1053)

Bale, John, *The Actes of Englysh Votaryes* (Antwerp, 1546 (false imprint); STC: 1270)

    A Brefe Chronycle Concernynge the Examinacyon and Death of the Blessed Martyr of Christ Syr Iohan Oldecastell the Lorde Cobham ([Antwerp], 1544; STC: 1276)

    A Comedy Concernynge Thre Lawes, of Nature Moses, & Christ, Corrupted by the Sodomytes (Wesel, 1538; STC: 1287)

Chapman, George, *The Blinde Begger of Alexandria* (London, 1598; STC: 4965)

Dent, Arthur, *The Plaine Mans Path-way to Heauen* (London, 1601; STC: 6626.5)

Drayton, Michael, *Matilda. The Faire and Chaste Daughter of the Lord Robert Fitzwater* (London, 1594; STC: 7205)

Ferne, John, *The Blazon of Gentrie* (London, 1586; STC: 10825)

Foxe, John, *Actes and Monuments* (London, 1563; STC: 11222)

Fuller, Thomas, *The History of the Worthies of England* (London, 1662)

Fulwell, Ulpian, *An Enterlude Intituled Like Wil to Like Quod the Deuel to the Colier* (London, 1568; STC: 11473)

Greene, Robert, *Greenes Farewell to Folly* (London, 1591; STC 12241)

Haughton, William, *English-men for My Money: or, A Pleasant Comedy, Called, A Woman Will Haue Her Will* (London, 1616; STC: 12931)

Heywood, Thomas, *The First and Second Partes of King Edward the Fourth* (London, 1599; STC: 13341)

Holinshed, Raphael, et al., *The First and Second Volumes of Chronicles* (London, 1587; STC: 13569)

The Third Volume of Chronicles (London, 1587; STC: 13569)

Ingeland, Robert, *A Pretie and Mery New Enterlude: Called the Disobedient Child* (London, 1570; STC: 14085)

Lodge, Thomas, *Rosalynde. Euphues Golden Legacie: Found after His Death in His Cell at Silexedra* (London, 1590; STC: 16664)

Marlowe, Christopher, *Tamburlaine the Great* (London, 1590; STC: 17425) and Thomas Nashe, *The Tragedie of Dido Queene of Carthage* (London, 1594; STC: 17441).

Meres, Francis, *Palladis Tamia: Wits Treasury* (London, 1598; STC: 17834)

Middleton, Thomas, and Thomas Dekker, *The Roaring Girle* (London, 1611; STC: 17908)

More, Thomas, *A Dyaloge of Syr Thomas More Knyghte ... Wheryn be Treatyd Dyuers Maters, as of the Veneracyon & Worshyp of Ymagys & Relyques, Prayng to Sayntis, & Goynge on Pylgrymage* (London, 1530; STC: 18085)

Munday, Anthony, et al., *The First Part of the True and Honorable Historie, of the Life of Sir John Old-castle, the Good Lord Cobham* (London, 1600; STC: 18795)

Nashe, Thomas, *Pierce Penilesse His Supplication to the Diuell* (London, 1592; STC: 18371)

Oates, Titus, Εικων Βασιλικη Τριτη; *or, The Picture of the Late King James Further Drawn to the Life* (London, 1697)

Εικων Βασιλικη Τεταρτη; *or, The Picture of the Late King James Further Drawn to the Life* (London, 1697)

Peele, George, *A Farewell. Entituled to the Famous and Fortunate Generalls of Our English Forces* (London, 1589; STC: 19537)

Perkins, William, *A Discourse of the Damned Art of Witchcraft* (Cambridge, 1610; STC: 19698)

A Golden Chaine: or, The Description of Theologie Containing the Order of the Causes of Saluation and Damnation, According to Gods Word (Cambridge, 1600; STC: 19646)

Scot, Reginald, *The Discouerie of Witchcraft* (London, 1584; STC: 21864)

Shakespeare, William, *The History of Henrie the Fovrth* (London, 1598; STC: 22280)

A Most Pleasaunt and Excellent Conceited Comedie, of Syr Iohn Falstaffe, and the Merrie Wiues of Windsor (London, 1602; STC: 22299)

Stephens, John, *Essayes and Characters: Ironicall, and Instrvctive* (London, 1615; STC: 23250)

Stow, John, *The Annales of England* (London, 1592; STC: 23334)

Tatham, John, *The Fancies Theater* (London, 1640; STC: 23704)

Turner, William, *The Rescuynge of the Romishe Fox* ([Bonn], 1545; STC: 24355)

WORKS PUBLISHED AFTER 1700

Adams, Joseph Quincy, Jr., 'Captaine Thomas Stukeley', *Journal of English and Germanic Philology*, 15 (1916), 107–29

Ardolino, Frank R., 'Robert Greene's Use of the Lambert Simnell Imposture in *Friar Bacon and Friar Bungay*', *American Notes and Queries*, 20 (1981), 37–9

Armitage, David, Conal Condren and Andrew Fitzmaurice, eds., *Shakespeare and Early Modern Political Thought* (Cambridge: Cambridge University Press, 2009)

Arrell, Douglas H., 'John a Kent, the Wise Man of Westchester', *Early Theatre*, 17.1 (2014), 75–92

Ashton, J. W., '"Rymes of . . . Randolf, Erl of Chestre"', *ELH*, 5 (1938), 195–206

Assarsson-Rizzi, Kerstin, '*Friar Bacon and Friar Bungay*': *A Structural and Thematic Analysis of Robert Greene's Play*, *Lund Studies in English*, 44 (Lund: C. W. K. Gleepup, 1972)

Baldwin, T. W., *The Organization and Personnel of the Shakespearean Company* (Princeton: Princeton University Press, 1927)

Barber, C. L., *Shakespeare's Festive Comedy: A Study of Dramatic Form and its Relation to Social Custom* (Princeton: Princeton University Press, 1959)

Barker, Roberta, 'Tragical-Comical-Historical Hotspur', *Shakespeare Quarterly*, 54 (2003), 288–307

Barroll, J. Leeds, *Politics, Plague, and Shakespeare's Theatre: The Stuart Years* (Ithaca: Cornell University Press, 1991)

  'Shakespeare and the Second Blackfriars Theatre', *Shakespeare Studies*, 33 (2005), 156–70

  Alexander Leggatt, Richard Hosley and Alvin Kernan, *The Revels History of Drama in English*, vol. III: *1576–1613* (London: Methuen, 1975)

Bartels, Emily C., and Emma Smith, eds., *Christopher Marlowe in Context* (Cambridge: Cambridge University Press, 2013)

Bayer, Mark, *Theatre, Community, and Civic Engagement in Jacobean London* (Iowa City: University of Iowa Press, 2011)

Beaumont, Francis, *The Knight of the Burning Pestle*, ed. by Michael Hattaway (London: Ernest Benn, 1969)

Beckerman, Bernard, *Shakespeare at the Globe 1599–1609* (New York: Macmillan, 1962)

Belsey, Catherine, 'Love in Venice', *Shakespeare Survey*, 44 (1992), 41–53

Bentley, G. E., *The Profession of Dramatist in Shakespeare's Time 1590–1642* (Princeton: Princeton University Press, 1971)

Berek, Peter, '*Tamburlaine's* Weak Sons: Imitation as Interpretation Before 1593', *Renaissance Drama*, 13 (1982)

Berry, Edward, 'Laughing at "Others"', in *The Cambridge Companion to Shakespearean Comedy*, ed. by Alexander Leggatt (Cambridge: Cambridge University Press, 2002), pp. 123–38

Betteridge, Thomas, and Greg Walker, eds., *The Oxford Handbook to Tudor Drama* (Oxford: Oxford University Press, 2012)

Bevington, David M., *From 'Mankind' to Marlowe: Growth of Structure in the Popular Drama of Tudor England* (Cambridge, MA.: Harvard University Press, 1962)

Tudor Drama and Politics: A Critical Approach to Topical Meaning (Cambridge, MA.: Harvard University Press, 1968)

Black, Joseph L., ed., *The Martin Marprelate Tracts: A Modernized and Annotated Edition* (Cambridge: Cambridge University Press, 2008)

Bly, Mary, 'Bawdy Puns and Lustful Virgins: The Legacy of Juliet's Desire in Comedies of the Early 1600s', *Shakespeare Survey*, 49 (1996), 97–100

Queer Virgins and Virgin Queans on the Early Modern Stage (Oxford: Oxford University Press, 2000)

Bradbrook, Muriel, *The Growth and Structure of Elizabethan Comedy* (London: Chatto and Windus, 1955)

Themes and Conventions of Elizabethan Tragedy, 2nd edn (Cambridge: Cambridge University Press, 1980)

Briggs, K. M., *The Anatomy of Puck: An Examination of Fairy Beliefs among Shakespeare's Contemporaries and Successors* (London: Routledge and Kegan Paul, 1959)

Brody, Alan, *The English Mummers and Their Plays* (London: Routledge and Kegan Paul, n. d.)

Brown, Pamela Allen, *Better a Shrew than a Sheep: Women, Drama, and the Culture of Jest in Early Modern England* (Ithaca: Cornell University Press, 2003)

Brown, John Russell, and Bernard Harris, eds., *Early Shakespeare, Stratford-upon-Avon Studies, 3* (London: Edward Arnold, 1961)

Bruster, Douglas, *Drama and the Market in the Age of Shakespeare* (Cambridge: Cambridge University Press, 1992)

Bullough, Geoffrey, ed., *Narrative and Dramatic Sources of Shakespeare,* vol. I: *Early Comedies, Poems, 'Romeo and Juliet'* (London: Routledge and Kegan Paul; New York: Columbia University Press, 1957)

Burton, Dolores M., *Shakespeare's Grammatical Style: A Computer-Assisted Analysis of 'Richard II' and 'Antony and Cleopatra'* (Austin: University of Texas Press, 1973)

Butler, Chris, 'Religion, Cognition and Author-Function: Dyer, Southwell, Lodge and *As You Like It*', unpublished PhD thesis, Sheffield Hallam University, 2013

Calvo, Clara, 'Thomas Kyd and the Elizabethan Blockbuster: *The Spanish Tragedy*', in Ton Hoenselaars, ed., *Shakespeare and Contemporary Dramatists* (Cambridge: Cambridge University Press, 2012), pp. 19–33

Campbell, Gordon, *Bible: The Story of the King James Version* (Oxford: Oxford University Press, 2010)

Candido, Joseph, 'Captain Thomas Stukeley: The Man, the Theatrical Record, and the Origins of Tudor "Biographical" Drama', *Anglia*, 105 (1987), 50–68

Canny, Nicholas, 'O'Neill, Hugh, Second Earl of Tyrone (c.1550–1616)', *Oxford Dictionary of National Biography* (Oxford: Oxford University Press, 2004);

online edn, Jan 2008, www.oxforddnb.com/view/article/20775 (accessed 23 August 2015)

Carley, James P., 'Bourchier, John, Second Baron Berners (c.1467–1533)', *Oxford Dictionary of National Biography* (Oxford: Oxford University Press, 2004); online edn, www.oxforddnb.com/view/article/2990 (accessed 30 July 2015)

Cartelli, Thomas, 'Marlowe and Shakespeare Revisited', in Emily C. Bartels and Emma Smith, eds., *Christopher Marlowe in Context* (Cambridge: Cambridge University Press, 2013), pp. 285–95

Cathcart, Charles, '*Romeo* at the Rose in 1598', *Early Theatre*, 13 (2010), 149–62

Cerasano, S. P., 'Alleyn, Edward (1566–1626)', *Oxford Dictionary of National Biography* (Oxford: Oxford University Press, 2004); online edn, January 2008, www.oxforddnb.com/view/article/398 (accessed 29 July 2015)

'Edward Alleyn, the New Model Actor, and the Rise of the Celebrity in the 1590s', *Medieval and Renaissance Drama in England*, 18 (2005), 47–58

Chamberlain, John, *The Letters of John Chamberlain*, ed. by Norman Egbert McClure, 2 vols. (Philadelphia: American Philosophical Society, 1939)

Chambers, E. K., *The Elizabethan Stage*, 4 vols. (Oxford: Clarendon Press, 1923)

Champion, Larry S., '"Havoc in the Commonwealth": Perspective, Political Ideology, and Dramatic Strategy in *Sir John Oldcastle* and the English Chronicle Plays', *Medieval and Renaissance Drama in England*, 5 (1991), 165–79

Chapman, George, *An Humorous Day's Mirth*, ed. by Charles Edelman (Manchester: Manchester University Press, 2010)

The Plays of George Chapman: The Comedies: A Critical Edition, ed. by Allan Holaday (Urbana: University of Illinois Press, 1970)

Charney, Maurice, 'The Voice of Marlowe's Tamburlaine in Early Shakespeare', *Comparative Drama*, 31 (1997), 213–23

Cicero, Marcus Tullius, *De senectute, De amicitia, De divinatione*, tr. by William Armistead Falconer (London: Heinemann; New York: Putnam's Sons, 1923)

Clare, Janet, '*Art Made Tongue-Tied by Authority': Elizabethan and Jacobean Dramatic Censorship* (Manchester: Manchester University Press, 1990)

Shakespeare's Stage Traffic: Imitation, Borrowing and Competition in Renaissance Theatre (Cambridge: Cambridge University Press, 2014)

Clayton, Tom, Susan Brock and Vicente Forés, eds., *Shakespeare and the Mediterranean: The Selected Proceedings of the International Shakespeare Association World Congress, Valencia, 2001* (Newark: University of Delaware Press, 2004)

Coghill, Nevill, *Shakespeare's Professional Skills* (Cambridge: Cambridge University Press, 1964)

Collins, Arthur, ed., *Letters and Memorials of State*, 2 vols. (London, 1746)

Collinson, Patrick, *The Elizabethan Puritan Movement* (London: Jonathan Cape, 1967)

Cook, Ann Jennalie, *The Privileged Playgoers of Shakespeare's London, 1576–1642* (Princeton: Princeton University Press, 1981)

Corbin, Peter, and Douglas Sedge, eds., *The Oldcastle Controversy: 'Sir John Oldcastle, Part I' and 'The Famous Victories of Henry V'* (Manchester: Manchester University Press; New York: St. Martin's Press, 1991)

Cox, John D., *The Devil and the Sacred in English Drama, 1350–1642* (Cambridge: Cambridge University Press, 2000)

— and David Scott Kastan, eds., *A New History of Early English Drama* (New York: Columbia University Press, 1997)

Dean, Paul, *Friar Bacon and Friar Bungay* and *John of Bordeaux*: A Dramatic Diptych', *English Language Notes*, 28 (1980–81), 262–6

Deats, Sara Munson, 'Mars or Gorgon? Tamburlaine and Henry V', *Marlowe Studies: An Annual*, 1 (2011), 99–124

— and Robert A. Logan, eds., *Marlowe's Empery: Expanding His Critical Contexts* (Cranbury, NJ: Associated University Presses, 2002)

Dessen, Alan C., 'The "Estates" Morality Play', *Studies in Philology*, 62 (1965), 121–36

De Vocht, H., ed., *A Knack to Know an Honest Man* (Oxford: Malone Society, 1910)

Dimmock, Matthew, *New Turkes: Dramatizing Islam and the Ottomans in Early Modern England* (Aldershot: Ashgate, 2005)

Dorval, Patricia, and Jean-Marie Maguin, eds., *Shakespeare et ses Contemporains* (Paris: Société Français Shakespeare, 2002)

Dowd, Michelle M., and Natasha Korda, eds., *Working Subjects in Early Modern English Drama* (Farnham: Ashgate, 2011)

Dusinberre, Juliet, 'Topical Forest: Kemp and Mar-text in Arden', in Ann Thompson and Gordon McMullen, eds., *In Arden: Editing Shakespeare: Essays in Honour of Richard Proudfoot* (London: Arden Shakespeare, 2003), pp. 239–51

Dutton, Richard, *Mastering the Revels: The Regulation and Censorship of English Renaissance Drama* (Basingstoke: Macmillan, 1991)

— '"Methinks the Truth Should Live from Age to Age": The Dating and Contexts of *Henry V*', *Huntington Library Quarterly*, 68 (2005), 173–203

— ed., *The Oxford Handbook of Early Modern Theatre* (Oxford: Oxford University Press, 2009)

— Alison Findlay and Richard Wilson, eds., *Theatre and Religion: Lancastrian Shakespeare* (Manchester: Manchester University Press, 2003)

— and Jean E. Howard, eds., *A Companion to Shakespeare's Works*, vol. III: *The Comedies* (Malden: Blackwell, 2003)

Edelman, Charles, ed., *The Stukeley Plays* (Manchester: Manchester University Press, 2005)

Edwards, Richard, *The Works of Richard Edwards: Politics, Poetry and Performance in Sixteenth-Century England*, ed. by Ros King (Manchester: Manchester University Press, 2001)

Empson, William, *Faustus and the Censor: The English Faust-book and Marlowe's 'Doctor Faustus'*, ed. by John Henry Jones (Oxford: Blackwell, 1987)

Bibliography

Some Versions of Pastoral: A Study of the Pastoral Form in Literature (London: Chatto and Windus, 1935; repr. Harmondsworth: Peregrine, 1966)

Enos, Carol, 'Catholic Exiles in Flanders and *As You Like It*; or, What if You Don't Like It at All?', in Richard Dutton, Alison Findlay and Richard Wilson, eds., *Theatre and Religion: Lancastrian Shakespeare* (Manchester: Manchester University Press, 2003), pp. 130–42

Erickson, Peter, 'The Order of the Garter, the Cult of Elizabeth, and Class-Gender Tension in *The Merry Wives of Windsor*', in Jean E. Howard and Marion F. O'Connor, eds., *Shakespeare Reproduced: The Text in History and Ideology* (New York: Macmillan, 1987), pp. 116–40

Ettin, Andrew V., 'Magic into Art: The Magician's Renunciation of Magic in English Renaissance Drama', *Texas Studies in Literature and Language*, 19 (1977), 268–93

Fehrenbach, R. J., 'A Pre-1592 English Faust Book and the Date of Marlowe's *Doctor Faustus*', *The Library*, 2 (2001), 327–35

Fitzpatrick, Tim, *Playwright, Space and Place in Early Modern Performance: Shakespeare and Company* (Farnham: Ashgate, 2011)

Fleay, Frederick Gard, *A Chronicle History of the London Stage 1559–1642* (London: Reeves & Turner, 1890)

Fleck, Andrew, 'The Origins of *Englishmen for My Money*'s "Lover in the Basket" Episode in Doesborch's *Lyfe of Virgilius*', *Notes and Queries*, 57 (2010), 357–9

Forrest, John, *The History of Morris Dancing 1458–1750* (Cambridge: James Clark, 1990)

Franssen, Paul, 'George Chapman's Learned Drama', in Ton Hoenselaars, ed., *Shakespeare and Contemporary Dramatists* (Cambridge: Cambridge University Press, 2012),pp. 134–48

Freedman, Barbara, 'Shakespearean Chronology, Ideological Complicity, and Floating Texts: Something is Rotten in Windsor', *Shakespeare Quarterly*, 45 (1994), 190–210

Freeman, Arthur, 'Two Notes on *A Knack to Know a Knave*', *Notes and Queries*, 207 (1962), 326–7

Frye, Northrop, *A Natural Perspective: The Development of Shakespearean Comedy and Romance* (New York: Columbia University Press, 1965)

Garber, Marjorie, 'Marlovian Vision/Shakespearean Revision', *Research Opportunities in Renaissance Drama*, 22 (1979), 3–9

Gibbons, Brian, *Jacobean City Comedy*, 2nd edn (London: Methuen, 1980)

Gibson, James M., 'Shakespeare and the Cobham Controversy: The Oldcastle/ Falstaff and Brooke/Broome Revision', *Medieval and Renaissance Drama in England*, 25 (2012), 94–132

Grady, Hugh, *Shakespeare, Machiavelli, and Montaigne: Power and Subjectivity from 'Richard II' to 'Hamlet'* (Oxford: Oxford University Press, 2002)

Grav, Peter F., *Shakespeare and the Economic Imperative: 'What's Aught but as'tis Valued?'* (New York: Routledge, 2008)

Green, William, *Shakespeare's Merry Wives of Windsor* (Princeton: Princeton University Press, 1962)

Greenblatt, Stephen J., 'Marlowe, Marx, and Anti-Semitism', *Critical Inquiry*, 5 (1978), 291–307

Greene, Robert, *Friar Bacon and Friar Bungay*, ed. by J. A. Lavin (London: Ernest Benn, 1969)

Friar Bacon and Friar Bungay, ed. by Daniel Seltzer (London: Edward Arnold, 1964)

Griffin, Benjamin, 'Marring and Mending: Treacherous Likeness in Two Renaissance Controversies', *Huntington Library Quarterly*, 60 (1997), 363–80

Griffith, Eva, *A Jacobean Company and its Playhouse: The Queen's Servants at the Red Bull Theatre (c. 1605–1619)* (Cambridge: Cambridge University Press, 2013)

Guenther, Genevieve, 'Why Devils Came When Faustus Called for Them', *Modern Philology*, 109 (2011), 46–70

Gurr, Andrew, 'Henry Carey's Peculiar Letter', *Shakespeare Quarterly*, 56 (2005), 51–75

'Intertextuality at Windsor', *Shakespeare Quarterly*, 38 (1987), 189–200

Playgoing in Shakespeare's London, 2nd edn (Cambridge: Cambridge University Press, 1996)

The Shakespeare Company, 1594–1642 (Cambridge: Cambridge University Press, 2004)

Shakespeare's Opposites: The Admiral's Company 1594–1625 (Cambridge: Cambridge University Press, 2009)

The Shakespearian Playing Companies (Oxford: Clarendon Press, 1996)

'Three Reluctant Patrons and Early Shakespeare', *Shakespeare Quarterly*, 44 (1993), 159–74

'Venues on the Verges: London's Theater Government between 1594 and 1614', *Shakespeare Quarterly*, 61 (2010), 468–89

'Who Strutted and Bellowed?', *Shakespeare Survey*, 16 (1963), 95–102

Hackett, Helen, 'Introduction', in William Shakespeare, *A Midsummer Night's Dream*, ed. by Stanley Wells (London: Penguin, 2005), pp. xxi–lxxxvii

'*A Midsummer Night's Dream*', in Richard Dutton and Jean E. Howard, eds., *A Companion to Shakespeare's Works*, vol. III: *The Comedies* (Malden: Blackwell, 2003), pp. 338–57

Hamilton, Donna B., *Anthony Munday and the Catholics, 1580–1633* (Aldershot: Ashgate, 2005)

and Richard Strier, eds., *Religion, Literature, and Politics in Post-Reformation England, 1540–1688* (Cambridge: Cambridge University Press, 1996)

Hammer, Paul E. J., 'Devereux, Robert, Second Earl of Essex (1565–1601)', *Oxford Dictionary of National Biography* (Oxford: Oxford University Press, 2004); online edn, Oct 2008 www.oxforddnb.com/view/article/7565 (accessed 23 August 2015)

Hanabusa, Chiaki, ed., *The Famous Victories of Henry the Fifth* (Oxford: Malone Society, 2007)

Harbage, Alfred, *Shakespeare and the Rival Traditions* (New York: Macmillan, 1952)

Hattaway, Michael, *Elizabethan Popular Theatre: Plays in Performance* (London: Routledge and Kegan Paul, 1982)

Hawkes, Terence, ed., *Alternative Shakespeares Vol. II* (London: Routledge, 1996)

Haynes, Jonathan, *The Social Relations of Jonson's Theater* (Cambridge: Cambridge University Press, 1992)

Helgerson, Richard, *Adulterous Alliances: Home, State, and History in Early Modern European Drama and Painting* (Chicago: University of Chicago Press, 2000)

    Forms of Nationhood: The Elizabethan Writing of England (Chicago: University of Chicago Press, 1992)

Henslowe, Philip, *Henslowe's Diary*, ed. by R. A. Foakes [and R. T. Rickert], 2nd edn (Cambridge: Cambridge University Press, 2002)

    Henslowe's Diary, ed. by W. W. Greg, 2 vols. (London: A. H. Bullen, 1904–8)

Heywood, Thomas, *'Oenone and Paris' by T. H.: Reprinted from the Unique Copy in the Folger Shakespeare Library*, ed. by Joseph Quincy Adams (Washington DC: Folger Shakespeare Library, 1943)

    A Woman Killed With Kindness, ed. by Brian Scobie (London: A. & C. Black, 1985)

Highley, Christopher, 'Shakespeare, Spenser, and the Crisis in Ireland', *Cambridge Studies in Renaissance Literature and Culture*, 23 (Cambridge: Cambridge University Press, 1997)

Hodgdon, Barbara, *The End Crowns All: Closure and Contradiction in Shakespeare's History* (Princeton: Princeton University Press, 1991)

Hoenselaars, A. J., *Images of Englishmen and Foreigners in the Drama of Shakespeare and His Contemporaries: A Study of Stage Characters and National Identity in English Renaissance Drama* (Rutherford, NJ: Fairleigh Dickinson University Press; London: Associated University Presses, 1992)

    ed., *Shakespeare and Contemporary Dramatists* (Cambridge: Cambridge University Press, 2012)

Holbrook, Peter, 'Shakespeare, Class, and the Comedies', in Richard Dutton and Jean E. Howard, eds., *A Companion to Shakespeare's Works*, vol. III: *The Comedies* (Malden, MA: Blackwell, 2003), pp. 67–89

Holderness, Graham, *Shakespeare's History* (Dublin: Gill and Macmillan; New York: St. Martin's Press, 1985)

    Shakespeare: The Histories (London: Macmillan, 2000)

Holmes, Peter, 'Stucley, Thomas (c.1520–1578)', *Oxford Dictionary of National Biography* (Oxford: Oxford University Press, 2004); online edn www.oxforddnb.com/view/article/26741 (accessed 23 August 2015)

Holt, J. C., *Robin Hood*, rev. edn (London: Thames & Hudson, 1989)

Honigmann, E. A. J., '*John a Kent* and Marprelate', *Yearbook of English Studies*, 13 (1983), 288–93

    'Shakespeare's "Lost Source-Plays"', *Modern Language Review*, 49 (1954), 293–307

    ed., *Shakespeare and His Contemporaries: Essays in Comparison* (Manchester: Manchester University Press, 1986)

Hotson, Leslie, *Shakespeare Versus Shallow* (London: Nonesuch Press, 1931), pp. 111–22

Howard, Jean E., 'Gender on the Periphery', in Tom Clayton, Susan Brock and Vincente Forés, eds., *Shakespeare and the Mediterranean: The Selected Proceedings of the International Shakespeare Association World Congress, Valencia, 2001* (Newark: University of Delaware Press, 2004), pp. 344–62

Theater of a City: The Places of London Comedy, 1598–1642 (Philadelphia: University of Pennsylvania Press, 2007)

and Marion F. O'Connor, eds., *Shakespeare Reproduced: The Text in History and Ideology* (New York: Macmillan, 1987)

and Phyllis Rackin, *Engendering a Nation: A Feminist Account of Shakespeare's English Histories* (London: Routledge, 1997)

and Scott Cutler Shershow, eds., *Marxist Shakespeares* (London: Routledge, 2001),

Hunter, George K., 'Bourgeois Comedy: Shakespeare and Dekker' in E. A. J. Honigmann, ed., *Shakespeare and His Contemporaries: Essays in Comparison* (Manchester: Manchester University Press, 1986), pp. 1–15

English Drama 1586–1642: The Age of Shakespeare, Oxford History of English Literature, vol. VI (Oxford: Clarendon Press, 1997)

'*Henry IV* and the Elizabethan Two-Part Play', *Review of English Studies*, n.s., 5 (1954), 236–48

John Lyly: The Humanist as Courtier (London: Routledge and Kegan Paul, 1962)

Hutson, Lorna, *The Usurer's Daughter: Male Friendship and Fictions of Women in Seventeenth-Century England* (London: Routledge, 1994)

Hyland, Peter, *Disguise on the Early Modern English Stage* (Farnham: Ashgate, 2011)

Ioppolo, Grace, *Dramatists and Their Manuscripts in the Age of Shakespeare, Jonson, Middleton and Heywood: Authorship, Authority and the Playhouse* (Abingdon: Routledge, 2006)

Jackson, MacDonald P., 'Deciphering a Date and Determining a Date: Anthony Munday's *John a Kent and John a Cumber* and the Original Version of *Sir Thomas More*', *Early Modern Literary Studies*, 15.3 (2011); https://extra.shu.ac.uk/emls/15-3/jackdate.htm.

Jensen, Phebe, *Religion and Festivity in Shakespeare's Festive World* (Cambridge: Cambridge University Press, 2008)

Johnston, Alexandra F., 'The Robin Hood of the Records', in Lois Potter, ed., *Playing Robin Hood: The Legend as Performance in Five Centuries* (Newark: University of Delaware Press; London: Associated University Presses, 1998), pp. 27–44

Johnston, Dafydd, 'Siôn Cent [John Kent] (*fl.* 1400–1430)', *Oxford Dictionary of National Biography* (Oxford: Oxford University Press, 2004); online edn www.oxforddnb.com/view/article/15419 (accessed 30 July 2015)

Jones, Emrys, *Scenic Form in Shakespeare* (Oxford: Clarendon Press, 1971)

Jones, John Henry, ed., *The English Faust Book: A Critical Edition Based on the Text of 1592* (Cambridge: Cambridge University Press, 1994)

Jowitt, Claire, *Voyage Drama and Gender Politics 1589–1642: Real and Imagined Worlds* (Manchester: Manchester University Press, 2003)

Kastan, David Scott, '"The King Hath Many Marching in His Coats," or, What Did You Do in the War, Daddy?', in Ivo Kamps, ed., *Shakespeare, Left and Right* (New York: Routledge, 1991), pp. 241–58

Kenny, Robert W., *Elizabeth's Admiral: The Political Career of Charles Howard Earl of Nottingham 1536–1624* (Baltimore: Johns Hopkins Press, 1970)

Kermode, Lloyd Edward, 'After Shylock: The "Judaiser" in England', *Renaissance and Reformation*, 20.4 (1996), 5–26

— ed., *Three Renaissance Usury Plays* (Manchester: Manchester University Press, 2009)

Jason Scott-Warren and Martine van Elk, eds., *Tudor Drama Before Shakespeare, 1485–1590: New Directions for Research, Criticism, and Pedagogy* (Basingstoke: Palgrave Macmillan, 2004)

Kingsley-Smith, Jane, *Shakespeare's Drama of Exile* (Basingstoke: Palgrave Macmillan, 2003)

Kinney, Arthur F., 'Textual Signs in *The Merry Wives of Windsor*', *Yearbook of English Studies*, 23 (1993), 206–34

Knight, Stephen, ed., *Robin Hood: An Anthology of Scholarship and Criticism* (Cambridge: D. S. Brewer, 1999)

Knutson, Roslyn L., 'Marlowe Reruns: Repertorial Commerce and Marlowe's Plays in Revival', in Sara Munson Deats and Robert A. Logan, eds., *Marlowe's Empery: Expanding His Critical Contexts* (Cranbury, NJ: Associated University Presses, 2002), pp. 25–42

— 'Play Identifications: *The Wise Man of West Chester* and *John a Kent and John a Cumber*, *Longshanks* and *Edward I*', *Huntington Library Quarterly*, 47 (1984), 1–11

— *Playing Companies and Commerce in Shakespeare's Time* (Cambridge: Cambridge University Press, 2001)

— *The Repertory of Shakespeare's Company 1594–1613* (Fayetteville: University of Arkansas Press, 1991)

— 'The Start of Something Big', in Helen Ostovich, Holger Schott Syme and Andrew Griffin, eds., *Locating the Queen's Men, 1583–1603: Material Practices and Conditions of Playing* (Aldershot: Ashgate, 2009), pp. 99–108

— 'Strength Training for Tamburlaine's Weak Sons Through Repertorial Commerce', unpublished paper, Modern Language Association annual convention (2011)

— 'What's So Special about 1594?', *Shakespeare Quarterly*, 61 (2010), 449–67

Kocher, Paul H., 'The English *Faust Book* and the Date of Marlowe's *Faustus*', *Modern Language Notes*, 55 (1940), 95–101

Korda, Natasha, '"Judicious Oeillades": Supervising Marital Property in *The Merry Wives of Windsor*', in Jean E. Howard and Scott Cutler Shershow, eds., *Marxist Shakespeares* (London: Routledge, 2001), pp. 82–103

Kyd, Thomas, *The Spanish Tragedy*, ed. by J. R. Mulryne, 2nd edn (London: A & C Black; New York: Norton, 1989)

Lamb, Mary Ellen, *The Popular Culture of Shakespeare, Spenser, and Jonson* (London: Routledge, 2006)

'Taken by the Fairies: Fairy Practices and the Production of Popular Culture in *A Midsummer Night's Dream*', *Shakespeare Quarterly*, 51 (2000), 277–312

Laroque, François, *Shakespeare's Festive World: Elizabethan Seasonal Entertainment and the Professional Stage* (Cambridge: Cambridge University Press, 1991)

Leather, Ella Mary, *The Folk-lore of Herefordshire Collected from Oral and Printed Sources* (Hereford: Jakeman and Carver; London: Sidgwick & Jackson, 1912; repr. Hereford: Lapridge Publications, 1992)

Leggatt, Alexander, *Citizen Comedy in the Age of Shakespeare* (Toronto: University of Toronto Press, 1973)

An Introduction to English Renaissance Comedy (Manchester: Manchester University Press, 1999)

Leinwand, Theodore B., 'Shakespeare and the Middling Sort', *Shakespeare Quarterly*, 44 (1993), 184–303

Levinson, Judith C., ed., *The Famous History of Captain Thomas Stukeley* (Oxford: Malone Society, 1975)

Lewalski, Barbara K., 'Biblical Allusion and Allegory in *The Merchant of Venice*', *Shakespeare Quarterly*, 13 (1962), 327–43

Logan, Robert A., *Shakespeare's Marlowe: The Influence of Christopher Marlowe on Shakespeare's Artistry* (Farnham: Ashgate, 2007)

Lopez, Jeremy, *Theatrical Convention and Audience Response in Early Modern Drama* (Cambridge: Cambridge University Press, 2003)

Lunney, Ruth, *Marlowe and the Popular Tradition: Innovation in the English Drama before 1595* (Manchester: Manchester University Press, 2002)

MacFaul, Tom, *Male Friendship in Shakespeare and his Contemporaries* (Cambridge: Cambridge University Press, 2007)

MacLure, Millar, ed., *Marlowe: The Critical Heritage 1588–1896* (London: Routledge and Kegan Paul, 1979)

Maguire, Laurie, *Shakespeare's Names* (Oxford: Oxford University Press, 2007)

Manley, Lawrence, and Sally-Beth MacLean, *Lord Strange's Men and Their Plays* (New Haven: Yale University Press, 2014)

Marcus, Leah S., 'Levelling Shakespeare: Local Customs and Local Texts', *Shakespeare Quarterly*, 42 (1991), 168–78

Marino, James, *Owning William Shakespeare: The King's Men and Their Intellectual Property* (Philadelphia: University of Pennsylvania Press, 2011)

Marlowe, Christopher, *The Complete Poems and Translations*, ed. by Stephen Orgel, 2nd edn (London: Penguin, 2007)

'Dido Queen of Carthage' and 'The Massacre at Paris', ed. by H. J. Oliver (London: Methuen, 1968)

Doctor Faustus 1604–1616: Parallel Texts, ed. by W. W. Greg (Oxford: Clarendon Press, 1950)

Doctor Faustus: A- and B-texts (1604, 1616), ed. by David Bevington and Eric Rasmussen (Manchester: Manchester University Press, 1993)

The Jew of Malta, ed. by N. W. Bawcutt (Manchester: Manchester University Press, 1978)

Tamburlaine the Great, ed. by J. S. Cunningham (Manchester: Manchester University Press, 1981)

Marotti, Arthur F., 'Shakespeare and Catholicism', in Richard Dutton, Alison Findlay and Richard Wilson, eds., *Theatre and Religion: Lancastrian Shakespeare* (Manchester: Manchester University Press, 2003), pp. 218–41

Marx, Stephen, *Shakespeare and the Bible* (Oxford: Oxford University Press, 2000)

Matthews, David, and Gordon McMullan, eds., *Reading the Medieval in Early Modern England* (Cambridge: Cambridge University Press, 2007)

McCallum, James Dow, 'Greene's *Friar Bacon and Friar Bungay*,' *Modern Language Notes*, 35 (1920), 212–17

McDermott, James, 'Howard, Charles, Second Baron Howard of Effingham and First Earl of Nottingham (1536–1624)', in *Oxford Dictionary of National Biography* (Oxford: Oxford University Press, 2004); online edn, January 2008 www.oxforddnb.com/view/article/13885

Mcintosh, Shona, 'Recent Studies in George Chapman (1975–2009)', *English Literary Renaissance*, 41 (2011), 219–44

McMillin, Scott, and Sally-Beth MacLean, *The Queen's Men and Their Plays* (Cambridge: Cambridge University Press, 1998)

McNeir, Waldo F., 'Reconstructing the Conclusion of *John of Bordeaux*', *PMLA*, 66 (1951), 540–3

'Robert Greene and *John of Bordeaux*', *PMLA* 64 (1949), 781–801

McPherson, David C., *Shakespeare, Jonson, and the Myth of Venice* (Newark: University of Delaware Press; London: Associated University Presses, 1990)

Menzer, Paul, 'Shades of Marlowe', *Marlowe Studies: An Annual*, 1 (2011), 181–92

Middleton, Thomas, *The Collected Works*, ed. by Gary Taylor and John Lavagnino (Oxford: Clarendon Press, 2007)

Milward, Peter, *The Catholicism of Shakespeare's Plays*, Renaissance Monographs, 23 (Tokyo: Renaissance Institute, 1997)

Munday, Anthony, *The Death of Robert, Earl of Huntingdon*, ed. by John C. Meagher (Oxford: Malone Society, 1967)

The Downfall of Robert, Earl of Huntingdon, ed. by John C. Meagher (Oxford: Malone Society, 1965)

John a Kent and John a Cumber, ed. by Muriel St.Clare Byrne (Oxford: Malone Society, 1923)

Munro, Lucy, *Children of the Queen's Revels: A Jacobean Theatre Repertory* (Cambridge: Cambridge University Press, 2005)

'Early Modern Drama and the Repertory Approach', *Research Opportunities in Renaissance Drama*, 42 (2003), 1–33

O'Neill, Stephen, *Staging Ireland: Representations in Shakespeare and Renaissance Drama* (Dublin: Four Courts Press, 2007)

Orgel, Stephen, 'Shylock's Tribe', in Tom Clayton, Susan Brock and Vicente Forés, eds., *Shakespeare and the Mediterranean: The Selected Proceedings of the*

International Shakespeare Association World Congress, Valencia, 2001 (Newark: University of Delaware Press, 2004), pp. 38–53

Orlin, Lena Cowen, 'Shakespearean Comedy and Material Life', in Richard Dutton and Jean E. Howard, eds., *A Companion to Shakespeare's Works*, vol. III: *The Comedies* (Malden, MA: Blackwell, 2003), pp. 159–81

Ostovich, Helen, Holger Schott Syme and Andrew Griffin, eds., *Locating the Queen's Men, 1583–1603: Material Practices and Conditions of Playing* (Aldershot: Ashgate, 2009)

Palmer, D. J., 'Casting off the Old Man: History and St. Paul in "Henry IV"', *Critical Quarterly*, 12 (1970), 267–83

Patterson, Annabel, 'Sir John Oldcastle as Symbol of Reformation Historiography', in Donna B. Hamilton and Richard Strier, eds., *Religion, Literature, and Politics in Post-Reformation England, 1540–1688* (Cambridge: Cambridge University Press, 1996), pp. 6–26

Peele, George, *The Dramatic Works of George Peele*, gen. ed. Charles Tyler Prouty, 3 vols. (New Haven: Yale University Press, 1952–70)

Poole, Kristen, 'Saints Alive! Falstaff, Martin Marprelate, and the Staging of Puritanism', *Shakespeare Quarterly*, 46 (1995), 47–75

Pope, Maurice, 'My Kingdom for a Horse', *Notes and Queries*, 41 (1994), 472–7

Porter, Henry, *The Two Angry Women of Abington*, ed. by W. W. Greg (Oxford: Malone Society, 1912)

Potter, Lois, ed., *Playing Robin Hood: The Legend as Performance in Five Centuries* (Newark: University of Delaware Press; London: Associated University Presses, 1998)

Proudfoot, G. R., ed., *A Knack to Know a Knave* (Oxford: Malone Society, 1964)

Pugliatti, Paola, *Shakespeare the Historian* (Basingstoke: Macmillan, 1996)

Quarmby, Kevin A., *The Disguised Ruler in Shakespeare and His Contemporaries* (Farnham: Ashgate, 2012)

Rabkin, Norman, *Shakespeare and the Common Understanding* (New York: Free Press, 1967)

Rackin, Phyllis, *Stages of History: Shakespeare's English Chronicles* (London: Routledge, 1990)

Records of Early English Drama: Patrons and Performances Web Site, University of Toronto http://link.library.utoronto.ca/reed (accessed 29 July 2015)

Renwick, William Lindsay, ed., *John of Bordeaux; or, The Second Part of Friar Bacon* (Oxford: Malone Society, 1936)

Ribner, Irving, *The English History Play in the Age of Shakespeare* (Princeton: Princeton University Press, 1957)

Richards, Jennifer, 'Male Friendship and Counsel in Richard Edwards' *Damon and Pythias*', in Thomas Betteridge and Greg Walker, eds., *The Oxford Handbook to Tudor Drama* (Oxford: Oxford University Press, 2012), pp. 293–308

Riggs, David, *Shakespeare's Heroical Histories: 'Henry VI' and its Literary Tradition* (Cambridge, MS.: Harvard University Press, 1971)

Rossiter, A. P., *Angel with Horns and Other Shakespearean Lectures*, ed. by Graham Storey (London: Longmans, 1961)

Rutter, Carol Chillington, *Documents of the Rose Playhouse* (Manchester: Manchester University Press, 1984)

Rutter, Tom, 'Adult Playing Companies, 1603–1613', in Richard Dutton, ed., *The Oxford Handbook of Early Modern Theatre* (Oxford: Oxford University Press, 2009), pp. 72–87

'The Communities of George Chapman's *All Fools*', in Roger D. Sell, Anthony W. Johnson and Helen Wilcox, eds., *Community-Making in Early Stuart Theatres: Stage and Audience* (Abingdon: Routledge, 2017), pp. 218–238

'*Englishmen for My Money*: Work and Social Conflict?', in Michelle M. Dowd and Natasha Korda, eds., *Working Subjects in Early Modern English Drama* (Farnham: Ashgate, 2011), pp. 87–99

'Introduction: The Repertory-Based Approach', 'Issues in Review: Dramatists, Playing Companies, and Repertories', *Early Theatre*, 13.3 (2011), 121–32

'Marlovian Echoes in the Admiral's Men Repertory: *Alcazar, Stukeley, Patient Grissil*', *Shakespeare Bulletin*, 27 (2009), 27–38

'Merchants of Venice in *A Knack to Know an Honest Man*', *Medieval and Renaissance Drama in England*, 19 (2006), 194–209

'Repertory Studies: An Overview', *Shakespeare*, 4 (2008), 352–66

Work and Play on the Shakespearean Stage (Cambridge: Cambridge University Press, 2008)

Salingar, Leo, *Shakespeare and the Traditions of Comedy* (Cambridge: Cambridge University Press, 1974)

Sanders, Norman, 'The Comedy of Greene and Shakespeare', in John Russell Brown and Bernard Harris, eds., *Early Shakespeare, Stratford-upon-Avon Studies*, 3 (London: Edward Arnold, 1961), pp. 34–53

Schafer, Elizabeth, 'William Haughton's *Englishmen for My Money*: A Critical Note', *Review of English Studies*, n.s., 41 (1990), 536–8

Schalkwyk, David, 'The Impossible Gift of Love in *The Merchant of Venice* and the Sonnets', *Shakespeare*, 7 (2011), 142–55

Schelling, Felix E., *Elizabethan Playwrights: A Short History of the English Drama from Mediaeval Times to the Closing of the Theaters in 1642* (New York: Harper, 1925, repr. New York: Blom, 1965)

Schoone-Jongen, Terence G., *Shakespeare's Companies: William Shakespeare's Early Career and the Acting Companies, 1577–1594* (Farnham: Ashgate, 2008)

Scott, Sarah, and Michael Stapleton, eds., *Christopher Marlowe the Craftsman: Lives, Stage, and Page* (Aldershot: Ashgate, 2010)

Scoufos, Alice-Lyle, *Shakespeare's Typological Satire: A Study of the Falstaff-Oldcastle Problem* (Athens, Ohio: Ohio University Press, 1979)

Scragg, Leah, 'Shakespeare, Lyly and Ovid: The Influence of *Gallathea* on *A Midsummer Night's Dream*', *Shakespeare Survey*, 30 (1977), 125–34

Sell, Roger D., Anthony W. Johnson and Helen Wilcox, eds., *Community-Making in Early Stuart Theatres: Stage and Audience* (Abingdon: Routledge, 2017)

Shakespeare, William, *As You Like It*, ed. by Michael Hattaway (Cambridge: Cambridge University Press, 2009)

The First Part of King Henry IV, ed. by Herbert Weil and Judith Weil (Cambridge: Cambridge University Press, 1997)

Henry IV Part One, ed. by David Bevington (Oxford: Clarendon Press, 1987)

King Henry IV Part 1, ed. by David Scott Kastan (London: Arden Shakespeare, 2002)

King Henry V, ed. by Andrew Gurr, updated edn (Cambridge: Cambridge University Press, 2005)

King Richard II, ed. by Andrew Gurr, updated edn (Cambridge: Cambridge University Press, 2003)

Love's Labour's Lost, ed. by William C. Carroll (Cambridge: Cambridge University Press, 2009)

The Merchant of Venice, ed. by John Russell Brown (London: Methuen, 1955)

The Merchant of Venice, ed. by Jay L. Halio (Oxford: Clarendon Press, 1993)

The Merchant of Venice, ed. by M. M. Mahood (Cambridge: Cambridge University Press, 2003)

The Merry Wives of Windsor, ed. by T. W. Craik (Oxford: Clarendon Press, 1989)

The Merry Wives of Windsor, ed. by David Crane, updated edn (Cambridge: Cambridge University Press, 2010)

The Merry Wives of Windsor, ed. by G. R. Hibbard (Harmondsworth: Penguin, 1973)

The Merry Wives of Windsor, ed. by Giorgio Melchiori (London: Thomas Nelson and Sons, 2000)

A Midsummer Night's Dream, ed. by Harold E. Brooks (London: Methuen, 1979)

A Midsummer Night's Dream, ed. by R. A. Foakes, updated edn (Cambridge: Cambridge University Press, 2003)

A Midsummer Night's Dream, ed. by Peter Holland (Oxford: Clarendon Press, 1994)

A Midsummer Night's Dream, ed. by Stanley Wells (London: Penguin, 2005)

Romeo and Juliet, ed. by G. Blakemore Evans (Cambridge: Cambridge University Press, 1984)

The Second Part of King Henry IV, ed. by Giorgio Melchiori (Cambridge: Cambridge University Press, 1989)

Shapiro, I. A., 'The Significance of a Date', *Shakespeare Survey*, 8 (1955), 100–105

'Shakespeare and Mundy', *Shakespeare Survey*, 14 (1961), 25–33

Shapiro, James, *Rival Playwrights: Marlowe, Jonson, Shakespeare* (New York: Columbia University Press, 1991)

Sharpe, Robert Boies, *The Real War of the Theaters: Shakespeare's Fellows in Rivalry with the Admiral's Men, 1594–1603: Repertories, Devices and Types* (New York: Modern Language Association of America, 1935)

Shell, Alison, *Shakespeare and Religion* (London: Arden Shakespeare, 2010)

Simmons, J. L., 'Masculine Negotiations in Shakespeare's History Plays: Hal, Hotspur, and "the foolish Mortimer"', *Shakespeare Quarterly*, 44 (1993), 440–63

Simpson, Richard, ed., *The School of Shakespere*, 2 vols (London: Chatto and Windus, 1878)

Sinfield, Alan, 'How to Read *The Merchant of Venice* Without Being Heterosexist', in Terence Hawkes, ed., *Alternative Shakespeares Vol. II* (London: Routledge, 1996), pp. 122–39

Singman, Jeffrey L., 'Munday's Unruly Earl', in Lois Potter, ed., *Playing Robin Hood: The Legend as Performance in Five Centuries* (Newark: University of Delaware Press; London: Associated University Presses, 1998), pp. 63–76

Skura, Meredith, 'Anthony Munday's "Gentrification" of Robin Hood', *English Literary Renaissance*, 33 (2003), 155–80

Shakespeare the Actor and the Purposes of Playing (Chicago: University of Chicago Press, 1993)

'What Shakespeare Did to Marlowe in Private: Dido, Faustus, and Bottom', in Sarah Scott and Michael Stapleton, eds., *Christopher Marlowe the Craftsman: Lives, Stage, and Page* (Aldershot: Ashgate, 2010), pp. 79–90

Smith, Emma, '"So Much English by the Mother": Gender, Foreigners, and the Mother Tongue in William Haughton's *Englishmen for My Money*', *Medieval and Renaissance Drama in England*, 13 (2001), 165–81

Smout, Clare, 'Actor, Poet, Playwright, Sharer ... Rival? Shakespeare and Heywood, 1603–4', *Early Theatre*, 13.2 (December 2010), 175–89

Stallybrass, Peter, '"Drunk with the Cup of Liberty": Robin Hood, the Carnivalesque, and the Rhetoric of Violence in Early Modern England', in Stephen Knight, ed., *Robin Hood: An Anthology of Scholarship and Criticism* (Cambridge: D. S. Brewer, 1999), pp. 113–45

Stewart, Alan, *Close Readers: Humanism and Sodomy in Early Modern England* (Princeton: Princeton University Press, 1997)

Syme, Holger Schott, 'The Meaning of Success: Stories of 1594 and Its Aftermath', *Shakespeare Quarterly*, 61 (2010), 490–525

Taylor, Gary, 'The Fortunes of Oldcastle', *Shakespeare Survey*, 38 (1985), 85–100

Thompson, Ann, and Gordon McMullen, eds., In *Arden: Editing Shakespeare: Essays in Honour of Richard Proudfoot* (London: Arden Shakespeare, 2003)

Thorndike, Ashley, 'The Relation of *As You Like It* to Robin Hood Plays', *Journal of Germanic Philology*, 4 (1902), 59–69

Tillyard, E. M. W., *Shakespeare's History Plays* (London: Chatto and Windus, 1944)

Towne, Frank, '"White Magic" in *Friar Bacon and Friar Bungay?*', *Modern Language Notes*, 67 (1952), 9–13

Traister, Barbara Howard, *Heavenly Necromancers: The Magician in English Renaissance Drama* (Columbia: University of Missouri Press, 1984)

van Es, Bart, *Shakespeare in Company* (Oxford: Oxford University Press, 2013)

von Rosador, Kurt Tetzeli, 'The Sacralizing Sign: Religion and Magic in Bale, Greene, and the Early Shakespeare', *Yearbook of English Studies*, 23 (1993), 30–45

Virgil (Publius Vergilius Maro), *The Pastoral Poems*, tr. E. V. Rieu (Harmondsworth: Penguin, 1954)

Waith, Eugene M., *The Herculean Hero in Marlowe, Chapman, Shakespeare and Dryden* (New York: Columbia University Press, 1962)

Wall, Wendy, '*The Merry Wives of Windsor*: Unhusbanding Desires in Windsor', in Richard Dutton and Jean E. Howard, eds., *A Companion to Shakespeare's Works*, vol. III: *The Comedies* (Malden: Blackwell, 2003), pp. 376–92

Staging Domesticity: Household Work and English Identity in Early Modern Drama (Cambridge: Cambridge University Press, 2002)

Walsh, Brian, *Shakespeare, the Queen's Men, and the Elizabethan Performance of History* (Cambridge: Cambridge University Press, 2009)

Wells, Robin Headlam, *Shakespeare on Masculinity* (Cambridge: Cambridge University Press, 2000)

Wertheim, Albert, 'The Presentation of Sin in *Friar Bacon and Friar Bungay*', *Criticism*, 16 (1974), 273–89

White, Paul Whitfield, 'Holy Robin Hood! Carnival, Parish Guilds, and the Outlaw Tradition', in Lloyd Edward Kermode, Jason Scott-Warren and Martine van Elk, eds., *Tudor Drama before Shakespeare, 1485–1590: New Directions for Research, Criticism, and Pedagogy* (Basingstoke: Palgrave Macmillan, 2004), pp. 67–89

'Shakespeare and the Cobhams', in Paul Whitfield White and Suzanne R. Westfall, eds., *Shakespeare and Theatrical Patronage in Early Modern England* (Cambridge University Press, 2002), pp. 64–89

Theatre and Reformation: Protestantism, Patronage, and Playing in Tudor England (Cambridge: Cambridge University Press, 1993)

and Suzanne R. Westfall, eds., *Shakespeare and Theatrical Patronage in Early Modern England* (Cambridge University Press, 2002)

Wickham, Glynne, Herbert Berry and William Ingram, eds., *English Professional Theatre, 1530–1660* (Cambridge: Cambridge University Press, 2000)

Wiggins, Martin, 'A Choice of Impossible Things: Dating the Revival of *The Battle of Alcazar*', in Patricia Dorval and Jean-Marie Maguin, eds., *Shakespeare et ses Contemporains* (Paris: Société Français Shakespeare, 2002), pp. 185–202

'Marlowe's Chronology and Canon', in Emily C. Bartels and Emma Smith, eds., *Christopher Marlowe in Context* (Cambridge: Cambridge University Press, 2013), pp. 7–14

Shakespeare and the Drama of His Time (Oxford: Oxford University Press, 2000).

'Things That Go Bump in the Text: *Captain Thomas Stukeley*', *Proceedings of the Bibliographical Society of America*, 98 (2001), 5–20

Williams, Deanne, '*Friar Bacon and Friar Bungay* and the Rhetoric of Temporality', in David Matthews and Gordon McMullan, eds., *Reading the Medieval in Early Modern England* (Cambridge: Cambridge University Press, 2007), pp. 31–48

Wilson, Richard, *Secret Shakespeare: Studies in Theatre, Religion and Resistance* (Manchester: Manchester University Press, 2004)

'"The Words of Mercury": Shakespeare and Marlowe' in Ton Hoenselaars, ed., *Shakespeare and Contemporary Dramatists* (Cambridge: Cambridge University Press, 2012), pp. 34–53

Withington, Phil, 'Putting the City into Shakespeare's City Comedy', in David Armitage, Conal Condren and Andrew Fitzmaurice, eds., *Shakespeare and Early Modern Political Thought* (Cambridge: Cambridge University Press, 2009), pp. 197–216

Womersley, David, *Divinity and State* (Oxford: Oxford University Press, 2010)

Yates, Frances, *Giordano Bruno and the Hermetic Tradition* (London: Routledge and Kegan Paul, 1964)

Index